MW00787710

Devils, Women, and Jews

The Mouth of Hell devouring damned souls. From The Hours of Catherine of Cleves, ca. 1440. (Courtesy The Pierpont Morgan Library, New York. M.945, f.47)

Devils, Women, and Jews

Reflections of the Other in Medieval Sermon Stories

Joan Young Gregg

SUNY Series in
Medieval Studies

Paul E. Szarmach, editor

STATE UNIVERSITY OF NEW YORK PRESS

Production by Ruth Fisher
Marketing by Fran Keneston

Published by
State University of New York Press, Albany

© 1997 State University of New York

All rights reserved

Printed in the United States of America

No part of this book may be used or reproduced in any manner whatsoever without written permission. No part of this book may be stored in a retrieval system or transmitted in any form or by any means including electronic, electrostatic, magnetic tape, mechanical, photocopying, recording, or other-wise without the prior permission in writing of the publisher.

For information, address the State University of New York Press, State University Plaza, Albany, NY 12246

Library of Congress Cataloging-in-Publication Data

Devils, women, and Jews : reflections of the other in medieval sermon
    stories / [edited by] Joan Young Gregg.
        p.   cm. — (SUNY series in medieval studies)
    Includes bibliographical references and index.
    ISBN 0-7914-3417-6 (hc : alk. paper). — ISBN 0-7914-3418-4 (pb :
alk. paper)
    1. Exempla—History and criticism. 2. Preaching—Europe—History—
Middle Ages, 600–1500. 3. Demonology—Europe—History of
doctrines—Middle Ages, 600–1500. 4. Women in Christianity—Europe—
History—Middle Ages, 600–1500. 5. Christianity and antisemitism—
History. 6. Europe—Church history—600–1500. 7. Europe—Social
life and customs.   I. Gregg, Joan Young.   II. Series.
BV4208.E85D48   1997
251′.08′0902—DC20   96-41503
                                                                CIP

10 9 8 7 6 5 4 3 2 1

Contents

Chapter Four   Jews in Medieval Sermon Stories • 169

Exempla about Jews

Preface

My fascination with the world of fairy tale and folk tale goes back to my childhood. As a youngster plowing my way through the yards of Grimm, Andrew Lang, and folk tales from around the world at the Fordham branch of the New York Public Library, I had no thought that underlying the narratives that so engaged me were serious, complex ideas that would someday draw my scholarly interest. Yet so it turned out, and this book is the result of one aspect of that matured fascination.

The importance of popular narrative as a representation of the "specific mentality of a given moment in history," to quote Sander Gilman, is a theme that has attracted a generation of brilliant writers such as Edward Said, to mention just one whose work has excited my admiration. In the medieval sermon story, where *marchen* and religious narrative meet, I found that "rich bounty" that Gilman describes as one key to decoding the values of a specific culture, in this case, that of the European Middle Ages. Yet these tales do more than reflect just the particulars of a designated place and period. They also provide a key to understanding a more universal circumstance, that of the encounter between opposing cultures and between those groups within a culture that are defined as the Other. The voices heard in these sermon narratives are not those of the margin but rather those in medieval society who defined the center. Hence, my introductions to the tales are an attempt to balance the voice of that center with an analysis of what shaped that voice and what influenced the representations that constitute its narrative core.

My primary aim in modernizing the sermon narrative exempla that conclude each chapter has been to render them accessible to the widest possible range of nonspecialist readers. Spelling and punctuation conform to current American usage. I have attempted to keep these exempla as faithful as possible to their originals. Thus I have retained medieval vocabulary except when doing so would obscure meaning, and I have adjusted syntax only in the interest of comprehensibility, preferring a literal, if somewhat stilted, sentence structure to any distortion of the original texts that might result from revision, omission, or paraphrase.

I am indebted to so many for this volume. I am grateful to New York City Technical College of the City University of New York for the Fellowship and Scholars' Leaves that made possible my extended periods of research and writing. My research was supported in part by grants from the City University of New York PSC-CUNY Research Award Program, to whom I am grateful; I would particularly like to thank Mrs. Miriam Korman for her assistance. I am also grateful to the National Endowment for the Humanities for supporting my participation in the summer seminar "Absence and Presence: The Jew in Early English Literature," which was crucial to my development of chapter 4. I want to thank Professor Stephen Spector, the inspiring director of that seminar and my seminar colleagues as well. I thank the New York Council for the Humanities for supporting my participation in its teachers' workshop "Women in American History and Religion," from which chapter 3 has benefited. I am grateful to the librarians at New York City Tech, who assisted my bibliographical searches. I also thank Inge Dupont, Head of Reader Services at the Pierpont Morgan Library for her assistance with the illustrations. My thanks to the reviewers of the manuscript, and especially to Timea Szell, whose insights on female hagiography I greatly appreciate. Thanks is also due Lillian Kristal for her bibliographic assistance regarding object relations. I also wish to thank Richard Kenefick for his invaluable computer support.

My professors at New York University's Graduate School of Arts and Sciences, particularly Lillian Herlands Hornstein, Jess B. Bessinger, Jr., Robert R. Raymo, and John Fisher, were exemplars of scholarly integrity and "the life of the mind" whom I shall never forget. For their encouragement of my work I would like to thank my family and friends, and most particularly the anthropologist Serena Nanda, whose support and crossfertilization of ideas have been indispensable.

1

Introduction

I do not care whether you expect some
well turned phrases today. It is my duty
to give you due warning by citing the
Scriptures. "Do not be slow to turn to the
Lord, nor delay from one day to the next,
for His anger shall come when you know
not." I cannot be silent; I am forced to
preach on it. Filled with fear myself, I fill
you with fear.

St. Augustine, *Sermon*

Illustration from a Latin Book of Hours from Poitiers, ca. 1480, depicting Anger, one of the Seven Deadly Sins instigated by the devil, a popular subject of sermon exempla. (Courtesy The Pierpont Morgan Library, New York. M.1001, f.88)

In 1214 the Fourth Lateran Council of the Roman Catholic Church met under the direction of Pope Innocent III to consider the spread of heresy, the decline in the quality of the priesthood, and its spiritual neglect of the laity. The council promulgated some seventy canons, a number of which dealt with sacramental obligations, those rites considered to have been established by Christ as a channel for grace. In regard to the sacrament of penance, all Christians were bound to make confession and receive the Eucharist at least once a year. The tenth canon asserted that in order for the laity to be properly prepared for this duty, they were to receive adequate religious instruction in their own tongue through the medium of more frequent preaching; and it stipulated that bishops appoint qualified men to assist them in preaching to the masses. The focus of the preaching was to be on the Seven Deadly Sins (pride, avarice, gluttony, lust, sloth, envy, and ire), the Seven Virtues, the Seven Gifts of the Holy Ghost, the Ten Commandments, the Twelve Articles of the Faith, the Seven Sacraments, the Seven Works of Mercy, and the Seven Petitions of the Pater Noster.[1]

Homiletic exempla, or instructive sermon stories, played a central role in the revitalization of the art of preaching.[2] In sermons to both clerical and lay audiences, in both Latin and the vernacular, the exemplum reinforced the doctrinal matter of the homily with concrete illustrations, providing religious instruction and effectively, if indirectly, inculcating the largely unlettered medieval populace with the societal norms of European Christianity.

Closely linked to the cultural, mental, and social life of the thirteenth through the fifteenth centuries, the sermon exemplum was characteristically grounded in a contemporary reality and often depicted realistic figures in ordinary situations. Theology was made vivid, and palpable life was given to the concepts of sin, contrition, and penance by descriptive—and often gory—details of the devil, hell, and the punishments meted out to the damned both in life and after death. In furnishing his exempla with mundane details from everyday life and creating scenarios of recognizable social behavior, however, the medieval preacher was not aiming for historical or sociological verisimilitude. Rather, his purpose was to show that there was no situation, regardless of how trivial or banal it appeared, that did not engage the issue of eternal life. What makes the popular homiletic exemplum irreplaceable as a cultural artifact is not so much that it depicts for us the material world of medieval life, for the incidental glimpses it offers us are more tantalizing than complete, but that it allows us to witness the interchange between popular and scholarly theology and, in doing so, permits us to discover those unselfconscious cultural notions that, by their frequent hearing and retelling in narrative context, became imprinted on the medieval mind.

In giving voice to these notions as they regard the devil, women, and Jews, medieval homiletic narrative speaks to us of an unholy trinity, a dark and distorted reflection of the orthodox trinity of Christian doctrine. Through popular sermon story, echoes of the medieval mentality, which linked these figures together and viewed them from a perspective of otherness, still resonate today.

Development and Diffusion of Exempla

While the term *exemplum* as used in the medieval preaching manuals was applied to a wide variety of illustrative materials such as biblical quotations and allegorically interpreted metaphors, the term in modern scholarship is generally limited to those relatively brief narratives incorporated into sermons that have the following characteristics: they are persuasive and didactic in aim and tone; they teach lessons of good conduct not only as the means to earthly happiness but, more importantly, as the means of eternal salvation; and they are told on the authority of recognized spiritual leaders as "true" events, either historical or contemporary, which supposedly took place as narrated.[3] It is these exempla, conveying the details of medieval life, reflecting the cultural notions of medieval society and permitting useful comparisons with their variants in other religious and secular sources, that form the basis of this study.

The use of illustrative narrative in moral discourse was not a creation of the medieval Christian pulpit. Greek and Roman writers of antiquity commonly employed historical and biographical anecdote in political and philosophical discourse, but there its use was largely to contrast the glories of past golden ages with the moral decline of the writer's own time or to persuade one's judicial or legislative colleagues to form or reverse certain opinions. The first methodical use of narrative exempla in Christian doctrinal writing is generally attributed to Tertullian, the third-century North African ecclesiastic in whose works, the first Christian tracts in Latin, we find examples of antique pagan anecdote—legend, history, or even animal fable—adapted to Christian purpose.

Like Tertullian, the fathers of the church writing from the third to the fifth century found brief narrative illustrations useful to make their presentations of doctrine more accessible to their audiences. Most of their anecdotal illustrations were pious tales of Christian hermits dwelling in the Egyptian deserts, whose lives were witness to the means by which spiritually advanced persons triumphed over demon-inspired desires of the flesh or religious doubts. By the fourth century, these rudimentary narratives of Christian holy men were elaborated into more formal, if still brief, stories and were anthologized with a variety of chronicles and saints' "Lives" to form a collection that was first called the *Vitae patrum* (Lives of the fathers) by Saint Jerome. By the fifth century, this amorphous compilation, now ten volumes of narrative and nonnarrative material with an affinity of theme and treatment, had become a basic resource of Christian preachers seeking edificatory narrative to enhance their homilies, and it continued as a staple of the medieval pulpit until the end of the Middle Ages.

With the expansion of Christianity and the Benedictine monastic reforms of the sixth century, sermon discourse shifted its focus from the relationship between a spiritual master and his disciples, such as we see in exempla about St. Macarius, to the reflection upon religious doctrines applicable to monastic groups or individual layfolk. The narrative exempla utilized in this new context were still almost wholly pious in setting and characters. This second stage of homiletic narrative development produced one significant volume which also became a popular resource for later medieval homilists: the *Dialogues* of Gregory the Great, a purported colloquy between Pope Gregory (d. 604) and his deacon Peter, whose purpose was to inspire and instruct the populace during the difficult period of Lombard invasion, plague, and social decay in Italy at the end of the sixth century.[4] Book 4 in particular, composed primarily of visions illuminating various questions of eschatology and related topics, contributed much to the popular medieval conception of hell, devils, the nature of damnation, and the like.

From the seventh to the twelfth centuries, the monumental changes that took place in the thrust of church dogma and the dynamics of religious instruction influenced the development of homiletic narrative in important ways. The geographical expansion of Christianity, with its conversion of new peoples and its concomitant need for appropriate teaching materials; the continual reexamination of church dogma in its struggle against repeated, if various, forms of heresy; the rise in veneration of the Virgin Mary and a multiplying number of saints; and the growth of distinct vernacular languages impelled a reexamination of church principles and policies regarding the spiritual needs of the laity. During this period Christian theologians expanded and systematized various doctrines pertaining to the sacraments, and clerical officiation in marriage, which took on sacramental status, increased. The doctrine of transubstantiation—the literal transformation of the communion wafer and wine offered at the Mass into the body and blood of Christ— and penance as a sacrament took on heightened significance. The theology of confession underwent expansion and refinement: there was a great movement towards the private examination of conscience; and secret confession, adopted in the seventh century, was required to be taken at least once a year. All of these concerns are reflected in the composition and compilation of the homiletic narrative of this era.

A host of tracts minutely defining and classifying such topics as the Commandments, the Creed, and the Deadly Sins were circulated to acquaint clerics with the new pastoral knowledge they required. In addition, with continuing monastic reform and expansion, a number of exempla collections were composed for the instruction of monastic novices. Sermons preached at the great monasteries also drew large lay audiences, for whom the exempla were an effective tool as well. Such sermons added to the eremetic and early monkish narratives of the *Vitae patrum* and Gregory's *Dialogues* a new stock of stories with wider appeal. Prominent among these were Miracles of the Virgin, emphasizing her role as an intercessor with Christ and protector of those who were faithful in their veneration to her. Composed by clerics devoted to the Marian cult such as Peter Damien, an eleventh-century Benedictine monk, these tales were widely circulated in both homiletic and secular contexts and were influential in shaping models of behavior for women in real life and female characters in popular vernacular *marchen*, or folk tale.

The growth of trade; the Iconoclastic controversy, which made refugees of dissenting Eastern clerics; and the Crusades also made this period one of enormous interchange between the cultures of western Europe and the Middle East, both Christian and non-Christian. Through this culture contact a fascinating store of fables, animal stories, and other non-Christian narratives was introduced to the homiletic literature of western Europe. The *Disciplina clericalis* (Guide for clerics), for example, was an anthology of thirty-four animal fables, folktales, and fabliaux modelled on Arabic literary patterns written by the Cistercian monk Petrus Alphonsi (d. ca. 1140), a Spanish convert from Judaism serving as a scholar-physician to King Alphonso I of Aragon. The tales were set in a frame of advice from a father to his son, a structure ultimately derived from older Indian, Persian, and Jewish sources, but Alphonsi Christianized them by adding appropriate moralizations. A similarly Christianized collection of originally secular tales was the *Parables* of the English Cistercian monk Odo de Cheriton (d. 1240), who reinterpreted his collection of Aesopian animal fables and beastiary material for the medieval pulpit by appending appropriately Christian allegories to them.

Thus, by the early thirteenth century, when the Fourth Lateran Council articulated the importance of homiletics in pastoral care, a climate conducive to the compilation, composition, and dissemination of illustrative homiletic narrative, both narrowly religious and more broadly moralistic, had already been established. The two streams of exempla literature, pious and secular, melded with each other in ecclectic encyclopedias of narratives compiled to benefit succeeding generations of popular preachers. The most prominent example of such volumes was the *Speculum historiale* (The Mirror of history) of Vincent de Beauvais (d. 1264), a French Dominican with access to the French royal libraries, who brought together scriptural allusions, hagiographies, Marian miracles, and quasilegendary anecdotes into an enormous hodgepodge frequently utilized, though not often acknowledged, by later homilists. Another enormous work whose material was commonly excerpted for pulpit use was the *Legenda sanctorum sive historia Lombardica*, usually cited by medieval homilists as *Legenda aurea* (Golden legend). This compendium of almost 350 saints' lives, many of which include motifs from folktales and secular romances, was written by Jacobus de Voragine, the Dominican bishop of Genoa

(d. 1298), and translated into Middle English by Caxton. The *Gesta Romanorum* (Tales from the Romans), a collection of romances and pseudoclassical tales written and allegorized for a Christian audience by the French Benedictine Pierre Bercheur (d. 1362), also underwent a medieval English translation and was immensely popular as a source of homiletic narrative.

The formation of the preaching orders of Franciscans and Dominicans in the 1220s and the continuing increase in the monastic movement gave an additional impetus to the composition and collection of homiletic narrative. While one branch of pulpit literature flowered through the Christianization of folktale, fabliaux, and romance, another blossomed with spiritual narratives of a more contemporary cast involving individualized characters both lay and clerical in recognizable life situations. These ostensibly true anecdotes, while largely concerned with apparitions of devils, visions of hell, and similar supernatural occurrences reminiscent of the tales of the *Vitae patrum* and Pope Gregory's *Dialogues*, were more concretely drawn than their formulaic ancestors and often took on a local flavor as they were circulated across Europe by preaching clerics crossing national borders, young men entering monastic establishments far from their native parishes, or travellers enjoying the hospitality of monasteries and convents along their routes.[5] In these socially contextualized exempla we find mirrored not only the religious tenets of the day but the cultural norms as well. One of the foremost exempla books conveying these sociocultural realities was the *Dialogue of Miracles*, a guidebook for young Cistercian monks at Heisterbach in Germany, written by the master of novices, Caesar of Heisterbach (d. 1240).

Another accumulation of contemporary tales enhanced by acutely observed social detail was the body of exempla incorporated into the sermons of Jacques de Vitry (d. 1240), a canon of Oignies in France and later bishop of Acre. De Vitry's fame as a raconteur of pious narrative was based on his homilies against the Albigensian heresy and in support of the crusade against the Saracens in 1214, and especially those directed to specific ranks and classes of both clergy and laity. Generally, two or three narratives were embedded in these sermons, seventy-four of which were collected under the title *Sermones vulgares* (Popular homilies). The extant manuscripts of de Vitry's exempla suggest that not only did his homiletic narratives circulate in conventional written volumes but that clerics in his audiences would take notes of his stories as he told them to compile their own collections.[6]

A new society was taking shape in the thirteenth century, one which was becoming increasingly diverse socially and economically. Its heterogeneous nature was acknowledged from the pulpit by apposite texts and exempla addressed to various emerging social groups, highlighting the sins to which, as the church perceived, they were most susceptible. Thus, for example, attacks on vanity in dress and sharp trading practices or usury are found in every exempla book of the period.

Yet in this era of social turbulence and transition, the popular sermon did not so much address social reform directly as focus on personal spiritual conversion as the root of all social improvement. The primary aim of the homily and its accompanying exempla was to bring about the spiritual correction of individuals in a public audience by exhorting fear of the devil, love of God, and sincere participation in the activities of confession, contrition, and penitence, which had moved to the center of the scheme of personal salvation. Sermon story reinforced homiletic material with unambiguous lessons on the wages of sin, the irrevocability of condemnation at the Last Judgment, and the everlasting tortures of hell that no member of the audience could fail to absorb. More than ever, as preaching was teaching, the exemplum played an indispensable role in the church's didactic program.

In one generation after the publication of the Fourth Lateran Council's directives, therefore, the less creative preacher working the pulpit *ad populum* had available a considerable and diverse store of moral anecdote upon which he could draw for pointed and engaging illustration of his homily proper. Notes taken at the sermons of master preachers passed from one cleric to another, fragmentary sermon collections containing exempla were copied and recopied, manuscripts were circulated that included illustrative narrative among other religious material. One refinement was necessary, however, before this potentially rich treasure of sermon stories could be conveniently utilized: the exempla had to be logically organized so that individual anecdotes were linked to corresponding religious topics. To meet this need, a new generation of ecclesiastical writers turned to the compilation of homiletic narrative under alphabetically arranged, cross-referenced rubrics pertaining to the penitential process and other standard subjects of pastoral care.

With fresh cadres of knowledgeable homilists provided primarily by the preaching orders, the composition of manuals on the art of pulpit discourse and the compilation of anthologies of exempla sensibly arranged for the specific use of the working preacher were not long in arriving. One of the best known of these exempla anthologies was the *Liber de septem donis* (Book of the seven gifts) of the Dominican preacher and inquisitor Etienne de Bourbon (d. 1261). This volume of basic religious instruction contained not only conventional patristic anecdotes but also more interesting contemporary tales, many supposedly heard at first hand. Piggybacking on Etienne's tract was the *Liber de dono timoris* (Book of the gift of fear) of Humbert de Romans, the fifth master general of the Dominican Order (d. 1277), whose compendium drew about four-fifths of its exempla from its predecessor and was prefaced, as was the earlier work, with suggestions for preaching to the masses and the appropriate employment of pulpit exempla.[7]

In the Dominican generation following Etienne and Humbert, Arnold of Liège, a master of theology at Paris, produced another volume similar to these, the *Alphabetum narrationum*. Arnold's 805 exempla, ranging from hagiographical and patristic anecdotes to contemporary *exempla terrible* (grisly cautionary anecdotes featuring details of the punishments accorded sinners), fables, and legends, almost all derived from standard written sources, were arranged under alphabetized topics from *Abbas* to *Zelotipa*, with the final narrative under each rubric followed by a cross-reference to other tales on the same subject listed under different headings. This efficient arrangement, whose use Arnold described in his prologue with the hope that it would prove convenient for preachers on a variety of occasions, undoubtedly contributed to the *Alphabetum narrationum*'s immense popularity over the next century and a half.[8] The work is cited both in later exempla handbooks and in actual sermons throughout England and Europe, and uniquely among such encyclopedia, the entire compendium was translated into English in the middle of the fifteenth century as *An Alphabet of Tales*.

From the mid-thirteenth century on, the same enthusiasm for the moral and didactic function of art that found expression in the stained glass, frescoed walls, and carved portals of the medieval church was embodied in homiletic narrative. The sermon story, at once edificatory and entertaining, carefully crafted for its purposes by highly regarded churchmen, was regarded as a legitimate means of making profound and complex theological doctrines more accessible to the untutored. Illustrative narrative served almost as a catechism in story, revealing the medieval Christian conception of the universe and the individual's role in it. Pulpit tales provided a stock of images and events that linked personal morality, religious dogma and social mores, and anchored the medieval masses in their culture by binding them together in a similar world view. The widespread dissemination of a common fund of homiletic exempla over many generations helped to perpetuate a perceptual and psychological mindset that became deeply ingrained in the popular imagination.

Exempla as a Genre: Form and Function

A rationale and analogy for the use of pulpit narrative in preaching to *"omne genus hominum"* (all manner of men), to the *"simplices"* (untutored) as opposed to the men of *"alte sapiencie"* (high learning), was provided by Christ's use of parables to express great truths to the folk of his own time. By the dramatic telling of a cautionary tale, those who slept during the sermon proper could be awakened, and those who were diverted from the sometimes dry and dull homiletic text by gossiping or doing business could be brought back to the spiritual matters at hand by the announcement of an illustrative story to come. Jacques de Vitry compared the use of exempla in the sermon to the blowing of the trumpets that alerted the Hebrew people to move out of Egypt and begin their Exodus. "Believe my experience," de Vitry wrote, "I preached a sermon one day and saw the multitude of people bored and sleeping. One little word and immediately they woke and paid attention to me. Thanks to the exemplum."[9] Robert Mannyng of Brunne, an English preacher whose sermon tract *Handlyng synne* was half filled with illustrative narrative, also justified the use of exempla by referring to the "vulgar people's" love of tales.[10]

While the entertainment value of the homiletic narrative was by no means despised, and even bawdy tales found a place in some preachers' repertoires, certain limits were articulated regarding exempla use.

Tales should not be offensive, asserted Robert Mannyng, and he, for one, would not speak of "pryuytees" (intimate acts). Gross, obscene, and explicit sexual or scatological references were to be avoided, especially descriptions of sexual activity that might awaken sin in the listeners that they would not have thought of themselves. One preaching manual cites a narrative of Gregory the Great about father-daughter incest as one that should not be preached *ad populum* lest it plant a hitherto unthought of sin into the minds of its listeners; another homiletic tract, the thirteenth-century Franciscan *Liber exemplorum* (Book of examples), states that while a certain dialogue between Alexander the Great and Denes the Philosopher denotes man as a "vessel of excrement," the preacher utilizing this exemplum should substitute the description of man as a "small [insignificant] thing," thereby capturing the meaning of the original without its rude language.[11]

Other instances of the necessity for tact are discussed as well. The *Liber exemplorum*, for instance, dictated prudence in depicting religious figures. It admonished the homilist to avoid negative characterizations such as the English ecclesiastic Bede's reference to a vicious-living monk: since a "monk" is a "man," the *Liber* suggests, a substitution of terms can be made without deceit.[12] The *Liber* further advises preachers to avoid the naming of recognizable political figures in their exempla; for homiletic purposes it is sufficient to describe the situation and the character in general terms.

While in the earlier centuries of Christianity, the exemplum had the nearly uniform structure of a battle between good and evil in which the chief opponents, a saint and the devil, appeared to be playing symbolic as much as literal roles, by the the thirteenth century an evolution in the sermon story had taken place. The exemplum's didactic purpose impelled every aspect of it in the direction of concreteness. Narrative action became particularistic and anecdotal, limning recognizable instances of sinful conduct and scenarios of vice. Exempla delineated tavern sins such as gambling and drunkenness through dramatic conflict and dialogue; warnings against lust and avarice were enhanced by tales of adultery and usury; preachers fulminated against vanity by describing exaggerated dress trains or a cleric's compact with the devil for arcane knowledge. In the exemplum the spiritual weight of a sin became a   physical burden: a sack of sand bowing down a corrupt abbot's back or a burning cloak enveloping an ambitious scholar. Vividly depicted physical punishments tortured the damned in hell: limbs were torn off or draughts of liquid fire were ingested until the flames poured out of the ears. No longer mere symbols of good and evil, exempla characters became distinctive human beings functioning in clearly recognizable social contexts.[13]

Yet, as has been noted, the elaboration of the exemplum was not introduced for its own sake. The pedagogic nature of the sermon story was clearly marked, was indeed a defining characteristic of the genre. The exemplum interpreted for the masses an ideological system which viewed human beings as feeble creatures continually beset by devil-inspired temptations, incapable of choosing or even desiring their true happiness—eternal life in heaven—without the constant instruction of the church. The realistic details of the sermon story were part of the didactic technique that illustrated for its listeners why and how to carry out the precepts crucial to the irrevocable disposition of their souls: whether to salvation with God, Christ, the angels, and the saints, or to the eternal torments of damnation in hell with Satan and his devils, unchaste women, Jews, and other sinners.

The *exemplum terrible* in particular mirrored the genre's purpose as more than an illustrative appendage supporting an abstract theological lesson. Its structure was in itself a rhetorical argument that impelled the listener to confession as the first step towards penitential reconciliation with God. The central portion of the *exemplum terrible* was the story, usually an anecdote relating a simple, purportedly true occurrence. The usual elements were the devil's temptation of the sinner in specific situational terms, the sinner's acceptance of or resistance to that temptation by specific actions, and the evaluation of his or her behavior as meriting reward or retribution. Thus, in a sense, the narrative exemplum recapitulated the penitential process itself.

The straightforward story line of the homiletic exemplum conveyed the singlemindedness of the homilist's aim. As a culminating exhortation to convert the listener to the specific conduct articulated in the sermon proper, the exemplum was required to have a single, unequivocal meaning. Ambiguity in character or situation that permitted multiple interpretations would have clouded the eschatological issue at hand and diminished the drama of the tale. The exemplum was intended to be not a multilayered, densely populated social narrative but rather a

focused, linear unrolling of action shaped to illuminate a specific theological precept. Its scheme opposed good and evil in simple terms:
the Virgin aided sinners to defeat the devil; lustful women were
severely punished unless they underwent sincere contrition and confession; Jews assaulting the Host were struck mute or blind until they
acknowledged Christ's grace and miraculous powers. While a sermon
audience was composed of many disparate social elements, all were
expected to resonate equally to the shorthand of received notions presented in the exemplum. The relative brevity of the didactic narrative
assisted this objective, for greater length or development might have
opened the way for misunderstanding, thus vitiating the narration's
impact. Yet despite its brevity, the exemplum had to appear as a complete rhetorical object; its structure had to convey a sense of closure
leading logically to its moral. It is this structure, rather than length,
which is an important criterion of the genre.

For the medieval sermon audience, the fusion of religious ideology
and human experience represented in the sermon exemplum was
given added weight by the introduction of a voice of authority.
References to respectable authorities—Humbert de Romans states that
bishops and cardinals, for example, are witnesses whose tales would
be worth repeating—gave an exemplum credibility, an aspect not to be
slighted, since many sermon stories involved supernatural occurrences or legends of the past whose veracity might be open to question.[14] Whether extended and localized like the citations of Caesar of
Heisterbach or attenuated to *pro forma* phrases such as "I read,"
whether incomplete, garbled, or erroneous, the citation provided a
meaningful perspective for the exemplum's events: here was an
engaged observer so struck by the spiritual significance of what he
heard or saw that he felt compelled to communicate it to others as a
warning. Rhetorically, too, like "Once upon a time" or "A funny thing
happened to me on my way here" in other narrative genres, the citation functioned to prepare its listeners psychologically for entrance
into another world of reality. Although John Bromyard, a prominent
fourteenth-century English homilist, advised preachers to tell their
audiences only of "notable and believable things" and to avoid the
"incredible" in their exempla, in fact it was a suspect supernatural
event upon which the sermon story turned.[15] The citation, therefore,
provided a link between two realities and assisted the preacher in

deflecting or rebutting skepticism, such as that exhibited by the peasant who interrupted a homilist's description of hell by calling out that the preacher had never been there.[16] The trenchancy of a tale was strengthened by a belief in its "truth," and that "truthfulness" was enhanced by the constant repetition of its motifs and notions under the authority of some respected figure. Whether the "truth" of the exemplum was factual was not at issue. For the medieval preacher and his audience, "that which [was] transmitted by a tradition . . . constant and multiple [was] assimilated under the name of history."[17]

From a comparison of exempla in their anthologized form with their analogues set in actual sermons delivered to live audiences, it is clear that the medieval preacher, having put his audience on notice that an illustrative narrative was in the offing, brought an active storytelling sense to his source material.[18] By his deliberate choice of diction and detail and the introduction of dialogue, the preacher *ad populum* made his tales more dramatic, more colorful, and more appropriate to lay-folk than were his originals. Syntactic structures in the exemplum were simpler than in the sermon proper; alliterative and rhythmical collocations were frequently employed; and verb, noun, and adjective doublets were used to impart emphasis and memorableness to certain pieces of information. Even versification was introduced. A colloquial lexicon which included a rich occupational vocabulary, the imaginative use of homely metaphor, and the employment of proverbs and other folk phraseology marked the vernacular pulpit story in contrast to its written Latin sources.

As oral literature, the exemplum required a redundancy and belaboring of points that was often supplied by the preacher's conclusion to the narrative. An exemplum's "truth," its moral or lesson, was usually generalized on one or more levels. The preacher might end his narrative with a straightforward commentary on the behavior of the *dramatis personae*, whether virtuous or sinful, as a reinforcement of the doctrine of the sermon itself, or he might extract from the narrative a rule of action which more or less explicitly advised the listener how to behave in the future. On an allegorical level the homilist might spin out a symbolic interpretation of his narrative, keying each discrete element to some aspect of Christian teaching. This Christian application would be particularly important if the narrative base were a secular romance or non-Christian legend, as is evident in the *Disciplina clericalis* and the

Gesta romanorum. For the medieval preacher, the urgency of his message warranted the exploitation of the same homiletic ground in several ways. His exemplum was not a perfunctory adjunct to his sermon but a vital part of his instruction, inferior in grandeur, perhaps, but not in purpose or impact, to those visual media of painting, carving, or stained glass that adorned the church in which the homily was being delivered.

The Medieval Mentality and Its Notions of Otherness

Despite the efforts of the medieval church to exert its hegemony over every sphere of human experience, such totalization was never possible.[19] The church hierarchy itself did not think with a single mind or speak with a single voice on the issues of the day, nor could it defend itself against the energy of heresy, clerical laxity, or the lethargy of the laity with equal success everywhere. Spiritual doubt assailed both the untutored and the highest representatives of the church, and skepticism existed even among the untutored. The sacramental status of matrimony was often breached in practice: marriage without benefit of clergy, irregular unions, adultery, and priestly concubinage were apparently common enough to fuel homiletic ire throughout the Middle Ages. Nor, if we take as evidence the many ecclesiastical documents attempting to regulate Jewish-Christian relationships and the implicit evidence of the exempla themselves, was the church wholly successful in segregating members of the two communities.

Yet through the revitalization of preaching, the church was largely successful in its efforts to bring all segments of society into closer conformity with desired social and religious practices. Like the sorcerer who drew a magic circle around those enchanted, from which outsiders were excluded, the preacher attempted to articulate a clear, simple, and achievable set of core beliefs and behaviors that would mark off the Christian, with his hope of life eternal, from the condemned Other.[20] The rebellion of Satan and his devils, which had thrust them into a liminal state, forever rejected by God and shut off from their former angelic bliss, operated as a referent for otherness in the human society addressed by the homilist. As the original and archtypical Other, the devil was forever and irretrievably alien to the community of Christ, but the sinners whom the devil instigated could, through sincere contrition, confession, and penance, be repeatedly salvaged.

While the ecclesiastic authority could never entirely stifle the voices of dissent or disbelief, and figures from the margin were continuously, to a greater or lesser degree, disrupting the hegemony of orthodox ideology, there was, nevertheless, no alternative guide to conduct or system of information that could successfully compete with that of the church. Its dogma became received notions through popular preaching; its rituals and feast days and the ubiquitous didacticism of its plastic arts dominated the quotidian life of prince and peasant alike. One's interpretation of the world and one's effort to make some sense of emotional turmoil, disease, misfortune, and evil derived almost entirely from the instruction of the church. While Christianity may have been superimposed on a non-Christian folk strata, which still ran deep in certain areas, whatever social dynamics had been derived from pagan or folk belief were, by the Middle Ages, either transmogrified into acceptable Christian forms or became occasions of sin and the subject of constant homiletic fulmination. Certainly through fear, as the preponderance of sermon narrative suggests, as much as by logical argument or the presentation of exemplars of virtue, the medieval church compelled all stations of society, if not all individuals, to acceptance of its central tenets.

The axis of medieval religious thought by which the homiletic exemplum was informed was the paradoxical notion that a just God created a world manifestly evil. The resolution of that paradox lay in God's offering to human beings the free will to choose between virtue and vice, thereby either ensuring the salvation of their immortal soul in heaven or consigning it to eternal damnation in hell. Once having accepted eternal salvation as the only rational purpose of existence, it followed then that the avoidance of sin (that is, specific human transgressions against divine law) and the practice of spiritual cleansing by confession, contrition, and repentance if one had fallen into sin became the only rational behaviors to pursue.

Devolving from this view was the constant, almost obsessional concern of medieval homiletics and their exempla with the literal battle of good against evil.[21] No compromise was possible between these two forces, understood actually, not merely symbolically, as the heavenly host and the horde of Satan and his devils. By this conflict, under the ever present threat of the Last Judgment, in which all of an individual's acts would be weighed, medieval humankind was held in a continual spiritual tension characterized by pairs of opposites: body and soul, heaven and hell, life and death, angels and devils, men and women, Christians and nonbelievers. Within each of these seemingly polarized categories, however, there was a contiguousness as well as a separation; perhaps they might be viewed as obverse sides rather than opposites of each other. Devils both possessed angelic power and were wicked beyond redemption; women might be either dangerous temptresses or imitations of the Virgin Mary; Jews might be both forerunners of Christianity and its archenemy. But the ultimate paradox which resolved all others was that evil was necessary so that man might choose good and be found worthy of salvation on the day of Judgment.

Humanity's free will was the key to the seemingly contradictory core of Christian theology. Through the freely chosen desire to know good and act in accordance with it, human beings could accrue the points that would tilt the scales of the Last Judgment in their favor and gain them access to the gates of heaven. Sin and evil were encompassed within God's scheme as the necessary instruments by which people were tested and ultimately earned or lost salvation.

In the uncompromising hierarchal universe construed by the medieval mentality, where all phenomena were assigned fixed places in a grand chain of being, those things not holding to their designated places or partaking of two realms simultaneously were monsters, ominous departures from the accepted structure and purpose of their kind with a potential for mischief-making that could threaten an individual's mortal soul. Yet these same alien forces were not without their appointed roles in the salvatory scheme. Devils, women, and Jews embodied an otherness that threatened one's redemption and necessitated one's constant vigilance and opposition, but in the very threat they posed they were an instrument of God's will, for it was by struggle against the evil they generated that Christians proved their steadfastness to their faith.

The alterity which characterized devils, women, and Jews in the medieval mind was the inescapable result of the origin and inherent nature of these figures as viewed by the medieval eye.[22] Satan and his devils, formerly angelic in being and power, had been thrust out of heaven into hell for the sin of pride; their brilliance literally and metaphorically extinguished, they now kept to the the shades or dark places on the margin of human existence; iniquitous themselves and instigators of sin in human beings, they garnered souls only through recourse to stealth, disguise, and dissimulation.

Women too, like devils both potent and inferior, embodied the paradoxical oppositions central to the medieval imagination. Born in paradise from the body of the male, and responsible thereafter for giving life to humankind, it was, nevertheless, the female sex, inheriting its disobedience and seductiveness from Eve, that lost us our blissful state and brought work, misery, and death to the human race. While the female saints, and preeminently the Virgin Mary, were present in the exempla as the church's model of the feminine ideal, the genre in the main depicts the female sex as vain and corrupt, vulnerable to damnation by their nature and a threat to the salvation of the male. The Jew, similarly, was an alien figure in the landscape of salvation. Although some ancient Hebrews might be acknowledged in theology and the popular religious arts as prophets and the progenitors of Christ, the post-Christian Jew, by his rejection of Christ's invitation to grace and the message of the Gospels, and by his stubborn adherence to the literalism of the "Old Law," inevitably became the third point on the nexus of alterity.

Linked by pride, disobedience, and carnality, devils, women, and Jews found a preeminent place as figures of both fear and scorn in the medieval exemplum. Like a catechism, over a long period of time, pulpit exempla simplified and reiterated a very narrow range of images of women and Jews, demonizing them through continual association, both explicit and implicit, with Satan and his minions. In sermon story, Christian doctrine mingled with popular piety to imprint these notions on the medieval mind.

The medieval triangulation of devils, women, and Jews germinated in the origins of Christianity itself, in the history of its ideological development and in various social, political, and economic circumstances that took shape in that period we call "the Middle Ages." Specific aspects of these connections will be explored in the introductory sections to the exempla. However, one phenomenon underlying this triangulation must be examined, albeit briefly, at this juncture: the mechanism of projection. Through this unconscious psychological process, the individual, having been taught that certain feelings or desires are unworthy, becomes conflicted over them, and to escape the pain this conflict engenders, he or she denies such feelings by detaching them from the self and projecting them on to an external Other.[23] It is neither fanciful nor frivolous to accord this phenomenon centrality in the medieval perception of devils, women, and Jews. Indeed, as one of the most insightful of modern scholars on the subject of otherness has asserted, it may be that the recognition of the unconscious, which leads us to discover the Other in ourselves, is the dividing point between the medieval and modern mentality.[24]

Indisputably, the medieval exemplum, in throwing a harsh spotlight on human transgressions in order to promote a saluatory course of conduct, illuminates a medieval conception of wickedness that owes much to this psychic process. Medieval folk, having been taught that particular impulses of the flesh were "bad," unconsciously repressed them by attributing them to the external Other, embodied, through the instruction of the church, as the devil. With the image of woman drawn from the Hebrew Bible's story of Eve's surrender to the serpent's/devil's temptation in the Garden of Eden and her persuasion of Adam to join her in sin, and through the association of the Jews with the death of Christ and their rejection of Christ's redemptive grace, both women and Jews emerged in the Middle Ages as concomitant objects of hostility linked to the devil. The devil, the woman, and the Jew became an unholy trio, a dark reflection of unresolved doubt and anxiety projected as obstacles to salvation that were legitimate targets of enmity.

On the heels of projection inevitably followed rationalization and justification for excluding, belittling, harming, or exterminating these Others. Within the ambit of an omnipresent and nearly omnipotent church, clerical influence moved these Others to the margin, determining for women and Jews, without their consent, how they could lead their lives. They were perceived not as people living by legitimate social rules and values imposed by their gender or religion, but as imperfect versions of dominant Christian masculinity. In the medieval mind, the blame for the spiritual marginalization of Jews and women lay within these sinners themselves. They were freely able, should they have desired, to move into the orbit of God's grace by the performance of simple, concrete acts of assent. If they persisted in remaining aloof from spiritual enlightenment and right action, as manifested on earth by the doctrines and directives of the church, then by their perverse and sinful conduct they would remain, like the devils who voluntarily cast themselves out of heaven, liminal creatures properly subjected to the opprobrium and opposition of those who made up the center.

Eluding, and thereby disturbing the fixed classifications that medieval Christian doctrine assigned to all elements in nature and society, demons, women, and Jews, like their counterparts in tribal societies, were frequently associated with wilderness, invisibility, darkness, and death. They partook of two natures: although originally infused with God's goodness they stubbornly rejected it, thereby removing the locus of their relationship to the Christian community from the center of authority to the margin. Christian hermeneutics concretized in homiletic narrative made it abundantly clear that devils, women, and Jews, in their "natural" mode as tempters, deceivers, and corrupters, had closed themselves out from the desirable possibilities of Christian life. In its content and imagery, the medieval exemplum reflected and reinforced these fundamental beliefs in which medieval European Christendom was grounded.

Like a popular medium in any age—Hollywood of the 1930s and 1940s and television in our own day immediately come to mind—the homiletic exemplum was an artifact that both mirrored and shaped the cultural notions of its audience. It was a witness to the assumptions and prejudices, the cognition and unconscious projections of its society. On a conscious level, as an instrument of salvation, the pious narrative was a manifestation of its society's continual striving to give concrete shape and iconographic form to the abstract notions central to the Christian scheme of salvation. The exemplum proved to be remarkably well suited to this ideologic purpose. It may be said of the exemplum that it was both "fact," that is, an event in the actual world, and metaphor, or a figure of a spiritual concept, with one aspect inextricable from the other. The exemplum, therefore, had power not only as a constructed artifact illustrating both desirable and undesirable behavior but also as a spiritual act in and of itself, a moral lesson by its very nature, its context and the part it played, not figuratively but actually, in the conversion of the listener to Christ. Because the occurrences described in the exemplum were believed to be "history," that is, "facts" that really happened, they were believed to have future applicability and thus were appropriate for repetition and reflection, since the future so often repeats the past. The exemplum, when successful, was a step in the penitential process. What it conveyed, therefore, about the interconnectedness of devils, women, and Jews, and their pervasive role in iniquity and unrighteousness, was accepted with the same trust and became as deeply ingrained as the sacramental principles enjoined by the homily itself.

2

Devils in Medieval Sermon Stories

Caesar of Heisterbach tells us that a fiend
who was in possession of a man was
asked by someone, "Tell me, devil, what
would you give to come again into that
bliss which you lost, if it were possible to
regain that joy?" The fiend answered,
"Were it in my power to choose, I would
rather go to hell with a soul I had
deceived than return to heaven." Those
who heard him were astonished at this,
so he explained to them, "My malice is so
great, and I am so stubborn and froward,
that I cannot wish for anything that
might be good or profitable to me."

Jacob's Well

Illustration from The Hours of Catherine of Cleves, ca. 1440, depicting a Guardian Angel and a Demon struggling for possession of a corpse's "Book of Deeds," a common motif of *exempla terrible*. (Courtesy The Pierpont Morgan Library, New York. M.917, p.206)

"The devil made me do it," tittered Flip Wilson's mischievous Geraldine on the television screens of America in the late 1960s, and from the secular American viewer it always drew a laugh. In medieval Christendom, however, while the claim would have been as readily asserted, mirth would have been the last response. Through centuries of famine, armed conflicts, and sudden, violent, and unexplained death, all aspects of socioreligious practice and belief, in every estate from the laboring and agricultural masses to the most erudite theologicans, were rooted in an acceptance of a devil as the generator of disorder and maleficence.[1] Medieval Christians were born, lived, and breathed their last in the grip of the devil. During Europe's Middle Ages, few alternative systems of either knowledge or succor existed outside the church, whose tenets permitted no doubt about the reality of the devil. What homiletic tracts and their exempla conveyed about the devil was received literally; Satan and his minions were actual beings belonging to an invisible nether world, but capable of interacting with people in their daily lives in the visible world just as the Evangelists had described in the Gospels. Apparitions of the devil during one's waking hours or in dreams were not fantasies but real occurrences whose consequences would be discernible in the awakened state.[2] The appropriately violent deaths that devils inflicted on sinners and the torturous pains of hell reported by those who were suffering there for their transgressions were taken as serious warnings by the living to amend their behavior.

In the mentality of the Middle Ages, distinctions between religious and social values, as we understand them today, had no application; the value systems of the two realms were blended, with sin and social disruption intimately connected. Incest, gambling, or vanity, for example, as well as religious doubt or disbelief, not only transgressed God's laws, but rent the social fabric. The devil's hand in sin, therefore, was directed against God, man, and the state. Not to believe that potential or actual harm could be perpetrated by Satan and his devils was both religiously unorthodox and socially disjunctive, for if social cohesion was menaced by demonic instigation of sin, it was also maintained by the pervasive fear of the devil that was preached from every pulpit.

The devil had not only his public uses but his private psychological uses as well. Through the mechanism of projection, the intolerable strains put upon the individual—in whom forbidden libidinous impulses coexisted with the dictates of God's laws—were eased, for by attributing one's unworthy desires to the devil, one could absolve oneself from the blame attached to such feelings. In addition, the belief in devils permitted the ordinary person to comprehend the existence of evil in a world created by a good and just God, who held authority over every creature. For if God created the devil, as was believed, then there must be some beneficent divine purpose in the devil-instigated misery to which most medieval folk were prey. This message was embedded in popular homiletics and the sermon story. The personal temptations by which the devil assaulted one were a testing ground for the salvation of one's immortal soul. To believe in the devil was to believe in the possibility of victorious struggle against him and the ultimate reward of a seat in heaven. To disbelieve in or to mock the devil was to thwart God's will and plan. By assenting to such notions, a person's desires and rage were replaced by anxiety and terror, which were encouraged by the homilist on behalf of the individual's soul. Interposed as a being between God and the individual onto which every negative impulse, moment of disbelief, and misfortune in life could be projected, the liminal figure of the devil was inestimable in its service to both the religious and social establishments.

A host of archaic folkloric beliefs and remnants of pagan religion lay behind the figure of the devil inherited by the medieval world. St. Augustine, whose writings were probably the most influential in the medieval conceptualization of the devil, suggests that while the pagans of Greece and Rome did differentiate between gods, who were good and worthy of sacrifice, and evil, air-dwelling demons who could feel the same emotions as men, but who shared immortality with the gods, all the supernatural beings of pagan belief and the powers that emanated from their shrines and statues were demonic and pernicious.[3] Thus, several of the characteristics of the medieval devil, most notably his cloven hoofs, horns, tail, and hirsuteness, probably owe their existence to the Greek god Pan and the satyrs of Greek myth.[4]

The ancient Gaulish and Germanic societies predating Christianity in Europe also held beliefs about the supernatural world that became conflated with popular Christian piety. Occupying a hidden realm with fairies and nature spirits were varieties of demons to whom were attributed such behavior against communal solidarity as disloyalty or non-payment of debts. Similarly, in agricultural pre-Christian eastern Europe, there existed the belief in domestic spirits or imps, mischievous beings similar to some described in homiletic narrative, who could punish those who angered them. In addition, many pagan cultures believed in punitive and potentially harmful spirits of the forest, waters, and fields who were held responsible for kidnappings and drownings. Like the devil in Christian belief, these mean spirits were shapeshifters who could assume any animal or human guise to accomplish their destructive aims. Notable among them were the Rusalki, beautiful female numens, comparable to sirens and reminiscent of the demonic temptresses of the patristic and medieval exempla, who led men to their doom.[5] With the introduction of Christianity, these malignant pagan spirits were not eradicated but incorporated into Christianity and its characterization of the devil.[6] Medieval *exempla terrible*, narratives intended to terrify the listener with depictions of devils, revenants, visits to hell, and mysterious happenings in connection with the dead, undoubtedly rest on a substratum of pagan and animistic culture.

This is not the place for a detailed history of pre-Christian and non-Christian devil and demon figures; here, we need only point out briefly that influences of Babylonian, Chaldean, and Persian religion, especially the latter in the form of Zoroastrian doctrine, which articulated a dualistic conception of the world as a struggle between the powers of light and the powers of darkness, are apparent in the figure of our medieval Christian devil. Yet despite the tangle of folklore and pagan and Middle Eastern religion that obscures the origin of the devil of medieval Christendom, this malevolent figure preserved a relatively constant aspect across the Middle Ages. Basically, he owed his conception as the embodiment of evil to the Christian interpretation of scriptural allusions. Two of the devil's defining characteristics, which would be fleshed out by numerous homiletic anecdotes, are illuminated by etymology, which offers the Greek *diabolos*, "slanderer" (literally, "one who throws something across a path") as the precursor of "devil," and the Hebrew "Shatan," or "adversary," as the original form of "Satan."[7] The Greek word for lesser evil spirits, *daimonion*, "demon," was sometimes utilized in the medieval exemplum to distinguish the inferior demonic figures from the chief devil, he whom the Christian Scriptures called Satan or Lucifer, a creature uglier and more frightening than other devils, who is sometimes accorded an elevated position

as judge over his minions or as the prince of hell presiding with authority over the disposition of the damned souls.[8] The exempla, however,
rarely call the chief devil either Satan or Lucifer, and his former angelic stature is only infrequently mentioned. The most common homiletic
appellation in English is "fiend," derived from the Anglo Saxon *feond*
or "enemy" and related to the Gothic and Anglo-Saxon verbs for
"hate" and "blame." This term acquired general meaning, which is evidenced in the exemplum, as an implacable and malicious foe.

Only a seed of the conception of the devil of the medieval exemplum
exists in Jewish religious books. While the Hebrew Scriptures do refer
to Satan—most importantly in the Book of Job (1:6, 12; 2:1), where he is
named as the accuser who is admitted into the presence of God and the
heavenly host for the purpose of testing men—they do not recount a
fall of the devils from heaven. Nor does the ancient Hebrew concept of
'Sheol' as the abode of the dead involve the notion of the devil's punishment of miscreant souls as later developed in Christian eschatology.

Notions about the devil as the supreme evil spirit and tempter of
mankind emerge in Christianity primarily through fragmentary references in the Christian Scriptures.[9] The lengthiest of these is in
Revelation (12:3–17), where it is told that a pregnant woman, having
given birth to a boy child destined to "rule all nations with a rod of
iron" was confronted by "a great red dragon" who cast the mother and
child down to earth. Of this dragon, foiled in his attempt to devour the
child, who ascended to heaven, the following narrative is recited:
"And there was war in heaven; Michael and his angels fought against
the dragon; and the dragon fought and his angels, and prevailed not;
neither was their place found any more in heaven. And the great dragon was cast out, that old serpent, called the Devil, and Satan, which
deceiveth the whole world; he was cast out into the earth, and his
angels were cast out with him . . . the accuser of our brethren is cast
down, which accused them before our God day and night . . . Woe to
the inhabitants of the earth and of the sea! For the devil is come down
unto you, having great wrath, because he knoweth that he hath but a
short time." The narrative continues by relating that the dragon, now
cast down to earth, "was wroth with the woman, and went to make
war with the remnant of her seed, which keep the commandments of
God, and have the testimony of Jesus Christ" (12:7–10, 12, 17).

Here, then, we have some of the basic attributes that would continue to be ascribed to the devil throughout the Middle Ages: his origin
as a fallen angel (although here it is a fall to earth, not yet that subter-
ranean place that would become elaborated in the medieval exemplum as a hell of eternal, cunningly contrived tortures); his physical
shape as a serpent/dragon; his role as the accuser of the innocent; the
war between him and his minions against the archangel Michael and
his angelic troupe; and his perpetual wrath and battle against the witnesses of Christ, descendants of the woman in the wilderness.

According to St. Augustine, whose exegesis of Christian Scriptures
provided the baseline for medieval thought, sin began with the devil,
"the secret instigator and prompter of those who sin," and it was the
devils who "strive by their example to lend, as it were, a divine authority to crime."[10] Like all else created by God, the nature of the devil was
not evil, but was, rather, "made evil by being perverted."[11] By the perversion of his nature the devil sought to overturn God's original
design of human harmony on earth and to obstruct God's plan for the
eternal salvation of the human soul after death.

This diabolical perversity was seen as the inevitable outcome of the
devils' rebellion against heaven and their descent from the light to the
nether regions, where the ambiguity of their status disposed them to
employ the remnants of their angelic powers in a vengeful and vin-
dictive ensnaring of men away from God. They were, asserts
Augustine, "spirits most eager to inflict harm, utterly alien from righteousness."[12] Unlike the angels, who held their knowledge and power
over the temporal world less than their love of God, the devils used
their arcane knowledge and the traces of their angelic abilities to
undermine God's mercy, which extended the potentiality of eternal
bliss to every sinner.[13] Having voluntarily exchanged their seats in
heaven for the limen of the nether world, yet, according to some exempla, envying the eternal joy they had relinquished, the devil and his
minions were so perverse as to prefer to act as the "assassins of man"
even though this behavior precluded their return to heaven.[14]

The demons operated in a perpetual fury against the saints of God's
church in particular, and nothing pleased them more than to corrupt
the soul of a man who had dedicated himself to the service of God. In
the pious tales of the early desert saints there are a plethora of anec-

dotes, later utilized as exempla in the medieval popular sermon, which narrate the assaults of devils in various forms upon the spirit, or in more modern terms the psyche, of the monks or hermits in their lonely cells. Today, we would ascribe the visions and dreams reported by these early Christians to hallucinations induced by the extreme hunger, thirst, and sexual abstinence of their ascetic regimens, for such illusions of the imagination typically arise when a person is in a state of low physical resistance, but the medieval world accepted these anecdotes as literal in every regard: the monk did indeed *see* the bread, meat, or beverage proffered by the devil, and that devil was no phantom but a material figure carrying a cup or a bottle or seductively disguised as a beautiful woman. Those saintly men who became too proud of their asceticism were punished by a fall into temptation until humility was added to their repertoire of virtues, a theme that informs the tale "St. Macarius Defeats the Devil as Physician" (D2). Here, the highly acclaimed purity of one Theocrite is shown as vulnerable to the devil's offerings, but in this case the devil's boasting backfired when Macarius used this information to seek out the sinner and reconvert him.

Following the patristic period, from the seventh to the thirteenth century, as the great monasteries replaced the desert cells of the isolated hermit, homiletic narrative showed the devil shifting his base of operations to these religious houses. To lust and gluttony were added the sins of pride and avarice, to which clerics were deemed most susceptible. Monastic rule apparently was no more impregnable to the temptations of the devil than eremetic isolation and asceticism had been. The exempla of the monastic sermons, composed primarily by spiritual masters to warn novices against vice, attest to the effort thought necessary to inculcate virtuous behavior into young men, often hardly more than adolescent boys, who, like the ordinary folk from whom they sprung, were filled with spiritual weaknesses. Lacking sleep, substantial food, and the familiar surroundings of their homes, such boys were highly susceptible to demonic hallucinations, nocturnal visitations from the dead, and visions of the tortures of hell. As in the days of the *Vita patrum*, such visions were not taken as a sign of mental illness but rather legitimated as a means by which persons in need of spiritual chastisement could establish contact with another world which escaped normal perception.

Exempla images of the devil, then, were compounded from a variety of sources: Christian scriptural references to Satan and his demonic legions as fallen angels; a hodgepodge of folk beliefs and pagan religious notions with which Christianity had collided, incorporating, modifying, and reinforcing these as it proselytized across Europe and the Near East; evangelical and patristic writings including the highly influential commentaries of St. Augustine, the anecdotes of the *Vitae patrum*, the biographies of such protomedieval saints as Benedict and the *exempla terrible* of Gregory the Great; and the homiletic writings of monastic novice masters and other ecclesiastics intended for popular consumption.

By a recombinant of motifs from many sources, the popular exemplum added its own vocabulary of demonic images to those of the plastic arts, working alongside the visual media to make recognizable and accessible what had been obscure and remote in erudite theological tomes. Eschewing explicit descriptions of the fiend, the popular sermon story for the most part preferred to delineate the devil's ubiquity in human life under a variety of guises or with symbolic accoutrements, and it portrayed his powers and machinations through anecdotes of his encounters with recognizable people in everyday situations. Using its own tools of familiar settings and characters, citations of "impeccable" authority, and terrifying supernatural experiences that were yet as thoroughly acceptable to the laity as they had been to the monks of the desert and the inhabitants of the monastery, the popular exemplum became a vehicle of the greatest importance in the formation of the medieval imagination regarding the devil.

In the illuminations of both religious and secular manuscripts, and in the church that rang with the preacher's declamations against the devil were frescoed walls and carved portals and pulpits that gave full play to the iconic elements of the devil—his hairy body, cloven or clawed feet, rudimentary tail, pointed ears, horns, and ribbed wings—as well as a myriad of even more grotesque representations.[15] These depictions, like the figure of the devil conveyed by the exempla, were individual and even idiosyncratic in their detail, but they embraced a general conception of the fiend that illustrated both his similarity to and difference from human beings. His face was a distortion of a human face, and his body, though multilimbed, with distended organs, fantastically colored, and with orifices spewing out or devouring damned souls, was recognizably human. It is interesting to note that, unlike exempla and most of the plastic arts, stained glass windows rarely played a role in spiritual instruction through terror; the association of the glass with light seems to have dictated that primarily positive lessons—depictions of biblical scenes, saints, and the heavenly kingdom—rather than negative, serve as their content. It was as if the various didactic media divided among themselves the elements crucial to the Christian scheme of salvation, each appropriating those aspects best suited to the materials.

The most significant symbolic cluster pertaining to the devil in both the plastic arts and the popular exemplum was the dichotomy between light and darkness, the former associated with the angels, the latter with Satan and the devils.[16] This dichotomy, originating in the scriptural tradition of devils as fallen angels and, thereby, the obverse of angelic nature, had been elaborated upon by St. Augustine and subsequently became firmly established in medieval theology and folk belief.[17] A connection between the extinguishing of angelic light in Satan's legions and spiritual obscurity—the dark stain or blot on a sinner's soul—became inevitable. The imagistic link between darkness and the devil was thereby inaugurated.

A dark complexion in medieval Christian imagery did not in and of itself necessarily have negative connotations.[18] In the preponderance, though not all, of the depictions of the Three Magi, one is a black man; and the mythic kingdom of the legendary priest and king, Prester John, was variously placed in Asia or Africa, presuming a dark skinned or black population. In general, however, the pious tales of the desert monks and the early theologians present dark skinned or "blue" men as imps or demons challenging the practitioners of Christian virtue.[19] A dark complexion became conflated with the darkness symbolic of the devil from biblical references and with paganism, and especially projected onto these dark skinned, nonbelieving Others was the hatefulness associated with the urges of the body that Christianity sought to suppress. We find, for example, in the earliest hagiography and Christian exempla, the devil as "Ethiope" putting burning coals instead of the Host into a communicant's hand, a demon depicted as an Ethiopian "blacker than soot," and little "blue men of Inde" disturbing Christian worship.[20] In the *Golden Legend's* Life of St. Gregory, John the Deacon reports a miracle in which the saint blackened an "adversary's mouth and face . . . until he looked like an Ethiopian" and set his outer garment aflame so that underneath "he was seen to be totally black. 'We have blackened him enough,' [St.] Peter said to Saint Gregory, who replied: 'We haven't blackened him. We showed that he really *is* black.' "[21] The gods of the "pagan" lands visited by early Christian proselytizers were transformed into demons, as John Mirk, the fifteenth-century homilist writing in English for a popular audience suggests in his *Festial* sermon for the Feast of St. Bartholomew, where, following the *Golden Legend*, he describes "the fiend" as a god of an Indian people thusly: "like a man of India, black altogether as pitch, with a sharp nose and a loathsome face, with a beard down to his feet, black as soot, with eye burning as doth iron in the fire, sparkling on each side and blowing out of his mouth flames of burning fire."[22]

Although in church painting the legions of the devil were colored in a broad range of hues from red through green, brown, and black (compare our current image of the devil as a red-skinned or red-clothed figure), in medieval homiletic narrative the devil, his accoutrements, and his companions were always black. The exempla linked blackness, sin, death, and damnation together. In Gregory's *Dialogues* the devil is described as a black boy; elsewhere he is a black man as in our tale of "The Skeptical Knight and the Devil" (D15).[23] Black animals such as crows, sheep, cats, and dogs, and particularly black horses, were closely associated with demons, as in the exemplum by Jacques de Vitry in which a demon on a black horse pursues a sinner to carry him off to hell.[24]

As sin darkened the purity of the soul, homiletic narrative shows persons or properties associated with sin turning black in consequence: a sinner's arm turned black, another sinner's body became black at the commission of his sin, a man signing a compact with the devil acquired a black spot on his hand that was erased only at confession, a damned usurer appeared after death to his wife in black robes, a monk of Oxford who unauthorizedly gave his shoes to his nephew was punished for this symbolic act of nepotism by having his feet turn black after death, Satan's book where sins are recorded was black.[25]

For medieval folk, the foulness of the devil's deeds was represented not only by his darkness, with its implication of events best hidden from the light of day, but by his repulsiveness as well. Called deformed, alleged to have no back, and reputed in various exempla to be so hideous in his real form that to view him was enough to cause sickness or even death, the devil was frequently depicted as a creature dissolving the boundaries of natural species, a monster, humanoid in appearance but grotesquely deviating from the shape of man, or an anomaly with features both human and animal or with the features of various animals in combination, a descendant of that "beast rising up out of the sea, having seven heads and ten horns . . . like a leopard, his feet . . . like the feet of a bear, and his mouth like the mouth of a lion" of whom Revelations (13:1–2) speaks.[26]

The most common transmogrifications of the devil in homiletic narrative were the toad, the serpent, and the dragon, creatures perceived as capable of transcending environmental boundaries and living in all the elements, in the dark reaches of the earth such as caves and forests or in the marges of water and land such as fens and swamps; as able to slither up trees or fly through the air; and as scaly skinned and beady eyed. The toad, already in folklore a shapechanger under whose repellent form might or might not lie that of a handsome prince, is in nature a creature who takes up a deceptively passive pose, a curious and repulsive parody of human patience, before satisfying his appetite. This squatting inhabitant of those places where the land and water meet, puffed out and waiting to snatch his dinner from the course of insects across his view, was a fit disguise for the devil, as in Caesar of Heisterbach's tale of the fraudulent tavernkeeper whose treasure was buried in the earth by a devil in the shape of a toad.[27]

The serpent, infamous from biblical stories as the instigator of original sin, was also readily conflated with the figure of the devil in exempla, although of the reptiles, it is the dragon who appears more frequently than the snake. The dragon as a form of the demon also enjoyed scriptural authority, and the exempla sometimes borrow from folklore his depiction as a guardian of ill-gotten treasure. Frequently in the sermon story we find this devil-demon poised at the deathbed of a sinner, ready to grasp the damned soul or in the act of devouring a transgressor, motifs aptly mirroring the psychological state of a sinner, whose gnawing conscience, symbolized by the powerful jaws and teeth of the dragon, reminds him that just as he gorged on sin and illicit pleasure, so will the dragon feast on him. While the exempla do not match the church frescoes in delineating the repulsive aspects of the devil in his reptilian forms, homiletic narrative sustained and reinforced the plastic arts by explicating through episode and anecdote the symbolic connection between the grotesque ugliness of the devil, the perversity of his nature, and the foulness of his acts. It is precisely in this concatenation of traits that the devil becomes fused in the popular exemplum with those other two figures of alterity, women and Jews.

The perverse nature of Satan and his demonic legions originates in their arrogant decision to abandon the light of God's love for a lower region, just as Adam and Eve would cause their expulsion from the Garden of Eden, distancing themselves from God's grace by their disobedience. The diabolical perversity that marked the devil was the inevitable outcome of the ambiguity of his chosen state. Degraded as bestial hordes retaining only sufficient of their former powers to remind them of their previous angelic state, fitly associated only with the marges and dark abysses of the earth, devils nevertheless share certain features with human beings as they do with angels. St. Augustine cities with approval the pagan characterization of devils as partaking of both human and supernatural aspects, explaining that while demons are not mortal, as human beings are (so that their period of earthly suffering may have an end) demons are like men in having souls capable of suffering—which will never end, since they are unworthy of God's pity.[28]

Devils, then, were quintessentially liminal creatures. Essentially of a "spirit" nature as are angels and possessing some, though diminished angelic powers, they could, at the same time, take material form, though being without flesh, and they were capable of feeling pain, both physical and psychic. Ambiguous, amorphous, outside any fixed category of being, the inhabitants of the demon world were able to maintain themselves and promote their ends in a world of men based on stable categories of sex, rank, and role only through disguise, fraud, and dissimulation. Whereas in the plastic arts of the Middle Ages the devil was shown in his naked being, intimidating the sinner by his terrifyingly ugly appearance and his poses of devouring and expelling that so perfectly captured the spiritual anxiety of the viewer, the exemplum exerted its cautionary influence by exposing the seductive and coercive powers of the fiend through narrative illustrations of his trickery.

Popular homiletic narrative reveals a devil ubiquitous in the every-day life of layman and cleric alike, a shapeshifter who pandered to the human appetites for food, drink, sex, gain, and status by presenting himself under a multiplicity of forms. Exempla portray male devils in human shape uniting with women or female devils with men; such unions supposedly produced a child of exceptional powers.[29] One of the most frequently used guises of the devil was that of a companion or traveller of the road, as in "The Devil Disguised as a Pilgrim" (D5).[30] Given the dangers, discomfort, and loneliness that rendered the medieval traveller vulnerable, the figure of a companion was under-standably welcome. The stability and familiarity of recognized and trusted categories in human social life are the basis of the human com-munity, but the devil took advantage of trust-inspiring contexts only to seduce mankind. He assailed the dignity of the human form by employing it only in a masquerade to trap the soul into sin, as in the exemplum where he acts as an advisor to a priest, counselling him to lighten a widow's penance for a sin, thereby tempting her to commit future sins more easily.[31] In other exempla, the devil becomes the ser-vant of a saintly man whom he wishes to tempt into sin, or a false con-fidant gleaning secrets from an individual that he later uses in mali-cious slander, or a seemingly innocent bystander who causes quarrels between people.

No role or rank was so elevated that the devil would not fraudu-lently assume it to thwart and undermine man's noblest intentions. Devils were able not only to imitate any human form and behavior perfectly, but, according to the the exempla, even successfully took on the guises of saints, angels, the Virgin Mary, and even Christ.[32] Such deceptions enabled the devils to instigate sin and retard confession and penance, creating spiritual havoc among well-intentioned indi-viduals.[33] A deluded sinner's trespass was not necessarily mitigated because his action was taken in error, although, depending on the cir-cumstances, some divine intervention might save him. Perhaps, in the nick of time, the devil would be unmasked and dispelled by the sign-ing of the cross or the saying of the Ave Maria, or God might reverse the sinner's damnation out of mercy, but frequently the exemplum has these betrayed souls as much damned as any other. In such cases some narratives may return the condemned soul to earth for the practical purpose of cautioning others about the need for constant vigilance against the fiend.

The modern reader wonders how a person could recognize the devil in his many guises and ward off his assaults. Was not an intolerable anxiety the continual state of medieval folk, unable as they were to distinguish spiritual friend from foe? Addressing this anxiety, homiletic narrative warned that a stance of constant alertness was the only way to defeat the devil's wiles. Since mankind is always in need of happiness, all situations that brought personal pleasure, joy, or the thrill of pride in success demanded scrutiny for the devil's hand. Following the hint in Revelation (12:9–15), the thrust of sermon story was that the devil was first and foremost a deceiver. It was given that the devil would veil his true ugliness and offer his temptations under a pleasant mask, operating on man's imagination by presenting attractive images and objects that would please human appetites and desires.

From the medieval Christian perspective, human nature was susceptible to the devil's wily temptations because of its innate corruption that began with original sin. The presence of the potential for sin was strong within every person, but sinful *action* could be curbed by man's free will to restrain himself and choose virtue over vice in specific situations. Thus, the commission of sin was the result of man's freely chosen complicity with the devil. By exposing himself to places and occasions of sin, man showed his willingness to enter the devil's realm and align himself with the forces of wickedness. "When man commits sin," stated St. Thomas Aquinas, the most influential theologian of the Middle Ages, "he . . . becomes a child of the devil, in so far as he imitates him who was the first to sin."[34] The storytelling novice-master Caesar of Heisterbach explicated the same notion in one of his homiletic narratives, drawing an analogy between the captive bear or lion who turns and worries on the end of a chain but cannot harm anyone as long as it is tied within a confined space and the devil, whose power is limited by the chain of divine constraint so that he can not force anyone to sin so long as that person does not approach him and thereby consent to evil.[35]

The existence of man's free will to choose sinful conduct was essential to the development of the exemplum, for this tenet compelled a person to acknowledge his or her guilt for committing a specific sinful act, and the feeling of guilt for a *particular* thought or action was the first necessary step in the remediation process of confession, contrition, and penance. Thus, the thrust of popular sermon story was not so much that man could expunge vice from his nature all at once and forever but that as each inclination to or occasion for sin presented itself, one could discipline oneself to resistance. Virtue, like vice, took practice and needed constant reminder and repetition to become a habit. Hence, as the exempla show, even seemingly minor lapses such as clerical slovenliness were an invitation to the devil, as in the exemplum where the devil gathers up words spoken carelessly in the Mass. Invoking the devil in irritation, as did the subject of "A Sinful Clerk's Cloak of Feathers" (D10), or using his name to curse objects or people, put one and one's possessions into the devil's power. Similarly, apparently innocuous pastimes such as dancing were to be avoided as occasions that attracted the devil's attention. Sins of the tavern such as drinking and gaming also made men vulnerable to more serious devil-instigated sins, as in the exemplum of the gambler who wanted so much to win that he took the devil for his partner, for which the devil himself rebuked him, saying that the man cared more for the state of his shoes than the state of his soul.[36]

While the "vices of the flesh" were those most commonly associated with the devil from St. Augustine onwards, "vices of the mind" such as wrath and avarice were also viewed as devil inspired.[37] The popular wisdom of the exempla regarding wealth was that in and of itself the possession of riches was suspect. Theft, holding back tithes, nonpayment of debt, and uncharitableness were seen as forms of avariciousness stemming from the love of money; and usury was a coin undeniably minted by the devil.[38] In one exemplum, for instance, it is said of a peasant refusing to give alms to two clerics that he would rather give his money to the devil; in another, we find the saying that "a usurer leaves his soul to the devil, his body to the earth and his riches to man."[39] Surprisingly, usury in the exempla is rarely connected with the Jews; rather it is linked to the devil in such motifs as angels and devils fighting over a usurer's corpse (D21), a usurer's corpse being fed his money by toads, and usurers being punished in hell by such appropriate tortures as being forced to consume their gold and silver pieces.[40]

Thus, whereas the medieval sermon proper inveighed against sin in relatively formal, abstract, and declamatory fashion, the exemplum's impact lay not in rhetorical denunciation of sin in general but in the illustration of concrete cases of sin sufficiently representative of experience to win instant recognition and instill an immediate, deep, and hopefully, abiding fear of the devil in the listener. The devil had to be seen to be ubiquitous; this belief, which took place on an unconscious psychic level was fueled by ignorance and the hard life that was the lot of nearly every ordinary person. The exemplum's business was not to grant excuses for the desire of the flesh or miserly avarice by acknowledging the harshness of life nor to empathize with the peasant's, artisan's or housewife's need to drink, socialize at the tavern, or exchange gossip with neighbors. It was, rather, to harp on the ability of the devil to corrupt people through human weakness. To avoid corruption, it behooved one to be continually pricked by conscience and remain vigilant against occasions of sin.

Because the fostering of individual responsibility and guilt played such an important role in the psychological dynamics of the exemplum, demonic possession was only a minor theme in exempla literature. Through possession, which could occur without seeming cause and might afflict the innocent, it was as if the devil had stepped through the looking glass reflecting man's darker nature to become a "doppleganger," or true double of the possessed, literally dwelling inside him and impelling him to antisocial or sinful behavior. Since this possession diminished or eliminated entirely the sinner's blame for his or her conduct, such motifs were not particularly useful as cautionary tales, for they undermined the vital role played by the individual's complicity in sin. Furthermore, exorcism, the cleansing ritual that restored the demon-possessed person to a state of relative innocence, obviated the salvatory rituals of confession, contrition, and penance that were promoted by the church.

By their *exempla terrible* dramatically depicting an implacable, ubiquitous, nearly invincible enemy stalking individual souls, the medieval preacher deliberately stirred up psychic insecurity for the

sake of man's eternal salvation. But in doing so, the homilist intensi-
fied hidden fears and delivered a message of such menace that some
folk, in their anxiety, turned to sorcery, attempting to combat the devil
by partaking of his power. Many pulpit stories dwell on this theme,
instructing their listeners that Satan must inevitably acquire the soul of
those who abandoned themselves by partnership or compact with
demons. Those people who were so deluded as to think that they
could obtain their sinful desires and then outwit the devil and cheat
him of his due were inviting disastrous consequences, which only
began with violent death and continued through bizarre and grue-
some tortures in hell. One exemplum treating this theme compares the
devil to a cardsharp who allows his rival to win at first but in the end
gathers up the pot.[41]

Many exempla show the devil failing to deliver on the promises he
makes to his "marks." It was one of the signs of the devil's otherness
and lack of fixed status, as was also held true of women and Jews, that
he could not be held to contractual agreements as could honest
Christian men. Cynical and callous, the devil often used verbal loop-
holes to escape his side of the bargain, but even when he delivered on
what he promised, the horrible fate awaiting his partner in sin would,
to the faithful, hardly be worth the trade. Thus, for example, one sermon story relates that a knight gambled with the devil and won, but
the devil flew off with him through the roof.[42] While some exempla
depicting occult practices may have unwittingly popularized the very
conduct that they hoped to combat, the thrust of such stories, that
damnation inevitably and irrevocably lay ahead, would perhaps have
deterred all but the most ambitious or desperate.

The Christian theology that rested on a core belief in a powerful,
often successful agent of evil wrestling souls from their potential seats
in heaven did not insist, however, as did its Manichean competitor,
that sin and wickedness were irremedial. For, if in Christian belief, the
devil had gained his rights over humankind by Adam's fall from grace
through willful disobedience, it was also a centerpiece of Christianity
that man's own free will, which gave dignity to the human species,
could lead him to reject sin, to do battle with the "life" threatening
enemy, the devil. The belief in the devil as a distinct entity, a physical
embodiment of both the vices of the mind and the body, provided a

psychologically useful Other, alien yet familiar, upon whom man could displace or project his suppressed feelings and illicit carnal urges as, by manipulating light and shadow, one may project an external image upon a screen at a distance from oneself. Life would be intolerable if one felt continual self-loathing for those libidinous urges or skeptical thoughts which rose unbidden in one's psyche, but if one could displace self-hatred onto the devil, one would receive social acceptance. Moreover, illicit feelings of lust or envy might more easily be resisted if one could detach them from oneself and ascribe them to the instigation of the devil, since struggle with an external foe is less conflictual than a struggle within.

On a case-by-case basis, then, the exempla pointed out how the devil, by assailing humankind with every enticement of the flesh and the mind, was presenting tests which one could pass or fail *by one's own efforts*. By naming the devil aloud and by limiting his wickedness to specific circumstances framed by the narrative, the exemplum articulated the comforting notion that by avoiding places and behaviors conducive to sin, one might inhibit the devil's power. As a complete dramatic offering it provided its audience with a means of catharsis for its psychic unease and empowered the individual listener to shatter the obscure reflection in the mirror that represented his sinful soul.

It is true that popular sermon story included a wide range of hagiographical material that presented models for virtuous behavior as well as illustrations of sin. Exemplars of resistance to the devil such as the saintly abbot Macarius or St. Mary of Oignies demonstrated the potency of meditation, prayer, and humility to exorcise devils and "conquer all the temptations of the adversaries." But the preponderance of *exempla terrible* in collections of sermon narrative suggests that the popular preacher had more confidence in the stick of fear than the carrot of persuasion. Even in an age accustomed to violence, the violent tortures of hell—to be dismembered, have the soul ripped from the body with burning forks, be immersed in a molten bath (each occurring literally and continuing forever)—were sufficient deterrent, at least in the short haul, for most folks.

If, like St. Augustine, the preacher *ad populum* felt "forced to preach [on God's anger] because filled with fear [he must] fill [his] audience with fear," he also elaborated in his tales on the mighty weapons of salvation

by which a sinner could regain a state of grace and retain his or her eli-
gibility for eternal bliss: confession, contrition, and penance. This
sacrament was an extremely complex act that required not only the
sincere and frank revelation of one's sin, and an almost ephiphanic
acknowledgment of regret for the sin, but also a sincere, not perfunctory repentance issuing from a conscious decision to accept God's
power to pardon and forgive. The cleansing process of this rite was
known to the devil and occasioned his best efforts to thwart it or retard
it until too late, a motif to which many exempla attest. In one, for
example, the chief devil, appearing at the moment of a sinner's death,
is prevented from claiming the man's soul because even his own
demons argue that the man is confessing in his heart; in others the
devil tries to invalidate the confessions of the dying by having them
made, through deceit, to himself.[43]

On the psychological level, through the concatenation of contrition,
confession, and penance, guilt could be assuaged. For believers, the
acts of penance imposed for one's sins, such as renunciations, punitive restrictions, or compensatory actions, were perceived as merited
and welcome protective measures against repeated assaults by an
aggressively hostile enemy, the devil. By their formulaic nature, the
church's multiple purificatory rituals reinforced the collective mentality that had been shaped by a thousand years of religious hegemony.
Popular sermon story supported theology with the idea that refusal to
confess and repent devolved from a devil-inspired pride and could
only result in a lifetime of sinful conduct. The exempla reserved some
of their worst punishment for those who, with their sins hidden and
unconfessed, were led into further sin and delayed repentance until
too late.

It is not an exaggeration, then, to describe the tug of tensions that
beset medieval folk as a "warrior vision," a state of war, where, on an
unconscious level a figurative duel was taking place between such
prohibited passions as lust, violence, avarice, and pride, and a strongly inculcated desire to love God and attain the soul's salvation.[44] This
conflict was rooted in a perceived dualism between the body and the
soul that had long been a part of popular Christian imagery, in which
the soul was viewed as dwelling with Christ while the body was associated with the devil. On the level of popular piety, an exemplum of a

devil possessing a woman's body makes this clear: as the demon receives the Eucharist he is asked whether he dwells with Christ. "No," the demon replies, "for Christ lives in the soul and the devil in the intestines."[45]

In addition to the open warfare between the devil and human beings on earth, there was also a continual battle between the forces of good and evil for possession of a person's soul at his death. On one side was the angelic host armed with its message of God's mercy, its powers of miraculous intervention and its complete knowledge of God's will. On the other side was the devil, whose authority in the disposition of souls at their death and at the Last Judgement was explicitly acknowledged in both popular religious literature and the plastic arts.[46] Many of the exempla motifs related to this theme stem from Revelation (3:5), where it is written that in the Book of Life there is a book of deeds which contains the destiny of the world. In popular medieval eschatology this reference became an account book of the bad and good actions committed by each soul. To one's deathbed might come the devil with his ledger—black as he was—while an angel appeared with his account book, and there was a debate for the possession of the soul based on the enrollments in each. Another exempla motif related to this deathbed competition was the weighing of sins and virtues on a scale to determine the disposition of the soul. Numerous sermon stories (as well as other popular didactic media) show each side arguing vociferously for its claim, often depositing a previously unregistered or last minute sin or good deed in an effort to shift the balance. In the exemplum, "The Devils Debate for a Usurer's Soul" (D21), for instance, a usurer who made a deathbed restitution is saved by four angels combatting four devils for his soul. In other cases the archangel Michael, Christ, or the Virgin Mary, invoked as a judge, may drop in the scales a tangible sign of his or her mercy in order to save the soul, as in one cautionary tale that relates how a nail from Christ's cross, deposited on the scales of judgement in a repentant sinner's favor, won him a reprieve from eternal damnation in hell.[47]

While the outcome of this battle between the angelic and demonic forces for the soul of each individual was not predetermined—a final act of charity or contrition could change the balance at the last moment as has been noted—it was foreknown by God and conduced, as all things on earth, to the fulfillment of his will and purposes. God, not the devil, was supreme. As St. Augustine had written, "But it is to be most firmly believed that Almighty God can do whatever He pleases, whether in punishing or favoring, and that demons can accomplish nothing by their natural power (for their created being is itself angelic, although made malign by their own fault) except what He may permit, whose judgments are often hidden but never unrighteous."[48]

Thus, paradoxically, the successful wiles of the devil become an instrument of God's justice in both the temporal and eternal world. Indeed, one of the most intricate yet significant aspects of the Christian belief system was that the devil, just as every other creature on earth, was a minion of God and subject to his authority. The apparent success of demons in transforming men into beasts, for example, is a phenomenon St. Augustine discusses at some length. While such transformations are quite "extraordinary," he asserts, they may take place, but only if God wills: "jugglings of this kind could not be difficult for demons *if permitted by the judgment of God*" (italics mine).[49] St. Thomas Aquinas similarly asserted the subjection of devils going about their malicious business to the will of God: "[while] the assault on men is due to the malice of the demons [who] through pride usurp a semblance of Divine power . . . But the ordering of the assault is from God, Who knows how to make orderly use of evil by ordering it to good."[50] Several sermon stories explicitly depict the devils' respect for the superior power of God and their acknowledgment that by their temptations of humankind they are performing God's work. In one exemplum told by a Polish Franciscan, for example, a usurer who would not make restitution is told by the devil who appears to him that he is one "who by the command [*precepto*] of God comes to you in this form."[51]

Thus, despite what appears at first glance as an unambiguous view of the devil as an agent of evil equipped with a variety of megapowers to bring about the damnation of humankind, there emerges from the vast body of medieval homiletic narrative a more complex portrait of the devil, some subleties regarding the extent of his powers, and some ambivalence about his character. Depicted on the one hand as evil incarnate and on the other as the executor of God's will; bearing something of the aura of a folkloric trickster, a manipulator of men's weaknesses who brings about confusion but stays aloof from it, the devil of the exempla, while rarely descending to the comic or satiric creation of the medieval stage, is not a wholly unsympathetic figure. Nor, though untutored medieval folk labored under that misapprehension, were his powers to work evil unlimited. Demons did possess such extraordinary abilities as speaking in different tongues, assuming different shapes, foreseeing the future, uncovering secrets, and transporting people through the air, and were to some degree able to change the appearance of temporal things and alter men's perceptions of phenomena, but they could not create anything new or actually transform one thing into another.[52] The real key to their success was, according to popular pulpit discourse, the complicity of humankind in the devil's pernicious aims. By committing sinful actions, human beings were consorting with an enemy who was most truly the Other, in that the devil is our darker intimate, a repellent reflection in himself of our evil impulses of which we wish to void ourselves.[53] The darker side of angelic nature as well as human nature, the instigating devil played an indispensible role in man's examination of his own conscience, a testing appointed by God to determine the disposition of every individual soul.

The revolution in social and economic life that was taking place in the thirteenth century was creating new ranks, increasing social mobility and exposing even ordinary folk to new ideas and customs. The material accoutrements of a new wealth were becoming diffused among a wider variety of people. The church saw the devil's hand in this more elastic order and its threat to the traditional values of which it had been, for so many centuries, the sole custodian and which it had a deep interest in maintaining. The religious and ideological doctrines of the medieval church blamed the social ills of the time on the sinful behavior of individuals, inspired by an external demonic enemy rather than on the established institutions that comprised the power base; hence, its remedy for social malady was spiritual rather than psychological or political. Encouraged after the Fourth Lateran Council to enhance pastoral care through the venue of the popular pulpit and to preach in the idiom of the folk, the medieval homilist found in the character of an iniquitous fiend a potent means of confronting the folk with the dire peril that threatened their souls and in the exemplum a dramatic method of providing the instruction that would save them.

Exempla about Devils

Tales D1 and D2 depict the spiritual prowess of Macarius (unnamed in the octosyllabic verse variant), the renowned fourth-century saint of the Egyptian desert who is portrayed in the *Golden Legend*'s Life as a man who can deal with the devil on equal terms because he has mastered his desires and thus cannot be snared into temptation.

D1. The Devil and St. Macarius in Church

One day a fiend said to the abbot Macarius, "Let us go to church together and see what is going on there." "Devil," replied the abbot, "What have you got to do with people going to church?" The fiend answered, "Just let us go and you will see what happens." So the abbot went into the church and everywhere in the building he saw diverse fiends, small as children, blue as men of India, running about the place, mocking all the congregants by making faces. The devils put their fingers into some people's eyes, and these folk went right to sleep; and when they awoke the fiends greased their lips with ointments from their boxes and then these people began to chatter and tell tales. After that the fiends skipped around in front of them in the forms of women, so that men found their hearts stirred to lechery. In front of some congregants the fiends drove cattle, and these folk were distracted by thoughts of their animals. Before others, the fiends counted money, and these men turned their minds to their treasures. In front of other men the fiends appeared as merchants, and these folk thought about buying and selling. To other people the fiends appeared with their horses and carts, and these began to think about their household business, their land and their tithes due, their houses and their worldly goods. Thus the fiends made these churchgoers idle in their thoughts and inattentive with chattering and other vanities. Abbot Macarius said to the fiend, "Why do you do this to men in church?" The devil answered, "On work days men serve the world and their business, not God; therefore on holy days, when they should be serving God, we prevent them from doing so, and make sure of getting their souls, for they that serve God neither workday nor holy day serve us, the world, and their flesh."

D2. St. Macarius Defeats the Devil as Physician

Of the seed that Satan sows,
A good tale St. Jerome tells us
Of a hermit, a holy man [St. Macarius],
Who lived in the desert with him for a year;
And as he sat in his cell,
He saw a fiend go by the gate
Carrying on his back bottles
And ampules such as leeches bear.
Near the hermit was an abbey,
Towards which the devil was taking the road.
The holy man who saw this fiend
Asked him where he was going.
"To yonder abbey," he said "I go,
For I have been away too long."
And this hermit thought with fear
About the devil's vials, and asked why
He bore such bottles with him.
"With these," he said, "I shall treat
All the brothers of yonder abbey,
This will be a good game for me,
And whoever shall refuse one medicine,
Another shall I make him swallow;
If he does not take gluttony,
I shall treat him with envy,
Or with some other concoction,
Of pride, hatred, crime,
Or with some other delicious drink
That may goad him to think of sin."
This hermit let that fiend go on his way
And bade him pass by again on his way back,
And prayed that God should help in this matter,
To prevent the fiend from these deeds.
This fiend went along to that abbey
To see how his plan might work.
He met with little success
And soon returned to this hermit
With woeful face, sore and unhappy.
The hermit asked him, "So soon

Have you returned, how have you done?"
The fiend said, "I have done very poorly,
For none of them would do my will,
None would try my wares
Except one named Theocist,
Whom I found ready to do
My will when I approached him."
    When this was said he went away
    And the hermit went to the abbey.
The monks all gathered around him
For they were happy at his arrival.
He asked about Theocist
And they pointed the way to his dwelling,
For he lived in a distant cell
As was the rule of their order.
With Theocist this hermit met
And they greeted each other warmly.
The hermit asked if Theocist was aware
Of having carnal thoughts,
And he answered and said, "No,"
For he was loathe to tell the truth.
And the hermit answered him then
And said, "I am myself a very old man
and yet not a day goes by
That I do not feel desires of the flesh;
How is it that you, who are in your youth
Do not know stirring of the flesh?"
The hermit spoke to Theocist in this way
To get him to reveal his sinful thoughts,
And Theocist asked for mercy
And said, "I am also
So beset with lechery
That I cannot control my fleshly desires."
This hermit told him, then, how he
Should stand firm against Satan,
And when this monk was once more pure
The hermit went back home again.
Soon thereafter he saw
The fiend going towards the abbey again
And quickly returning,

And the hermit began to
Needle Satan, asking how he had fared.
And he answered as if he were mad.
Saying, "Alas, oh woe
That I ever came to that abbey,
For I cannot win at my game
Against any of those knaves,
For none of them like my wares,
And they got rid of me.
I cannot get any of them to play
Despite all my lures,
Even Theocist, whom I had won
Is now shamefully wrest from me,
He who was won is now my bane,
He is steadfast against me.
Thus there is no profit
In going to that abbey any more."
   This hermit praised God almighty
   Who defeated the devil's craft.
This tale shows us clearly
What seed of hell the devil sows
And we must pray now that God help us
And keep us from the devil's crop.

Tales D3 and D4 turn on the devil's appearance in the form of various loathsome animals such as a toad and a serpent. Tale D4 includes the motif of a sinner's empty boast that he can successfully take on the devil.

D3. A Devil in the Form of a Toad

Caesar of Heisterbach tells us that once, in the diocese of Cologne, a man named Theodoric injured a toad, which, when it was harmed, stood up against Theodoric on its hind feet. Theodoric, becoming very angry, took an iron bar and slew the toad, but, amazing as it may seem, the toad came to life again and tried to revenge itself on Theodoric. It ran after him, but he picked up a spade and smashed it once or twice, cutting it in half; then he burned it. None of this, however, could prevent him from being so overcome by fear of this toad that he could hardly sleep nights anyplace near the ground, and so finally one night he put his bed up on a high platform.

Now one day, when Theodoric was out riding with a friend, he decided to tell his story about the toad, hoping that it would end his spell of fear. Suddenly he looked behind him and saw the toad climbing up on his horse's tail. The animal was almost close enough to touch him, so he cried out; and at the same time his companion called loudly, "Beware! the devil is in your horse's tail and is almost upon you!" The friend quickly alighted from his horse and slew the toad. Sometime later, as Theodoric sat among his friends, he became aware of this same toad sitting on a post in the side of the wall. As soon as he saw it, he cried out in anguish, "Lo, sirs, there yonder is a fiend that will never leave me alone until it revenges itself on me." His friends advised him to uncover one leg and let the toad come to it. He did so, and the toad came up to him and bit him; after it did his, Theodoric pushed it away with his hand. Then he took a razor and cut out the part of his leg which the toad had bitten and threw it away. At once this piece swelled up as huge as a football and burst, and then at last Theodoric was delivered from this devil.

D4. An Ungrateful Son

Caesar of Heisterbach tells us that once there was a young man named Henry whose mother was a rich widow. The time came when the young man began to pester his mother for her money, saying, "Give me all your goods so that through my reputation as a wealthy man I may marry well and get a rich wife; then I shall return your money. And in the meantime I shall provide well for you." The woman agreed and did as her son suggested. The son got married, but a little while after the wedding his bride nagged him to put his mother out, and soon the old woman had nothing to eat but what she begged. When she came to complain to her son, he closed his ears and would not listen to her. One day, while the son and his wife were sitting at dinner together, his mother knocked at the door and asked for meat for the sake of God. The son said, "Lo! See how the devil cries at the door."

His mother came in and begged him to take mercy on her and give her some food, but he screamed at her as if he were mad. At last he bade a boy go fetch the remains of a pullet that was lying in a box and give it to her. The boy went to the kitchen, found the box, and lifted its lid, but instead of a pullet on the platter he found only a writhing serpent. Afraid, he ran back and told his master what he saw. The son then sent a serving-girl to fetch the pullet, but she, too, came running back, pale-faced, and told him that she saw the same thing. Finally the son rose up angrily himself and said, "Should the devil be lying on the platter, I will fetch him out here." So he lifted up the lid of the box and stooped down to get the pullet off the platter. As he did so, the serpent lying there clasped him about the throat and wound itself around his neck, strangling him. The more he labored to free himself, the tighter the serpent clung, until it made his face swell out so that his eyes fell onto his cheeks. In this state he lived for fourteen years and more, blind, with the serpent hanging around his neck. He was taken from one place of pilgrimage to another but could get no relief. At last, his mother had compassion for his pain and forgave him his sins, and then he died.

Tale D5 illustrates that the devil could be so convincing in his disguises that only constant vigilance was an adequate defense against his wiles. Here, the deceived man is punished rather than rewarded for his apparently charitable act because his charity, falsely based on rumor, was misplaced.

D5. The Devil Disguised as a Pilgrim

According to St. Gregory, there was once a holy bishop named Fortunatus who drove an evil spirit out of a man, and the next day this same spirit, disguised as a pilgrim, walked about the city streets crying, "Oh Fortunatus, you who are deemed a pious man and a good bishop, why did you put a pilgrim out of your house? Nowhere in this city may I be lodged now; I can find no place to stay." Hearing this, a certain man who was sitting in his house by the fire with his wife and children came out and asked the pilgrim what the bishop had done to him. When the pilgrim told him, the man took him into his own house and gave him lodging for the night. That same evening, as he and the lodger sat talking by the fire, this same fiend suddenly picked up the man's child and threw him into the flames where he was burned to death. Then the evil spirit flew away with a fearful din. At this, the poor father realized that he had received into his home not a pilgrim, but a fiend who was slandering the good bishop Fortunatus.

Tale D6, a grisly sample of the *exemplum terrible*, indicates how people put themselves in the devil's grasp by their love of luxury, selfishness, and spiritual neglect. The background of tale D6 suggests how such narrative melded historical and fictional material, transferred anecdotes about one figure to another, and provided verisimilitude by dramatizing supernatural events with contemporary social details and dialogue. The exemplum's history begins in a twelfth-century German chronicle which describes the punishments after death of two corrupt archbishops. One hundred years later these two narratives were combined into a single exemplum of a fictional archbishop, Udo of Magdeburg, whose account was widely disseminated in a number of variants. Udo's punishments were shaped to suit his reputation: the molten bath of hell was retribution for a supposed love of hot baths, and his pinioning to a hot griddle was an apt torture for his reputed love of soft beds. For its authority, this exemplum cites Udo's canon Frederick, who woke from a revelatory vision to find Udo's severed head on the altar of the church of St. Maurice, which retained the blood-stain ever after. The exemplum reports that the townspeople tossed Udo's corpse into a bog, where it was torn apart by infernal monsters, and then burned the remains, strewing the ashes in the river Elbe, from which the fish disappeared for the next ten years.

D6. The Torment of Bishop Udo

Once, in Saxony, there was a bishop named Udo who continued in his religious estate the lecherous and luxurious life he had led before becoming a bishop. God wished to end these sins, so one night Udo heard a voice chastise him, saying, "Udo! End your play, for you have played enough, I say." After Udo heard this voice, he reformed for a while, but then he was tempted back into his former life and fell into sin again. A second time he was warned by the same voice, saying, "Udo! Make an end to this, for you have played enough, I say." And once more, Udo reformed for a short time only. The third time Udo was chastised by the voice it happened as before, and he returned to his life of sin after a short period of reformation.

One night, when Udo had been merrymaking and had gotten drunk and gone tipsy to sleep, his assistant saw two devils take the soul of the bishop from his bed and bring it before the prince of devils, who was sitting in his court as a judge, with a great multitude of other devils around him. The master devil said to the bishop's soul, "Welcome, my child; now speak blasphemies." But the soul stood still and ashamed and would not speak. The devil said again, "Speak now, my own child, for I am he whom you have served, and therefore I shall reward you for your service." But the soul stood still and said nothing. Then the prince of devils said to the demons who had brought the soul, "Go, put him in a bath, and then he will speak." So they took the soul and put it in a cauldron full of boiling pitch and brimstone, and then they took it out and brought it before their master who again bade it speak. But it would not speak. Then the master devil said, "Give it a drink from my own cup and it shall speak." His minions took the cup, filled it with the most abominable and stinking liquids and then made the soul of Bishop Udo drink it, but still the soul would not speak. The leader of devils then said, "Stew him, and then he will speak." So the fiends took off the cover of a pit out of which arose the foulest-reeking smoke (with a smell that would corrupt all the world, thought the observer), and into this pit they cast the soul. And when it had been there a little while, they took it out and brought it before the master, who said, "Now speak, my child." Then the bishop's soul finally spoke, blaspheming all those he knew. "Cursed and cursed again be they who begot me!" he cried. "Well said," announced the master devil. "Speak on." "Cursed and cursed again," said the soul "are my God and the hour I was conceived and cursed be those who begot me." Then, when the prince of devils urged the soul to continue, it added, "Cursed and cursed be my good father and mother who made me Christian." "Speak more," encouraged the chief fiend. "Cursed and cursed be Christ and his mother and all the saints of heaven!" cried the soul. Then the prince of the devils said, "Now you have spoken wisely and I shall reward you for your service." So they took the soul and put it at the bottom of the pit where it had been before and they covered the pit.

All this the bishop's assistant saw, and when he awoke he was sweating because of the anguish he felt. He rose and went to the bishop's chamber and asked the prelate's valet, "How fares my lord?" "Let us go and see," replied the chamberlain. They went into the room and looked around, and then they found the bishop dead, and they sought the devil's cup but could not find it.

In tales D7 and D8 the devil as shapechanger is permitted to punish sinners who do not heed warnings to reform. Typical elements of the *exemplum terrible* are the adulterer's punishment by a cancer eating away a part of his body, symbolic of sin eating away at the soul; the devil's appearance as a man's servant, a reminder of the devil's intimacy with those disposed to sin; and the devil's association with a black horse.

D7. An Adulterer Punished by the Devil

Near Northhampton there was an eleven-year-old child who was so ill from the plague that he fell into a coma. When he awoke, he related many wondrous stories, mentioning among other things that a certain neighbor had a lover unbeknownst to his wife. When this adulterer heard of the boy's words, he determined to go and speak with the child himself. As he was proceeding there, he met a fiend in the likeness of his sweetheart, whom he kissed before continuing on. When he came to the child, the adulterer first inquired about his health. "I am well, sir," said the boy, "but you are ill, for you have a lover unbeknownst to your wife, a thing that is against God's law, and this lover, whom you think you kissed today on the way here was but a fiend in your sweetheart's guise. This devil has caused a cancer on your lip which shall eat right into your heart unless you mend your ways." But the adulterer took the child's words for fantasy and ignored them, and a cancer grew on him and ate into him as prophesied, and he died soon after.

D8. A Usurer Outsmarts Himself

Caesar of Heisterbach tells us that once in a certain bishopric a usurer took up the cross and resolved to go into the Holy Land on a crusade. Just as he was about to start on his journey, he found himself ill and anxious, and he decided that he would not go but would hire another to go in his place. He gave his substitute five marks, although he should have given forty. Afterwards, when those who were marked with the cross were sitting in a tavern preparing for their departure, the usurer joined them and announced scornfully, "You fools, now you are forsaking your wives and children, your friends, and all your goods, and putting yourselves in danger beyond the sea, while I shall sit home with my wife and children and all my treasures, and for my five marks have as much pardon as you do."

But God, who is righteous, showed how much the labor and expense of the pilgrims pleased him, and how much the deceit and blasphemy of slackers displeased him. That night, he made the devil come to the usurer in the likeness of the man's servant; the devil was leading two huge black horses, and he bade the usurer dress himself warmly in his best clothes and gallop away with him on his horse. Now the cross that the usurer had taken up was sewn upon his outer garment and this man, thinking that if he dropped off the coat he might escape being led to the crusade, cast the coat away, then leapt on the horse. The devil leapt up on the other horse and within a short time he had led the usurer to the place of torments. The devil showed the usurer the seat of diverse pains reserved for him and said, "Now you may go back to your house, but within three days you shall die and return here." Then the usurer was brought home, and when he was asked where he had been, he related his story to all his questioners. A priest was brought to the usurer and counselled him to repent and confess, but the man refused. Then he fell into despair and died without the last sacraments and was buried in hell.

The allusion in tale D9 to the pilgrim's good angel reflects medieval folk and theological belief that each person had a celestial companion, a good angel assigned when the soul entered the body, whose function was to report all the person's actions to God and the angels in heaven.

D9. The Vision of a Drunken Pilgrim

Caesar of Heisterbach tells us that a certain pilgrim once exchanged his mantle for wine and drank so much that he got drunk out of his mind and walked about like a zombie. That night his spirit was taken to the place of horrible torments where he saw the prince of hell sitting on the side of a pit which was covered with a great log. In front of this creature was brought an abbot from Corbey whom the prince of devils welcomed warmly. He gave the abbot a fiery cup of burning brimstone to drink; when the sinful man took a draught, fiery liquid burst out of his eyes, nose and ears. Then the fiend uncovered the pit and cast the abbot into hell for his gluttony, drunkness, and self-indulgence. When the pilgrim saw all this, he was terrified. Then the prince of fiends bellowed out, "Now bring me that pilgrim who yesterday sold his cloak for wine." The pilgrim cried to his good angel to help him, and he promised never to sin again if his angel would deliver him from the fiend. At that moment, the spirit returned to the pilgrim's body and he awoke. When he returned to his own country, he found that the abbot of Corbey, a neighbor, had died at just the hour when the pilgrim had seen him cast into the pit of hell.

The central image of tale D10, a garment weighing down its sinful bearer—as sin weighs down the soul—was described in a variant by the acclaimed preacher Jacques de Vitry as a parchment cape inscribed all over with the letters of its clerical owner's "sophistries and subtleties" and heavier to bear on his neck than the nearby church of St. Germain.

D10. A Sinful Clerk's Cloak of Feathers

According to Helinandus a certain archdeacon who had to go to Rome begged his canon to allow a clerk named Nathaniel, a good servant, to accompany him on his journey. Although the clerk did not wish to go, the archdeacon insisted he come and made him the bookkeeper for the trip. When they arrived in Rome, the archdeacon, who was a parsimonious man, asked his clerk to total up the accounts and expenses of the

journey down to the last halfpenny. The clerk's account varied somewhat from the archdeacon's, but the clerk swore by the devil that his
total was correct. The two argued over the figures as they walked into
the city, and while they were thus disputing, they happened to pass a
bridge, where the clerk fell over the edge into the water and was
drowned.

Now it must be told that this clerk had made a pact with his master,
the canon, that whichever one of them died first would appear to the
other within thirty days to say how he was faring. On the night after
the clerk's death, as the canon lay awake in his bed, a burning lamp in
front of him, the clerk Nathaniel came to his side arrayed in a beautiful cape of feathers. The canon was unafraid at the clerk's appearance,
for he thought it was the living man whom he had been expecting
back from Rome. "Welcome, Nathaniel," the canon said, "Is the
archdeacon here with you?" The clerk answered, "No, sir, for I am here
as a result of the pact you and I made before I left. I am dead now, and
I pray that you will help me for I am in great torment." The canon
asked him why that should be, since he had lived honestly and decent-
ly, and the clerk replied, "Truly, sir, it would have been all right with
me except that on the day I died I was upset and swore on the devil. I
pray you, warn others by my example, for he who swears by the devil
gives himself over into the devil's keeping, as I did on the day I was
drowned. And, therefore I am in great pain."

The canon asked Nathaniel how, if he was in such torment, he could
be wearing such a lovely cloak. The clerk replied thusly, "Sir, this cape
is heavier on my back than if I were supporting the tallest tower in the
world. The beauty of the cloak symbolizes my belief that my sins may
be forgiven me if I am heartily prayed for." When the canon told the
clerk that he would pray for him as hard as he could, the clerk vanished away and was never heard from again.

Tales D11 and D12 illustrate various constraints on the devil's
power when the sinner's conduct is mitigated by certain circumstances: committing the sin unknowingly, heeding a supernatural
warning, maintaining devotion to a saint, or showing remorse and
performing the required sacraments. Tale D11 is notable for the
romance motifs—the abandoned wife, the token of a ring and the
magic journey that prevents an illicit wedding—that link such exem-

pla with secular popular tales. Exemplum D12 demonstrates that the
devil himself shares the theological view that he, like all creatures, is
subservient to God's will. The tale upholds the doctrine of transubstantiation, a sectarian issue in the Middle Ages. In one variant, which
concludes with the reconversion of a heretic to orthodoxy, the devil
explains to his companion that he knelt to the Host because "he is my
lord and thy lord, that made me and thee, and all things. He is in the
form of the bread passing by here and therefore I worship him."

D11. The Devil and a Knight's Charity

Caesar of Heisterbach tells us that once, in the town of Holyback, there
was a knight named Gerard who had great devotion to St. Thomas the
Apostle. Now it happened that the devil, in the guise of a poor man,
came to this knight and asked him for hospitality in the name of St.
Thomas; and of course, it was granted him. The knight sent up his best
fur gown to the poor man's bed so that he might keep warm, but during the night the devil stole the cape and disappeared with it. The next
morning the knight's wife was very angry with her husband and
berated him for taking in poor beggars, saying, "Don't do such good
things again." But the knight replied, "Never mind; St. Thomas has the
power to do me a favor worth as much as my gown."

A little while after this incident, the knight decided to go on pilgrimage to the grave of St. Thomas. He broke a gold ring in two pieces
in front of his wife and gave her one half, saying, "Trust this token
should it be sent to you, and wait for me five years." The wife
promised she would, and took the ring, while her husband went his
way. After several years the knight came to the city of St. Thomas,
where he went into the church, said his prayers to the saint, and commended his wife and children to St. Thomas's protection. Then he
became aware of a fiend walking up and down in what he recognized
as the fur gown he had given to the beggar years before. This fiend
came up to him and asked, "Gerard, do you know me?" The knight
answered, "I don't know you, but I know that gown well enough."
Then the fiend said, "I am the devil that took the form of a poor man
who stayed with you and then stole your gown; on that account I have
been sorely punished. Now I am commanded to get you right home

safe and sound, for this very day your wife is about to wed another man, since it is over five years that you have been away." At once, the devil lifted the knight up and took him from India to his own gate in Germany. The knight's wife and her betrothed were sitting at dinner when the knight came in and threw his half of the gold ring into his wife's cup. When the woman saw it, she took out the other half; and seeing that the two pieces matched, she knew it was her husband. She sent her betrothed away and took back her old husband again.

D12. A Devil Bows to the Host

In Devonshire beside Oxbridge there dwelled a holy vicar, one of whose parishioners, a woman, lay at the point of death about a half mile from where he lived in the town. This woman, at midnight, sent for him to give her the last rites. So this man made all the haste he might, got up and went to the church, and took God's body in an ivory box and put it in his vest-front, for at that time men used vests. Then he went off in the direction of this woman's house, which led through a meadow, for that was the path. As he went upon his way, without his knowing it, the box fell out of his bosom and dropped to the ground; and in so falling, the box opened and the Host fell on the green.

Later, after the priest had shriven this woman, he asked her if she would take Communion and she said that she would. So he put his hand into his bosom and looked for the box, and when he could not find it he was sorely afraid and said to the woman, "Madam, I shall fetch God's body and be back again as soon as I can." So he came to a large tree and cut himself a good switch and stripped himself naked and beat himself as fast as he could, saying to himself, "You foul thief that has lost this precious object, you shall be punished." And when he had beaten himself thus, he threw on his clothes and ran forth. At that moment he noticed a pillar of fire springing from the earth up to heaven. At first he was terrified, but afterwards he blessed himself and went closer to it and saw that all the beasts of the field had gathered within its glow. As he came near to this pillar it shone as brightly as any sun, and he became aware of the Host lying on the grass, with the fiery pillar springing from it up to heaven. Then he fell down on his knees and asked for mercy with all his heart, weeping sorely for his

negligence. When he had finished his prayer, he rose up and looked
about him and saw all the animals kneeling on both knees worshipping the Host. Only one black horse was kneeling on but one knee.
Then this good man said to the horse thusly: "If you are a beast that
can speak and answer me, I command you by the virtue of Christ's
body that lies here to tell me why you are kneeling only on one knee
while all the other animals are kneeling on both." Then the horse
answered and said, "I am a fiend from hell and would not kneel willingly at all, but I am compelled to do so against my will, for it is written that each man of heaven and earth and hell shall bow to Him."
Then the priest asked him, "Why are you in the likeness of a horse?"
And the creature said, "I go forth in this guise of a horse in order to
tempt men to steal me. And thus was one man from a certain town
hanged because of me, and after him another, and in yet another town,
a third." Then said this vicar, "I command you by the power of this
Host here that you go into the wilderness where no man steps foot and
remain there until Doomsday." And at once the horse vanished. With
all the reverence in his power, the priest took up the Host and put it
back in the box and then went back to the dying woman and gave her
communion and afterwards he rode home, thanking God with all his
heart for showing him this miracle.

Exempla D13 through D18 turn on the motif of compacts made with
the devil. The church's continual fulmination against the use of spells,
charms, and "the art of illicit superstition," as St. Augustine termed
magical practices, was never wholly successful in eradicating these.
Orthodoxy combatted sorcery and pacts with the devil by such exempla as these, emphasizing that the sinner could break the devil's contract by confession and repentance, and should never despair.

Several conventions concerning magic and necromancy are apparent in tales D13 and D14: the setting in Spain, a Moslem country often
associated with studies in sorcery; the devil's proffering of a magical
object that confers power; a magic circle drawn as a privileged portion
of space to protect the participants in necromancy from permanent
seizure by demonic forces; the devil's attempt to strong-arm a partici-
pant out of the enchanted space; and the physical changes in the person who has returned from the nether world. Tale D14's invoking of a
devil's council to judge a peer's actions and tale D15's depiction of the

devil as a huge black man are staples of sermon story. Folk belief that a person is in the devil's power so long as the fiend holds one of his possessions underlies the knight's rejection of the devil's request in tale D15. In tale D16, the knight's setting conditions for his bargain with the devil is not unique; in one exemplum of a widow turned prostitute who compacts with the devil for riches, the sinner lays down four conditions the devil must fulfill. Exemplum D17, given an eastern, pagan setting, implies an identification between the devil and pagan spirits, following St. Augustine. Exemplum D18's legend of a pact between the devil and Gerbert, Pope Sylvester (d. 1003), originated in Sylvester's reputation as an unusually learned man who had studied in Moslem Spain, a country associated with necromancy. A purportedly historical twelfth-century English account claims that as a resident in Spain, Gerbert stole a book of supernatural knowledge from a Saracen and made a pact with the devil to prevent the Saracen from capturing and punishing him.

The universal motif of animals leading human beings to a particular site, as occurred at Sylvester's funeral, informs other medieval pious tales. In the *Golden Legend*'s Life of St. Menas, the sixth-century patriarch of Constantinople, it is told that camels carrying his body for burial would not take it farther than the spot where a spring welled out of the ground. This site became known for its healing waters, and pilgrim flasks sometimes show the saint with two camels to commemorate this event. A related motif occurs in an anecdote embedded in John Mirk's homily on St. James in the *Festial*. Here, the Spanish queen has ordered St. James to be yoked to two bulls who will pull him to his death. When St. James makes the sign of the cross, however, the bulls refuse to move. When the saint releases them, they run straight to the queen's palace. Another form of the motif surfaces in a pious tale from a medieval Jewish diarist visiting the Holy Land. The rabbinical author states that after an exhumation of the body of King Baruch in the Holy Land, an attempt was made to rebury it at a distance from the king's spiritual master, the prophet Ezekiel. But this separation was thwarted when the horses and mules carrying the coffin stopped but a mile away and would go no further. (In another legend, from Japan, it is told that when the tenth-century noble Sugawara Michizane died in exile on the island of Kyushu, he was buried where the oxen stopped with his remains.)

D13. The Stone of Knowledge

Once there was in Paris a certain student whose dull wit and poor memory made it impossible for him to either learn or retain any knowledge. Everyone ridiculed him, calling him an idiot, and made him feel very unhappy. One day, the devil appeared to him and told him that if he would give himself into the devil's power, he would, in return, become able to learn any kind of subject he wished. The student refused the devil's offer, but the devil put a stone in his hand and said, "As long as you hold this stone you shall know all kinds of things." The student rose and went into his school where he asked such difficult questions and completed so many courses that everyone marvelled that this idiot should have become so smart. The student, meanwhile, told no one what had happened. Not long after the meeting with the devil, the student fell very ill. Then he shrove himself and threw away the stone and his newly gained but meretricious knowledge all together. When he was dead and the priests and clerks were singing psalms around his bier, the devils came and took his soul to a fiery valley where two teams of devils threw the soul from one side to the other as if playing handball; the fiends scratched the soul with their nails at each turn and hurt it in many other ways. At last, the Lord took mercy on the soul because it had been deceived by the devil, and He put it back into the body, and brought it back to life. Everyone around the corpse fled as the man rose up out of the bier. The former student entered a Cistercian convent as a monk and tormented himself with painful penances for the rest of his life.

D14. The Magician and His Student

Caesar of Heisterbach tells us that in the city of Toledo there was once a man skilled in necromancy whose pupils wanted their master to show them all that he knew on the subject. So their teacher, although he did not wish to do so, led them into a field, and with a sword drew a circle around them, and bade them that if they saw any living thing they should not give it anything nor take anything from it, but remain within the circle. Then he went a little ways off and began to recite his spells. Soon the fiends that he called up came to the students, some in the guises of men, some as women, and some making minstrelsy and dancing. Among the demons was one who looked like a lovely lady, fairer than all the others, and she proferred a gold ring to one of the students. At first he refused it, but when she persisted, he took it; at that moment the demon grabbed him out of the circle, ring and all, and spirited him away. His companions began to cry out for their teacher and they told him what had happened. The teacher called up the master fiend and told him that his student had been wrongly seized and asked that he be returned. The master fiend called all the other fiends into council and reproved the one who had done the deed, but that demon excused himself by saying that the seizure of the pupil was justified as the boy had disobeyed his teacher's instructions. Nevertheless, the sentence was passed that the student should be delivered again to his teacher, for he was a generally obedient fellow; and so it was done. From that day forward this boy's schoolmates thought that their friend's face seemed lean and pale, as if he had been taken out of the grave. The boy told his schoolmates that he had, indeed, been at hell's gates and implored them to give up the wicked arts they were learning at school. Then he became a Cistercian monk and lived a holy life.

D15. The Skeptical Knight and the Devil

Once there was a knight who would not believe that there was such a thing as devils. So he went to a magician named Phillip and asked that he show him some fiends, if such existed; and when the magician refused him, the knight pestered the man until he finally agreed. Thus, one day about noon, this Phillip had the knight bring his sword with him to a certain city gate, and with the sword he had the knight describe a circle about his body. The magician bade the knight remain firmly within the circle, for if any limb should go outside it, it might be lost until it could be restored by magic. Phillip told the knight further that if he saw anyone, he should neither give anything nor receive anything from that creature, for if he did so he would be thrashed and flayed; but if he followed the magician's directions exactly, nothing would harm him.

When the magician left the knight alone in the circle, there came a movement like a great flood, and then a noise like the grunting of pigs, and then blasts of wind. Then the knight thought he saw a man as high as the trees who came near the circle and told the knight to ask him anything and it would be answered. As the knight looked at this huge creature, so black of hue and monstrous in shape, he thought he could hardly stand to face him. But at last he gained courage to speak and he asked, "Why does everyone talk of your great wickedness? I have very much wanted to see you and ask you this." The devil replied, "Men often judge without reason, and I do no one ill unless he injures me. For example, Phillip, your teacher, is my friend, and I do all I can to please him; I have never hurt him yet, and as you see, I came when he called me." The knight then asked the fiend where he was at the time he was conjured, and the fiend replied that he had been as far beyond the sea as the sea was from the place in which they were standing. "And therefore," the devil added, "it seems only right that you should give a big reward for my labor." The knight asked him what he wanted and the fiend replied, "Your girdle or your gown, or a sheep from your flock, or a hen or a cock." The knight refused all these requests.

Then the knight asked the fiend how much knowledge he had. To this the fiend replied that there was no evil done in the world of which he was ignorant. "So true is this," he said, "that I can tell you that it was in such and such a town and such and such a house that you first had carnal knowledge of a woman, and that these and these and these are the sins you have committed." The knight could not deny a thing that the devil said. Then the devil put out his hand as if to grab the knight, and at this the knight became so afraid that he fell over backwards in the circle as if he were mad. He called out to his magician who came as soon as he heard his name and banished the phantom away. And forever after, from that moment on, the knight looked pale and ill, and believed in fiends. Then he reformed his life and became a virtuous man.

D16. The Devil Who Rode with a Knight

According to Caesar of Heisterbach, a Saxon knight named Albert Stobberd, happening to pass by a place inhabited by a girl possessed of the devil, heard the girl cry out, "Lo! Here comes my friend." As the knight drew near, the girl ordered everyone aside to allow room for him to pass. Although the knight was annoyed at this incident, he put on a smile and called out to the fiend in possession of the girl, "You, fiend, are a fool! Why do you bother an innocent maid like this? Leave her, and come with me to tournaments and battles." The fiend said that he would gladly do so if the knight would allow himself to be possessed. "Or," said the fiend, "you could let me ride on your saddle or bridle or some other thing which belongs to you." The knight, having great compassion for the noble maiden who was possessed, and wanting to rid her of the fiend, replied, "If you will leave the girl I will give you a pleat in my gown, on the condition that you do not hurt me, and that, when I want you to, you will leave." The fiend agreed, and with that, he left the maiden and went over to the knight, settling himself in a pleat of the man's gown. From that moment on the knight had such strength and power that no one could vanquish him; whomever he fought with, were they ever so swift, they could not defeat him.

After his battles were over, however, the knight began attending church, and here the fiend became restive and querulous. He complained that the knight tarried too long, and he warned him not to touch him with the holy water he was sprinkling on himself. Finally it happened that the knight attended mass at a church where the Crusade was being preached. Then the knight said to the devil, "Now I will leave you and go to serve God." "Why?" asked the fiend, "How have I displeased you? I never hurt you, and I have brought you safely through many adventures and into great wealth; and through me you have gained great fame." The knight answered him by saying, "Lo! Now I see the cross and I command you in the name of He who died on it never to come to me again." With this, the fiend left him and the knight served on the Crusade for two years.

D17. The Devil and a Clerk in Love

Once, in the city of Rome, there lived a senator who desired to make his daughter a nun so that she might pray for his soul. A clerk who loved this girl passionately from afar, but whose lower rank made him reluctant to profess his love openly, decided to see if a conjurer of devils could help him in his plight. He composed a letter describing his situation and

went to an unsavory place where pagans dwelt; there he read his letter aloud. At once a fiend came up to him and asked, "What do you
want me to do for you?" to which the clerk replied that he wanted to
have a certain maiden return his love. The fiend instructed the clerk to
deny the son of God, His mother, and the faith of the holy church; and
after the clerk readily assented to this, the devil added, "I will not
believe your denial unless you write it down for me in your own
hand." When the clerk had done so, the devil stirred up such love in
the senator's daughter that she now loved the young clerk more than
he loved her. She begged her father to make that man her husband, but
her father refused, saying, "Daughter, I thought that you wanted to be
a nun and pray for my soul; this is what you have always said. And
now you want to take a husband!" "Alas, father," the girl said, "I must
have this man or die." So at last they were wed. The young husband,
however, would not attend church like a Christian but scorned the
mass as would a man who despaired of God's mercy. When his wife
saw his troubled state, she asked him the cause of it, and he replied
with the whole story of his pact with the devil. She took him to a bishop to whom they repeated the tale; when they had done, the bishop
bade the husband to keep his faith, and then confessed him. After that,
he shut the young man up behind the altar of the church to do penance
for three days. The first day devils came and annoyed him, saying,
"Think, wretch, that you can elude us? See, here is your contract; you
came to us, we did not come to you." But the bishop visited him afterwards and bade him to fear not, but to remain in his penance behind
the altar until the third day. And so the young man did, despite the
harassments and threats of the devils. When the third day was over,
the bishop came back and asked the man how he fared. "Well," he
answered, "your holy prayers have overcome the devils, who were
unable to harm me." On the next holy day, the bishop led the young
man to the church and stood him at the head of the people's procession. The devils appeared for all to see and tried to drag the man out
of the bishop's grasp, but the prelate cried in a loud voice, "Wretched
devils, it shall not be so." And he urged all the congregants to lift up
their hands to heaven and remain in their places until the young man
was exorcised. It was done as he said, and the devils, afraid of the rite
to be performed, left the young man alone and let his contract fall out
of the air into the bishop's hands.

D18. Pope Sylvester and the Devil

In the Chronicles of St. Sylvester it is related that Pope Sylvester, who was first a monk, made a pact with the devil in which he promised to do everything the devil asked if the devil would, in return, give him everything that he desired. Sylvester met often with the devil and continually increased his knowledge in science and the magic arts until he became so famous that the emperor Otto and King Robert of France came to study under him. Later, through the efforts of the devil, Sylvester was made an archbishop, then a cardinal, and finally the pope. Now one time, when Sylvester was speaking with the devil, he asked him how long he would live, and the devil replied that he would live until he said mass in Jerusalem. At these words Sylvester was elated, for he thought it would be a long time before he would go on pilgrimage to the Holy Land and sing mass there. Sometime later, however, during Lent, Sylvester said mass in a church which, unbeknownst to him, was named Jerusalem. While he was at this mass he heard a din of devilish noise and fell so ill that he thought he must be going to die. Then, although he had led a wicked life, he felt contrite and sorely repented his sin. He sought mercy from God and refused to fall into despair. In front of a public gathering he made open confession of his sin, and then he ordered that when he was dead all the limbs with which he had served the devil should be cut off and the carcass of his body should be loaded on a cart to be buried wherever the draft animals should lead it. The people did as he commanded. The animals drawing the funeral cart led it to the Church of St. John Lateran, and there Sylvester's corpse was buried. In token that God had granted Sylvester His mercy, oils and small bones exuded from the grave.

The theme dominating exempla D19 through D26 is the battle between the devils and the angels for the human soul. The individual was to be judged by the careful tally of deeds recorded in the respective books of the devils and the angels, although at the last moment acts of repentance, restitution, contrition, and confession could tip the balance in a dying person's favor. Tale D19 depicts the devil's recordkeeping. Tale D21, with its rich verse debate between angels and devils for the soul of a repentant usurer, spells out the conditions for salvation for

Christians who practiced usury. The debate format had become popular through various medieval debates of the body and soul, written to
popularize the sacrament of penance. Tale D22 of Peter Toller (or
Taxcollector) became immensely popular from its inclusion in the
Golden Legend's Life of St. John Almsgiver, the sixth-century patriarch
of Jerusalem known for his charitable deeds. In Mirk's *Festial* version,
the Virgin intercedes with Christ for the usurer's soul, which she
claims merits salvation for the bread he threw to the beggar, while the
devils contend, justly but unsuccessfully, that the bread was "given"
involuntarily. Tale D23 mingles fact and fiction, ancient and medieval
history, in its account of St. Lawrence, a historical third-century deacon martyred for having refused to deliver the vases of the church to
the prefect of Rome.

D19. The Devil's Recordkeeping

Once there was a holy hermit who had a chapel dedicated to St. John in
his hermitage. On account of the hermit's reputation for piety, and in
order to worship St. John, many knights, ladies, and gentlefolk came to
the hermit's chapel for services. One time, when the chapel was filled
with congregants, as the hermit finished saying the gospel he turned
towards the people and saw that they were chatting and japing, talking
and wrangling with each other. As he looked at them and noticed their
foolish faces, he became aware that at each of their ears was a horrible
fiend writing down all that they said and ridiculing and mocking them.
The horrible black fiends went leaping on their heads and on the points
of the women's headdresses and all over their rich attire, just as the
birds that sit in the trees leap from branch to branch. The hermit was
greatly astonished at all this, but he went on with the mass. The people
continued their chattering, laughing, and quarrelling, until finally the
hermit smacked his hand loudly on his book to quiet them down. But
some did not become quiet, so then the hermit said, "Lord, if it is your
will, make these people hold their peace at mass and let them know
their foolishness." Suddenly all those who were making noise began to
cry like mad folk out of their mind, and it was a piteous thing to hear.
When the hermit finished the mass, he told the congregation how he

had seen the fiends of hell on their heads, headdresses, and clothing, and he warned them of the perils of such chatterings and vain talk, such joking and socializing during the divine service.

D20. The Devils' Competition

Once on a time there was a young holy man whom the devil, the enemy of mankind, stirred to sin. The young man continued in his sin throughout the many winters of his life. At last it happened that he fell ill and felt his end was coming, as it does to every man and woman, and then, as he lay in his bed, he saw four devils, one standing at his feet, one to the left and one to the right of him, and one at his head. When he saw this, he was full of fear. The devil that stood at his feet said to the others, "This soul is mine to present to our king, Satan, and receive his thanks, for it was I who first stirred him to sin." Then the devil on the left side of the man said, "I am more worthy to have this soul than you, for although you tempted him to sin, I made him commit the sin; therefore I shall have his soul to present to your lord and sovereign." Then the devil standing on the right spoke up, "I am more worthy to have this soul than either of you, for if you tempted him and made him commit the sin, I made him continue in it until now, and I have made his soul secure for us, for he cannot speak any longer to confess, as I am holding onto his tongue with my hand. Therefore, I shall present him to our worthy king, Satan, and receive his thanks." Then spoke the devil at the man's head, "You are all big fools." "Why?" asked the others. "For God is merciful and as long as this man's soul is in his body he may ask mercy and be saved." The devil on the right replied, "How can he ask mercy when he may not speak for my hands on his tongue?" The other returned, "Though you have his tongue in your hands, yet he may ask mercy with his heart. You stand to lose all your labor and be reprimanded by our prince." The young man heard all this and cast up his soul to God with great sorrow for his sins and asked for mercy. "Send me my speech," he prayed, and immediately he could speak. So he sent for his confessor, was shriven of his sins, and thus eluded the devils.

D21. Devils Debate for a Usurer's Soul

According to Caesar of Heisterbach there was once a man who had
become rich through usury and who repented of this sin while he lay
on his deathbed. Sincerely contrite, he told the abbot who confessed
him, "Sir, I bequeath all my goods to you and your monastery that you
may pray for me and help save my soul." But the abbot said, "To rob
Peter to pay Paul is not almsgiving, but sin. To take goods illegally
from other men and give them to us is damning to you and wrong for
us. All the prayers and masses of Christendom would not save you if
you died in this state. You must make as full restitution as possible to
all the people from whom you stole." So the dying man said, "Then,
abbot, take all my goods and restore them to their rightful owners, for
I am too near death to do so."

The abbot restored the usurer's goods as he was directed and he gave
other alms in the usurer's name. The remainder, a great sum still, the
abbot used for his own monastery as the usurer had permitted him.
Then he took the usurer's corpse to his convent where his monks said a
service for the repose of his soul. As this was being performed, four
fiends entered and stood on the left side of the corpse. The abbot and his
monks were terrified, and all, except for one, fled the scene. Then four
angels came in and stood at the right side of the corpse. The one monk
observing heard one of the four fiends say, "Our friend here is dead, and
therefore we four fiends will say our Psalter for him, and I will begin:

> "This sinner on his own did say
> That he would sin and evil pay.
> Never had he, day or night,
> Fear of God before his sight."
The second fiend then spoke:
> "The man has lived treacherously
> In the sight of Him on high.
> In his wickedness, early and late,
> His God has found only hate."
The third fiend added:
> "The words of his mouth were wickedness.
> He never did well, neither more nor less."

The fourth fiend concluded:
   "A wicked thought was in his head
   Each night he took himself to bed.
   Wicked ways he hated not,
   Malice and sin he always thought."

Then the first angel said to the fiends, "You fiends have said your service and your Psalter for this sinful soul. Now we shall say our Psalter for him, and I will begin:

   "Good Lord, your mercy is in heaven on high,
   Your truth on earth reaches the sky
   To save sinners who repent heartily."
The second angel then said:
   "Righteousness is God's will
   His judgments are good, not ill."
The third angel spoke these words:
   "You, Lord, both man and beast
   Save, and bring to rest.
   Your mercy is always shown the most
   And multiplied for men."
The fourth angel ended the Psalter:
   "The children of man's begetting
   Shall be protected under Your wings
   If they trust in You.
   Of humankind this dead man is;
   And though on earth he did amiss,
   Yet under Your wings of mercy he is,
   And can be helped with
     Your grace.
   To this sinful man
   Devils have no right,
   Therefore, fiends, depart,
   And leave him be."

At these words the devils disappeared and the angels bore the soul to heaven.

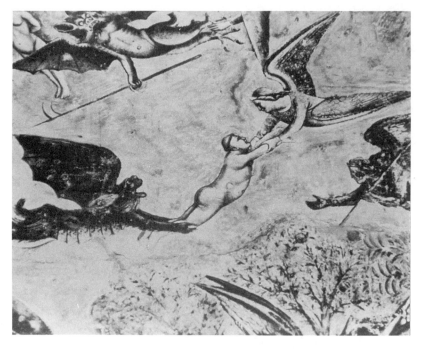

Devils and angels compete for a dead soul. (Fresco from the Campo of Pisa. Photo by Joan Gregg)

D22. The Judgment of Peter the Tax Collector

St. John the Almsgiver tells us that there was once a rich tax collector named Peter who had no charity towards the poor and would never give them alms; when they came to his house he would shoo them away and give them nothing. Now one time, when a group of poor beggars were talking together, they complained among themselves about how they could never get anything from Peter the tax collector. One of them rose up and said, "I will make a big bet with all of you that today I will be able to get some alms from this man." So he went to Peter's house and stood outside the door, begging. When Peter told him he would get nothing from him, and ordered him to get packing, the beggar cried ever more loudly for alms and would not stop. Peter became so angry with him that he looked for a stone to throw at him, but he could find none. Just at that moment, his servant was coming in the door with a basket full of rye bread, so Peter, in his fit of anger, grabbed one of the loaves out of the basket and threw it at the beggar, striking him smartly. The beggar took the loaf and returned to his fellows, claiming he had indeed gotten alms of Peter the tax collector.

Two days after this incident, Peter the tax collector fell ill and seemed close to death. Then he had a vision in which it seemed that he was brought before a judge, on one side of whom there were foul black men putting all his evil deeds in the balance of a scale. On the other side he saw fair men with despondent faces who said that they had no good deeds to put in the other balance except for a loaf of rye bread which Peter had, against his will, given to a beggar. They put that in the balance, but it was so much lighter than all the evil deeds that the black men said unless more good deeds could be found they would take Peter's soul. At this point Peter awoke and felt so contrite that he sent for a priest to whom he told the whole story. Then he said to himself, "If one rye loaf I cast at a beggar in anger protected me so much, I know that if I give all my wealth to the poor for God's sake, I will profit greatly." And so he did and ever after lived a virtuous life.

D23. The Devil and St. Lawrence's Pot

The *Golden Legend* tells us that the emperor Henry, who maintained a chaste marriage with his wife, Ranegunde, began, through the instigation of the devil, to suspect his wife of having a lover. He put his wife on trial by forcing her to walk barefoot on hot coals for fifteen feet, but as she was about to begin this ordeal, she made this prayer: "Lord, as you know that I am undefiled by Henry, my husband, and every other man, I ask your help." Her husband, resentful at her public prayer, struck her on the cheek with his knife. At that moment a voice was heard saying, "Mary, who was a virgin, will save you because you are a virgin," and then Ranegunde passed through the fire unharmed.

Sometime after this the emperor Henry died. On the day of his death, a great multitude of fiends came running by the cell of a hermit, who opened his window to ask them who they were. They answered him, "We are a legion of fiends on our way to the funeral of the emperor Henry to see if there is anything of his that belongs to us." The her-

mit asked the fiends to come back to him again and tell him how they
fared. So a little while later one fiend came back and told the hermit
that they had not done well. "For," he said, "as Henry's false suspi-
cions of his wife and all his other wicked deeds were being weighed in
a scale against his good deeds, St. Lawrence came by with a big gold
pot, and seeing that Henry's evil deeds were going to outweigh his
good ones, he threw the pot on the side with the good deeds and so
tipped the balance." "Now," the fiend continued, "when I saw that, I
got so angry that I grabbed the pot by its handle—it had been made
with two handles to lift it by since it was so heavy—but one of the handles broke off." This pot to which the fiend referred was a chalice
which the emperor Henry had given to the Cistercian order in honor
of St. Lawrence, and when the hermit went to look at the chalice later,
he saw that one ear had indeed been broken off just as the devil had
told him.

D24. A Pilgrim to St. James Saved from the Devil

> Since I told you that Satan
> Waits for us like a thief in the night,
> I will tell you of a pilgrim,
> How Satan deceived him.
> There was a man as I heard say,
> That to St. James's [shrine] would go,
> And on the day that he was departing
> He gave a feast to all his friends.
> At that time he was so joyous
> That he made Satan angry,
> And Satan tempted him to sin
> With a woman in that place.
> When he had done this sin,
> Upon his way he quickly went,
> And he that had tempted him to fall in blame
> Met him in the likeness of St. James,
> And asked him where he was going.
> The man knew not that it was the fiend,
> And said, "I am making a journey,

A pilgrimage to St. James."
The fiend quickly answered him,
"Don't you know what you have done
In lechery against me?
I am Saint James that speaks with you,
You are unworthy to seek my shrine,
Your pilgrimage is not worth a leek:
Think you your sin to hide from me?
When you did it, I was right beside you.
Your pilgrimage will have no merit
Except if you do as I bid you."
This man believed the fiend to be St. James
And said, "Lord, I am all yours,
Beholden to you
And will do all that you say to me."
"Go forth," the fiend said, "and geld yourself
That I may see your repentance.
And then immediately slit your throat.
Then you will have done my bidding,
And when you have done this dreadful act
Til heaven falls I will stand by you."
This pilgrim continued on his way to St. James,
And committed this shame,
Angrily shearing away
His genitals and his testicles both,
And then he cut his throat in two.
And as soon as he had done so
Satan was full ready
And took that soul greedily,
And made full great joy of his prey
And toward hell he went with it.
But Saint Peter and Saint James met him
And both blocked his way,
And Saint James said to the fiend,
"Where are you going with my pilgrim?"
And he answered and said, "To hell,
Where he shall for his sins dwell,
For he destroyed himself;

Therefore you have no business with him,
With right and reason he is mine,
To come with me to hell's pains."
Then answered Saint James for his man
And said, "You lie, traitor Satan,
You know well, thief, you are to blame,
For he slew himself in my name.
He truly thought that you were me,
When you tempted him to his folly.
Indeed, he was devoted to me
And therefore shall he come with me."
The fiend said, "That may not be,
With right and law you may see
That he is mine through this reasoning:
For when he went on his pilgrimage
He filled his deadly soul
With the filth of lechery,
And afterwards, with his own knife
He took his own life.
Why do you tell me, Saint James, for what reason
Should he not remain in my service?
Look whether I with right and law
May not take him with me to hell?"
Saint James answered and said to him,
"I will not do you any wrong,
But if we will test the truth,
Let us put our case before Our Lady,
And as she judges, so shall it be,
For that is fair, it seems to me."
And Saint Peter, his companion
Said, "This I think is right and law.
Mary," he said, "is a good judge,
She will never do wrong in any way."
   When they came before Our Lady,
   She deemed soon with her mercy
That the soul should to the body
Return, and do a worthy penance,

And said, "This soul, as it now is,
May not come to heaven's bliss,
Before it be cleansed in body
Of sin, with worthy penance.
Therefore, I give this judgment
That it return to the body,
And cleanse itself with worthy penance
And keep itself afterwards from evil."
The fiend at this judgment was bitter
And ill tempered that Our Lady
Had deprived him by her fair judgment
Of that man whom he would have snared.
   When this soul came again
   Into his body, this man was fain
To make himself a monk of Cluny
And told this tale to his abbot,
How he was damned through sin
And rescued by Our Lady.
Gerard he called himself, and from that time
That Satan had lost him,
He became a good and holy man,
And feared God with might and main.
But his throat was scarred by the knife,
He carried a red welt all his life,
And where his genitals were before,
He had afterwards only a hole.
By this tale here we may see
That it behooves us to be wise and wary
So that Satan can not turn us
From right conduct to sinful acts.

D25. The Devil Claims a Lecherous Priest

Caesar of Heisterbach tells us that once, in the bishopric of Saxony, as a priest named Henry sat in a tavern, a great stormy tempest blew up in the sky. The priest and his clerk ran quickly into the church to ring the bells, but just as they came to the church door, a dint of thunder

struck them both down so that the clerk, who was unharmed, lay
underneath the priest, whose body was also uninjured except for his
genitals, for this priest was guilty of the sin of fornication. The priest's
clothes were so torn that not a piece was left whole except that part
covering his left arm where his maniple usually hung. The new boots
he had on were all ripped to shreds as if animals had been chewing
them, and the soles looked as if they had been boiled in water.

When the clerk, who was very frightened at the spectacle before him,
looked around, he observed fiends fighting in the church, and he
noticed that two shrines which stood behind the altar had fallen on the
altar and broken. Then he saw the saints, statues, and relics of the church
give fierce battle to the fiends, who withstood them mightily. At last,
however, the fiends were overcome, and because they could not take the
priest's body away with them, they carried off part of the church's roof.
Then the clerk saw the priest borne off by devils to the steeple top, but
through the power of the saints he was brought down again.

D26. The Unrepentant Knight

There was a knight who for his wit and his cleverness was chosen to
be part of the king's council of the land. This knight thus chosen ruled
with great wickedness: he was a great blasphemer, he instigated false
quarrels and injustices and false judgments, and he disinherited many
rightful heirs. He took no heed of God nor of holy church nor of man,
but only thought of pleasing the king. Yet he displeased the king
because of his wicked speech and rule so that the king reproved him
and counselled him to stop his falsehoods and to shrive himself and
reform so that death should not take him unprepared. And the knight
said he would when he felt it was time.

Soon afterwards the knight fell sick and lay for a long time sorrow-
ing in his bed. The king came to him and visited him often and bade
him confess his sins and repent. And the knight said that as soon as he
recovered he would turn himself to God, for he would not be such a
coward as to reform himself in sickness only out of fear of death.

And the king came another time unto him and again gave him
counsel as before. The knight answered and said that now it was too
late for him to mend his ways. "For just now," said he, "at midday,

there came to me two fair young men, handsome and bright. And when I saw them, I thought that I was made well. And they laid before me a beautiful book to read, although it was amazingly small, and there I found all the good deeds that I had ever done or thought of, but certainly these were few and unimportant. Then suddenly and soon there came to me two people black and horrible to look at and I was greatly afraid when I saw them, and I turned every which way to see if I could hide from them, but wherever I turned, they were continually before me and in my sight. And when I saw no other choice I lay still. They sat themselves down and took forth a huge book that was quite black and horrible, and there, whether I would or not, I read all my evil deeds and all my ill thoughts; the least evil thought that ever I had had was not omitted. And then there came another who said to them, "Why are you sitting here? You know well that he is ours." And they said, "Yea, then take him with you unto the pain of hell without end." Then the two foul fiends took two knives of burning iron and one struck me on the head and the other pierced my feet, and now these awls are entering my body. And when they come together, then I know well that I shall die and go to hell. Why should I repent now who am so soon to die? No matter how long I might live, I could never amend my life. My sins have been so great and so foul that I can never have forgiveness for them."

Then the king went away, and this knight went to the devil as he had said he would.

Source Notes to Exempla about Devils

1. *JW* 237, from *AN* (*AT* no. 581). Original in *VP* col. 765, no. 43. *IE* no. 1665.

2. *English Metrical Homilies*, 148–51. Although unnamed here, the *VP*'s Life of Macarius contains the tale and he is named in other analogues. See *VP* cols. 769, no. 67; 981, no. 9; 1027, no. 8. *IE* nos. 210 and 3105.

3. *AT* no. 119. Original in *DM* 10.67. *IE* no. 4884.

4. *AT* no. 359. Original in *DM* 6.22. *IE* no. 970 omits this reference.

5. *AT* no. 394. Original in Gregory's *Dial.* 1.10. *IE* no. 1598 omits *AT*.

6. *GR* 65 (Addit. MS 9066) 380–82. *IE* no. 5015 omits *JW* 9 for a discussion of which see Gregg *Traditio* 376. For a full source analysis see Scholderer, "Archbishop Udo" 349.

7. *Festial* 293. *IE* omits this reference.

8. *AT* no. 231. Original in *DM* 2.7.

9. *JW* 157 from *AN* (*AT* no. 286). Original in *DM* 12.40. *IE* no. 2249.

10. *AT* no. 158. See JdeV (Crane) 31 and p. 145 for variant and discussion.
IE no. 1103 refers not to this precise motif, but to a parchment cloak, as in JdeV.

11. *AT* no. 620. Original in *DM* 8.59. *IE* no. 1580.

12. *Festial* 173. *IE* no. 2654 omits this reference.

13. *AT* no. 699. Original in *DM* 1.3. *IE* no. 4630.

14. *AT* no. 562. Original in *DM* 5.4. *IE* no. 1071a.

15. *AT* no. 551. Original in *DM* 5.2. *IE* no. 1071.

16. *AT* no. 490. Original in *DM* 10.2. *IE* no. 1585. See *IE* no. 3567 for widow
setting conditions in pact with devil.

17. *GR* 59 (addit. MS 9066) 375–76. See *IE* no. 1071b. A variant of an
Egyptian monk's lust for a Saracen priest's daughter appears in our volume,
exemplum W25. *IE* no. 3566 omits reference to a variant in *AT* no. 64, told of
St. Basil; the same anecdote appears in *GL*'s Life of that saint, 1.110.

18. *AT* no. 50. The original of this tale and its analogue in *JW* 31 following
the *AN* was probably Vincent de Beauvais's *Speculum historiale* (Strausberg,
1473), bk. 25, chaps. 98–101. *IE* no. 906. *IE* no. 375, motif of animals choosing a
gravesite omits *Festial* 211, which relates the Life of St. James the Apostle based
on the *GL*'s Life of St. James the Greater, 2,6. (St. James Apostle in *GL*, 1.269
refers to James the Less.) For a discussion of Sylvester's life in history and legend see Allen, "Pope Sylvester II." A full account of Gerbert's life, but omitting
the motif of animals choosing his gravesite, is found in William of
Malmesbury's *Chronicle of the Kings of England* 172–81.

19. *KTL* 27.40; see also p. 41. Sermon analogues appear in *Festial* 279 and
JW 232. *IE* no. 1630 omits reference to *AT* nos. 150, 581.

20. *GR*, 83 (addit. MS 9066) 403–4. *IE* no. 4902. See also *IE* no. 1656.

21. *JW* 138, from *AN* (*AT* no. 753). Original in *DM* 2.31. *IE* no. 232. The
verses in the English tales are direct translations from their Latin source, which
omits some the *DM*'s details of the usurer's wealth: "his chests full of silver
and gold, and also very many pledges in vases, books, and various ornaments,
much corn and wine and furniture, as well as a vast number of cattle."

22. *AT* no. 296 (erroneously printed by Banks as 316). Also in *JW* 192 (and
again in fol. 204) following *AN*. Original in *VP* Life of St. John the Almsgiver
(PL col. 356, chap. 21), which continues with later examples of the usurer's
conduct: he gives his cloak to a mariner, who refuses it, but is afterwards told
by Christ that this charity was not in vain; he sells himself to a man who pros-
pers through his new slave's humility; he refuses to allow friends to help him
escape from his slavery. Our tale also appears in St. John the Almsgiver's Life
in *GL* 1.113–14. *IE* no. 3727 omits reference to *Festial* 104, a variant probably

based on the *GL*. An analogue (with an unnamed rich usurer) is told in *MES* 152; in *The Northern Homily Cycle*, for which see Gerould *North English Homily Collection* 56 and *HS* lines 5572–694.

23. *AT* no. 434. The original is in the Life of St. Lawrence Martyr at *GL* 2.69. The *Festial's* version, 220, tells the second part of our exemplum as a separate anecdote. *IE* no. 1501d.

24. *English Metrical Homilies* 53–58. *IE* no. 3788 rubrics the tale under mutilation of "limbs," a substitution that appears in some variants. *GL* 1.8, in the Life of St. James the Greater, refers to the pilgrim's multilation of his "male member." *AT* no. 375 cites Hugh of St. Victor for the full tale; *AT* no. 376, a summary, cites Hugh of Cluny.

25. *AT* no. 744. Original in *DM* 10.29. *IE* no. 237 omits these references.

26. *MES* 144. Original in Bede's *Ecclesiastical History of the English People*, bk. 5, chap. 13, places the tale in the kingdom of Mercia in the time of King Coenred, hence its occasional title "King Coenred's Knight." In *IE* nos. 1501 b and c, *AT* no. 30 is this exemplum; *IE* omits reference to *Festial* 220 and *HS* lines 4361–509.

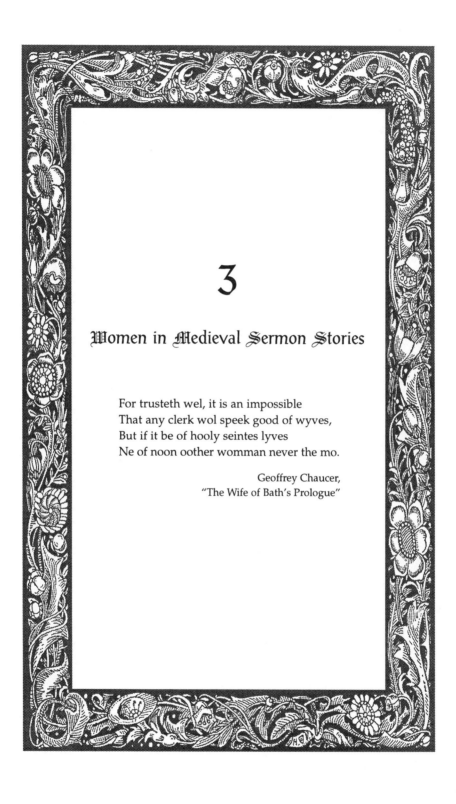

3

Women in Medieval Sermon Stories

For trusteth wel, it is an impossible
That any clerk wol speek good of wyves,
But if it be of hooly seintes lyves
Ne of noon oother womman never the mo.

Geoffrey Chaucer,
"The Wife of Bath's Prologue"

The original Eve and the "new Eve," the Virgin Mary stand on opposite sides of the tree of knowledge in this illustration from the Hours of Catherine of Cleves, ca. 1440. The clerical view of women is made explicit by the banderole above the tree: Eve authoress of sin; Mary authoress of merit. (Courtesy The Pierpont Morgan Library, New York. M.917, p.139)

While the greatest poet of the Middle Ages, Geoffrey Chaucer, was able to depict a wide range of feminine types that included "good women" of ordinary status, the bifurcated image of women complained of by Chaucer's Wife of Bath was a most accurate assertion as regards medieval homiletic narrative. Exempla rendered women within a very limited range of constructed images that conformed to the psychological apprehensions and religious convictions of an empowered clerical male authority that had developed along misogynistic lines from its inception. In the earliest Christian writings, the identity of women was scripted through a cluster of attributes which, like those assigned to Satan and his fallen angels, confounded the vulnerable Christian male and put the salvation of his immortal soul in danger at every turn. Like the devil, women were perceived as masking their perniciousness in attractive guises, and it was part of the exemplum's purpose to unveil their subtleties and sorceries in order to underscore the need for vigilance against them. While stories may serve as instruments of empowerment, as we know, they may also oppress, and towards this latter end, in regard to women, sermon narrative was clearly bent.

Furthermore, as we shall see in detail in the next chapter, homiletic antifeminism was supported and strengthened by clerical anti-Judaism.[1] Women and Jews together came to be viewed not just as the spiritual inferiors of the Christian male but, more specifically and perniciously, as the embodiments of carnality and sexual peril, with all that that implied for the damnation of one's eternal soul. Throughout homiletic narrative, the instigating devil, the lustful woman, and the carnal Jew emerge as destabilizers of Christian equilibrium, embodiments of seduction, deception, and contamination who laid siege to the faith and dogmas of the established church. As most medieval women, perhaps even more so than men, interpreted and evaluated their identities with reference to the tenets of the church, the voices of women in resistance to these constructed identities, even more so than that of Jews, were little heard outside their own sphere.

While religious literature did present a variety of narratives starring models of feminine virtue, these were largely hagiographical accounts of female martyrs or miracles of the Virgin, idealized women whose chastity, purity, and loving-kindness were contextualized by spiritual considerations far from those that dominated the lives of most medieval women. Apart from these models of unattainable perfection, homiletic narrative offered almost no exempla of ordinary "good women" to offset its string of witches, bawds, priests' concubines, adulterous lovers, and incestuous mothers. Even in one charming exception, a tale of a miner's wife who brings food to her husband trapped in his quarry, the woman is chided for having neglected her spiritual duties and thus inviting the devil to further imperil her husband.[2] The Wife of Bath's accusation against clerical stories, then, was not hyperbole, and, after the era of courtly love, it pervaded not only popular pulpit tales, but influenced secular literature as well.[3]

The medieval homiletic construction of the female identity served two struggling aspects of a troubled clerical masculinity. First, it enabled a projection of male sexual guilt onto an unempowered Other, women, just as Christian guilt about wavering faith was projected onto the Jew as perfidy. This in turn permitted the rationalization that women's inferiority and sexual aggressiveness required male governance, just as Christian authority rationalized its persecution of the Jews by the perfidy attributed to them through projection. As in the case of the Jews, the male clerical perspective on women became encoded in the social conventions, religious doctrines, and secular laws of medieval society for many hundreds of years, during which it exerted a powerful hold over many levels of society. Nor did this misogynist perception diminish in the period of the Reformation. Rather, it conflated the figures of women and the devil even more explicitly, inspiring and providing theological underpinnings to the witch-hunts of this period. Indeed, few would argue against the persistence of these views in influencing western sex and gender relations down to our very day.

The operative motif in the misogynistic medieval representation of womankind was Eve's disobedience to God and her betrayal of Adam in Genesis's account of the creation (Gen. 2:21–25, 3:1–24). As with so many personages and stories from the Hebrew bible, the problematic figure of Eve was interpreted by Christian theology to serve its own interests. Eve's creation from Adam's rib signalled her inferiority; her succumbing to the wiles of the serpent/devil demonstrated her vulnerability to pride, ambition and the vanities of the world; her role in Adam's fall and the consequent original sin of our species marked her as a source of evil, confusing man's reason, polluting his virtue and vitiating his loyalty to the God who created him, and Christ, who would save him. Utilizing Genesis's assertion that Adam and Eve covered their genitals when caught out by God, theological and popular Christian belief came to view Eve's temptation in a sexual light. Just as the biblical serpent—with its phallic connotations—was transmogrified into a sexually aggressive devil by centuries of Christian exegetes, so too, throughout the Middle Ages, was the figure of Eve employed to project a demonic sexuality. Articulated throughout centuries of Christian sermon literature directed to religious males and lay audiences alike is the judgment that both female desire and the desire that women aroused in men originated with the devil, who manipulated these passions to destroy both sexes.

Having established the leitmotif of Eve as a betrayer of Adam and of all mankind, medieval cautionary literature applied it to womankind in general, frequently elaborating it with accounts from the Hebrew scriptures of heroic male figures such as Samuel, Solomon, or David and whole communities of ancient Hebrews who were brought low through the sexuality and treachery of women. In *The Book of the Knight of Tour Landry*, for example, a fifteenth-century secular manual of conduct for women modeled along popular homiletic lines, a wide range of misogynistic cautionary tales is interspersed with biblical narratives of whores and harlots wreaking havoc upon their husbands and communities. In a concatenation of vanity and wantonness characteristic of popular pulpit narrative, Tour Landry presents, for instance, the account of the Midianite woman who seduced a lord of the Hebrews and caused his death, by "arra[ying] herself gaily . . . forto fulfelle her foule luste," and relates elsewhere how "lechery and the disguisying of youre array displesid God and . . . alle the world was stroied therfor, . . . Sodom and Gomor, and other v. citees was brent in stinking sulfure, and sank to hell."[4]

The Hebrew biblical image of the whore and the harlot as an emblem of irreligion, cultural treachery, and political disloyalty, such as we find in the books of Jeremiah (3:1, 20) and Hosea (2:1–10) exerted a powerful influence in the shaping of the identity of women from early Christian times. In the patristic and later medieval periods, women, like the Jews, for whom the epithets "whore" and "harlot" became common coin, were viewed as betrayers of their faith, subverters of the social order, and collaborators with the enemies of their nations.

Medieval exempla sit squarely within these early Christian tradition, although torturous deaths and such hellish pains after death as
the dismemberment or conflagration of the body largely replace the
biblical punishments of exile. In "The Collier's Vision" (W13), for
example, one of the most popular of medieval exempla, the tale's
male narrator relates with complacency that he saw a deceased male
adulterer hewing his partner into pieces and throwing them into a fire
"night after night . . . [because] she was the cause of [his] sin." Even a
humorous *fabilau* such as the Knight of Tour Landry's "A Roper's False
Wife" (W17) concludes its narrative of adultery with the community's
approval of the deceived husband's impaling of his wife and her lover
to their bed of sin; to both the man's neighbors and the law this was
viewed as "a proper way to punish them."

In addition to the derogations of women extrapolated from the
Hebrew bible, and such popular antifeminist folk traditions as the
Jewish myth of Lilith, two female images from Christian scriptures
were also significant in the exemplum's misogynistic construction of
its female personae.[5] The whore Babylon, as depicted in the Revelation
of St. John the Divine, strikes several chords that continue to be heard
in medieval sermon story. "The mother of harlots . . . arrayed in pur-
ple and scarlet, and adorned with gold and precious stones . . . having
a golden cup in her hands full of abominations and the filthiness of her
fornication . . . drunken with the blood of the saints . . . and the martyrs of Jesus . . ." (17–19) brings together motifs of irreligion, female
adornment, and a predatory sexuality directed towards the spiritually
pure male that resonated, albeit on a more domestic scale, throughout
sermon story.[6] The whore Babylon's carnality and the linking of her
worldliness to the aggressive commercialism of the Babylonian merchants also made her a compelling anti-Judaic as well as antifeminist
symbol for medieval Christendom. Like the Hebrew figure of Jezebel,
whom St. John also employs in Revelation (2:20), the whore Babylon
stood as an exemplar of women as murderous seductresses, which was
to become the subtext of much medieval homiletic narrative.

The theological crafting of the figure of Mary Magdalene was more
specific in its influence on medieval homiletic narrative. As the
"reformed harlot," Mary Magdalene became a stock figure of support
for Christianity's salvatory rituals of contrition, confession, and repen-

tance.[7] While the evangelist Luke names Mary Magdalene as one of "certain women who had been healed of evil spirits and infirmities . . . out of whom had come seven demons" (8:2), she is never identified there as a sexual transgressor. Nor is another female sinner in Luke's Gospel, the unnamed woman forgiven by Christ after she washed his feet with her tears and dried them with her hair (7:37–39), particularized as a sexual sinner. Yet over time, through conflation of Mary Magdalene with the unnamed sinner forgiven by Christ and through the attribution of carnality to the female gender as a whole, theological and popular tradition evolved the character of the Magdalene as a reformed prostitute. This prototype of the penitent harlot figures in several tales of saintly women, preeminently in the widely disseminated exemplum of the Egyptian prostitute Thais's encounter with the abbot Paphnutius ([Pascuncius] W31). In more generalized, domestic form, the figure of the penitent wanton abounded in medieval sermon story, with an increasing emphasis on the efficacy of the sacrament of confession as an element of her reform. As we shall later see, the motif of the reform of a lecherous woman also became a staple of Marian legend, where devotion to the Virgin was added as an instrument of spiritual conversion over and above the redemptive processes of confession, contrition, and penance.

While the concomitancy of male asceticism and misogyny is perhaps not inevitable, there is little argument that in Christianity, the praise for virginity and the antimatrimonial stance taken by St. Paul in his Epistles developed into a potent source for medieval clerical misogyny. These themes, which dot his letters of advice to the newly formed congregations of gentiles in Asia Minor, resonate strongly in the hagiographical exempla of the monks of the Egyptian desert and in the theology of the church fathers. Paul established the notion of an irreconcilable dichotomy between the spirit and the flesh: "Walk in the spirit and you shall not fulfil the lust of the flesh. For the flesh lusts against the Spirit and the Spirit against the flesh; and these are contrary to one another" (Gal. 5:16–17). He admonished that "It is good for a man not to touch a woman" (1 Cor. 7:1) and urges the unwed to remain so, as he himself will. He praised the spirituality of the virgin woman above the wife, for the "unmarried woman cares about the things of the Lord, that she may be holy both in body and in spirit. But she who is married cares about the things of the world—how she may please her husband" (1 Cor. 7:34) and lauds the celibate man as one who "[has] no necessity, but the power over his own will" and "does better" than the married man (1 Cor. 7:38).

Thus did woman became part of that cluster of appetites that had to be mastered and overcome; she became explicitly the Other, a being whose innate nature was in direct conflict with the highest Christian idea of the spiritual self. This notion informed a wide range of the new church's doctrines and beliefs, and found strenuous expression in homiletic narrative from the inception of the faith. The issue of the power of self-discipline to tame male desire became preeminent in the pious tales of early Christian ascetics, and numerous exempla from their literature, transmitted into medieval pulpit narrative, point to the paramountcy of this Pauline concept. The account of the desert monk who kept the dead body of his beloved in his cell so that her stench would remind him of the wages of sin is a most graphic, but by no means unusual, example of such narratives.[8]

Although certain of St. Paul's utterances imply a mutually respectful and even affectionate vision of marriage that was advanced for his time and place, explicit statements in the Epistles relegated women to a status inferior to men's and suggested that perhaps only in heaven might men and women be equal. On earth, "the head of every man is Christ, the head of woman is man . . . [the man] is the image and glory of God; but woman is the glory of man. For man is not from woman, but woman from man. Nor was man created for the woman, but woman for the man." (1 Cor. 11:3–9). Pauline commentary on womankind's weak reason and spiritual defectiveness would later lend support to the inferiorization and demonization of women that began in the patristic period and shaped the medieval perspective. For just as Satan's sin of pride led him to falsely equate himself with God, so too was Eve's weaker intellect responsible for her mistake in thinking herself God's equal in knowledge and her foolish belief that she could challenge his commandments with impunity. And as Eve was, so were all women.

By the patristic period and continuing into the Middle Ages, Paul's theme of woman's inferiority to man would become elaborated with issues of feminine pollution, specifically that women's innate lowliness as well as their impurity was manifest in their servitude to their menstrual periods.[9] Indeed, it was a subject of debate by the church fathers whether women should be permitted to take the Eucharist during their menses. Nor did Christian tradition fail to find another link between women and Jews in this myth of the menses as a signpost of female inferiority, for it was a commonplace of medieval sermon storytelling that Jewish males, like all females, were subject to genital bloodlettings at certain times. Thus, Jewish males, like all women, were "unmanned" and thereby inferiorized by their physiology.

While the Pauline tilt of early Christianity towards asceticism was not unique in the Near East of those times—Stoicism, with its emphasis on controlling the passions, for example, shared similar views—the denigration and even disgust that characterized patristic views of women is so obsessive as to merit a closer look. While other female appetites besides the sexual were condemned in early Christian literature, it was egregiously lust, or sexual desire, and the figure of women as sexual beings that excited homiletic revilement.

This disparagement of sexuality and, by extension, the female sex that was both its subject and its object was no mere adjunct to Christian theology: it was a central and enduring correlative of Christianity's redemptive theology. A persuasive psychoanalytic argument has been made that the roots of this development lie in the dynamics of the male unconscious. Specifically, according to this analysis, the male's guilt-inducing sexual desires resulting from an unsuccessful negotiation of the Oedipal complex became a widespread phenomenon in Christian lands during patristic times due to economic circumstances that left many families without fathers at home.[10] Thus, the son's wrongful sexual desire for his mother and his rivalry with his father could not be resolved normally thorough gradual identification with the male parent and the transfer of sexual desire to other, appropriate women. Unacknowledged, unexpunged, and repressed, this forbidden sexual desire evolved into an unassuagable guilt, with a corresponding obsession with bodily purity and a desire for punishment in the form of physical deprivation and pain. A further means of dealing with this psychically intolerable guilt was to project it onto the object causing it, that is, women, with accompanying rationalizations to justify male antipathy towards the female sex. This psychic content marked the utterances about women of the highest authorities of the early church, and it is to this nexus of personal psychology melded with church theology that we must look in order to rightly understand the reiterated cluster of misogynist motifs that permeate medieval pulpit narrative.

The theological psychodynamics of Christian misogyny were shaped most clearly and influentially in the writings of St. Augustine, the reformed sinner whose perspective on female sexuality became salient in the medieval church.[11] While Augustine declared that "the sex of a woman is not a vice but natural," he attributed original sin to the emission of semen in the sexual act, which tainted the child in the womb, thus condemning the female duties of "carnal intercourse and childbearing" as the contaminants of our species. He interpreted Eve's role in the Fall as a specifically sexual one, approving the sexual dimension of her punishment, "the curse of Eve," which was to bring forth children through painful labor. While on earth, this female duty was necessary for the propagation of the species, but in heaven, on the contrary, "the female members shall remain adapted not to the old uses, but to a new beauty, which so far from provoking lust, now extinct, shall excite praise to the wisdom of God."[12] Thus it was not the sexual act *per se* that was sinful but its initiating lust, or sexual desire, which the female excited in the male. This passion was the mainspring of the female nature and its inherent flaw from which sinfulness emanated. Under the spell of sexual arousal men could not achieve spiritual perfection, for lust drove out the love of God. Thus, in Christian hermeneutics, the quest for sexual satisfaction could not be reconciled with the quest for salvation.

To experience sexual desire, then, was to embrace death and the damnation of the soul that was eternal death, even to the Last Judgment. This theme, which necessarily pitted woman against man, is sounded in numerous medieval exempla. One such pulpit tale, which portrays this notion in literal form, is the *Speculum laicorum*'s anecdote of a mortally ill priest who cannot resist one last visit from his concubine. The concubine's form is taken by the devil, and, as the priest embraces her, he immediately falls dead.[13]

While the ubiquity of male sexual desire compelled acknowledgement, it was intolerable to the male psyche that his own concupiscence should condemn him. Culpability, therefore, had to be placed elsewhere: on women, who were the visible proximate source of sexual desire, and on the devil, who could serve as the instigator that would partially excuse women by presenting their lust-arousing conduct as involuntary. Women became the screen upon which the fleshly passions could be safely projected. Chaucer's Wife of Bath comprehended this phenomenon clearly: "By God, if wommen hadde writen stories, / As clerkes han withinne hire oratories, / They wolde han writen of men more wikkednesse / Than all the mark of Adam may redresse."[14]

But as Chaucer's Wife of Bath correctly asserted, it was "clerkes[']" stories that were privileged over women's, and for clerical stories to impart the desired object lesson, the image of women must be one that could plausibly absorb the unregenerate sexual passions of the male and manifest them in a way that men could rationally accept. With the shadow of Eve in the background, and the doctrines and homilies of the church fathers in support, we should not wonder at the medieval view of women as insatiable, ineradicably sexual creatures, those Others—not like "us"—composed of mysterious, almost nonhuman elements, like explosions of nature that imperilled a man's life by their forceful unpredictability. "It fareth with them as fyr and tunder," one medieval preacher intoned, nor could they leave any man alone but attempted to seduce "all who are made of flesh and bone."[15]

While Christian theology recognized that men succumbed to sexual temptation of their own free will, in the rhetoric of the church fathers and in the scenarios of the medieval exemplum, women are projected as the active agents of lust, men as the victims. Eve, again, in conjunction with the phallic, demonic serpent, is the prototype, the temptress of an innocent Adam. Man's passivity before woman's onslaught of sexuality is raged at by the third-century Christian rhetorician Tertullian, who accuses Eve of having "[broken Adam] as if he were a plaything," while John Chrysostom, the fourth-century patriarch of Constantinople known as "golden mouthed," drew a forceful if vituperative picture of sexual woman as both the literal and spiritual death-dealer of men in his analogy comparing her to "those who prepare the draught and concoct the envenomed potions" that poison men, exculpating man as the victim who drinks it.[16]

In medieval homiletic narrative and popular art, the images of women, as of the devil and the Jew, were marked by predatoriness, voraciousness, and assault. Denial of male complicity in sexual encounters necessitated the construction of fantasies in which

women—again like the devil and the Jew (male or female)—lured men
to their spiritual death, in this case through sexual arousal. Like the
devil holding his councils in the nether world or the Jew concocting his
plots against Christian artifacts or helpless children behind the walls of
his quarter, homiletic narrative frequently places women's sexual pre-
dation in dark or isolated spaces: the hidden chambers of the prostitute
Thaïs (W31); the barren fields where the fornication of "The Collier's
Vision" took place (W13); even within the curtained privacy of the con-
fessional, where the courtship of the adulterous wife and her monk
lover took place in "The Virgin Puts Devils in the Stocks" (W37).

This projection of the victimization of a hapless male by a sexually
aggressive female is particularly evident in the incest narratives that
appear in the medieval exempla collections, for these turn almost
entirely on incidents of mothers' illicit sexual relations with their sons
in the face of the contradictory reality that the reverse molestion is far
more common. While one well-known homiletic manual, in warning
preachers not to employ illustrations of incest that might give ideas to
the audience, conforms to reality in using an instance of father-daughter abuse as its sample narrative, most homiletic incest exempla turn
on a mother's sexual activity with her son.[17] When those in power pro-
mulgate a myth manifestly contradicting reality by placing the blame
that belongs to the privileged group onto its victims, such myths must
be carefully scrutinized for unconscious and unintended significa-
tions. What then, lies behind such mother-son incest exempla as "A
Mother Forgiven for Incest" (W22) and "The Virgin Defends a Matron
against the Devil" (W35), which are representative of the homiletic
treatment of this theme?

The psychodynamics of the exempla treatment of incest suggest an
ambivalence towards the female/mother figure that has already been
noted.[18] On the one hand, such tales indicate a deep anxiety of the male
narrators that even the mother role—the most beneficent one women
can play—is but another guise for the sexual corruption of men that is
an ineradicable element in the female nature. Such exempla warn that
beneath the loving female that the mother *ought* to represent lies a
"bad mother": an unregenerately sexual woman who leads the vulnerable male astray. Mother-son incest tales project the ultimate impurity of women, a projection that reverses the guilty secret of the male's

desire for his mother which he has not successfully resolved. Mother-
son incest motifs resonate to the same male victim fantasies that fueled
the notion of Eve as the "bad mother" tainting her progeny. On the
other hand, while mothers' violation of their sons is surely one of the
strongest taboos in western society, the matrons of our incest exempla
merit only relatively light punishments and are forgiven their sin after
sincere particpation in the penitential process. In this way some beneficence is returned to the maternal role, releasing the psychic pressure
of guilt that must accompany male hostility towards the women who
bore and reared them. Moreover, there was an institutional gain for the
church in these exempla, for they conveyed the crucial notion that no
sin is so heinous that it cannot be erased through the salvatory rituals,
the efficacy of which had been coming under increasingly hostile
scrutiny by all manner of heretics and the faithful alike.

    That motherhood might be just another cover for the threatening
female persona against which the male must be wary was consistent
with the misogynistic patristic notion that women's physical beauty
was not emblematic of spiritual purity—a symbolic conjunction
unique to the Virgin Mary and articulated about secular women in the
Middle Ages only in romance narrative and in the literature of courtly
love—but, rather, a trope for the mortality that Eve had brought upon
a susceptible Adam and the entire human race. A beautiful woman
was a diabolic paradox, commented the homilist Etienne de Bourbon,
"a fetid rose, sweet venom" that entrapped a man and killed him spri-
itually. To the influential "golden mouthed" church father John
Chrysostom, feminine loveliness was a casing over "nothing less than
phlegm, blood, bile, rheum, and the fluid of digested food."[19] The hidden subtext of female beauty was *Luxure*, or carnal sin, revealingly
depicted by one monastic author as "an Ethiopian woman of fetid and
ugly aspect," whose otherness was doubly manifest by her femaleness
and her identification with an alien culture.[20]

    In this construction of womanhood that emerged from the clerical
dualism between love of God and love of the world, in popular piety
and in numerous literary works, woman was projected as the embodiment of the material world and a symbol of all that was temporal and
corruptible, and would eventually wither and die. The impermanence
of feminine beauty, subject to the decay of age, contributed to man's

domestic as well as spiritual unhappiness, as Gower tells us in the *Mirror of Man*: "But most of all I mistrust / The old trot who used to be pretty, / When her breasts dry up: / It is my opinion, no matter what others say, / That with such a wife in bed, / A man is a fool if he pays her debts."[21]

Clerical disparagement of feminine beauty, a reaction formation that denied its appeal, was a true antifeminism in its antipathy to the enduring difference of the female, her physiology, which could not be changed.[22] The female appearance, even when innocent of vanity or intention to arouse male desire, was rationalized as a threat not only to men but to the woman herself, for it invited assault on her most important physical asset, her virginity. The widely disseminated pious tale, "A Nun Tears Out Her Eyes to Preserve Her Chastity" (W29), exemplifies these intertwined notions, for here, a nun whose beautiful eyes attracted the lust of her convent's patron, plucks out the offending orbs not only to save herself from an assault on her chastity but to rescue her suitor from the sin of lust as well. While in some analogues the nun is rewarded for her defensive mutilation by having her beautiful eyes restored, in others she remains permanently mutilated so that she will never again become an occasion of sin for men.

By the High Middle Ages, the psycho-religious matrix from which clerical misogyny had sprung had been overlaid with a specific aversion to the new affluence of the rising bourgeoise and enterpreneurial classes. In the increasing sumptiousness of feminine dress and adornment that reflected rising economic statuses (and, more directly threatening, a waning of clerical values), the homilist saw the familiar sin of vanity, which came under strenuous pulpit attack. This was especially true in the sermon tales of the newly instituted orders of Dominican and Franciscan preachers, who were strictly governed by values of austerity and humility and who were so influential in setting the tone of homiletic discourse *ad populum*. Just as the Virgin's raiment and accoutrements were viewed symbolically as manifesting her various virtues, the fashionable woman's attire also signalled her inner qualities: frivolity, spiritual insouciance, and even uglier vices. Alterations of her physical form for fashion's sake were particularly decried, for reshaping her hairline and coloring her face signalled her blasphemous usurpation of God's unique prerogative of creation and threw her in league with the devil. The Knight of Tour Landry, for example, related that a certain woman who "popped, painted, plucked, and fared her hede" was punished by having her visage transformed into such a hideous sight that no one could bear to look at her, and she died in poverty although she formerly had been a woman "made moche of" for her more than four score dresses. The high "cornes" of fourteenth-century women's headresses, characterized as devil's horns, figure in another homiletic tale, where a woman who missed part of the Mass in order to do her coiffure found the devil in the form of a spider so tightly locked on her head that she fell down as one dead.[23] The fashion for trains on dresses also aroused homiletic ire and was the subject of many cautionary tales. The trains were compared to the tails of animals that covered their shame and, as in "A Gown with a Train of Devils" (W1), were frequently reviled as infested with demons.

Women in medieval exempla, consistently deployed as cautionary figures, preeminently represented sexual appetite; and the sexuality of a woman, whether harlot, wife, spinster, or widow, unequivocally represented the potential for male diminishment. Consciously and unconsciously, men construed female sexuality as the one powerful weapon of an otherwise unempowered gender. While they might despise and dominate women, sermon story indicates that men also feared the spiritual injuries women might wreak upon them. Female fornication and adultery, which not only disrupted the established social order but, more importantly, obstructed man's spiritual progress, was viewed as a figurative castration or "umanning," which robbed males both of their masculine prerogatives on earth and their eschatological reward of heaven.

Two specific figures of ungoverned female sexuality whose potential for disuption excited clerical concern were bawds and witches. The bawd, a dissolute woman who pandered to male sexual appetites by providing female partners, threatened the sacred domain of marriage, an institution that the church had finally sacramentalized by the end of the Middle Ages but had never been able to fully control. By enabling female sexuality, the bawd violated the sacred space of marriage, undermining its ideals of monogamy and sexuality only in the service of procreation. The subtext of the illicit sexuality facilitated by the bawd was female independence, represented in the figure of the

bawd herself, who occupied an anomalous gender position uncon-
strained by the limits imposed on economically dependent wives,
maids, or nuns. Bawds cocked a snook at respectability, for which we
may read male authority, utilizing female sexuality to deceive clerical
and secular men alike, as such exempla as "A Bawd's Warning to Her
Husband" (W16) and "A Roper's False Wife" (W17) suggest. As the
former tale illustrates, the bawd's sexuality, like the prostitute's and
the adulteress's, should still be reined in and forgiven by the male
authority of the church through the reformed sinner's participation in
its priest-governed salvatory rituals.

A more serious threat to male authority and clerical ideas emanated
from women designated as witches. Although the witch hunting crazes
reflect the excesses of a period after the Middle Ages, and the *Malleus
maleficarum* (Hammer of witches), the church's authorized compendium of witchlore was published only at the end of the medieval period,
that work's derogation of and disgust with women in general, under
the rubric of witches, represents an attitude formed earlier and characteristic of homiletic narrative. Like the bawd, the witch did not fit any
of the designated spaces for women. Single or widowed, usually independent of the control of husbands or fathers, women of knowledge
were perceived as menaces to both clerical and secular male domina-
tion. As women became increasingly demonized in homiletic literature
through the Middle Ages, the accusations of sexual relationships
between witches and devils became more pronounced, and women
were increasingly viewed as the *voluntary* accomplices of the devil,
rather than as his victims. The chimerical accusation that witches sometimes committed sexual mutilation, that is, castration of men, and the
serious attention this issue receives in the *Malleus maleficarum*, indicates
the depths of masculine fear of women in the sexual realm.[24] Moreover,
the intimacy and authority that characterized the relationship between
women (as mothers and midwives) and children (particularly unbaptized infants), also positioned them as threats to male governance, occa-
sioning their suspicion as practitioners of withcraft; and homiletic literature cautioned midwives in particular about the spiritual considerations they must bring to their work.[25]

In earlier centuries of the Middle Ages, witch practitioners of "white
magic," which did not necessarily involve the cooperation of demonic
forces, were granted a certain measure of toleration, as we may see in

the folklore-based exemplum "The Witch and the Cowsucking Bag" (W18), where even a bishop is not above trying to winkle the secrets out of a female wonder-worker, although he ultimately concludes by urging her to discontinue her magical practices. By the later Middle Ages, however, as evidenced by the indictments in the *Malleus maleficarum* and the widespread dissemination of such *exempla terrible* as "The Witch of Berkeley" (W19), the involvement of the devil in witchcraft was taken for granted, and women were accused of willingly "embrac[ing] this most foul and miserable servitude" to Satan and his devils.[26] In retaliation for the witch's overturning of the world of orthodox piety and ritual with her own "topsy turvey" world of the devil, male clerical authority, through preaching and writing, sanctioned earthly and eschatological punishments of women including torture, execution, and hellpains after death.[27] In an age when the pains of hell were taken literally, homiletic reports of these punishments doubtless instilled terror in many listeners. Indeed, the creation of a climate of fear that rationalized the persecution of witches, as of heretics and Jews, was an important purpose of post–Lateran Council exempla.

The concatenation of femaleness, sexuality, and the demonic in the witch was but an extension of the demonization of women that informed the homiletic perspective of the Christian Middle Ages. As with the liminal constructions of the devil and the Jew, onto whom were projected forbidden sexual desires, guilty ambivalencies, or losses of faith, masculine clerical authority constructed an image of women as the evil Other as well. As both the object and stimulus of sexual desire, women presented a ubiquitous peril. Like the devil, drawing men to their spiritual death under a variety of ingenuous or pleasant guises, woman appeared to a celibate clergy as a perverse, demonic paradox. "What else is a woman," asks the *Malleus maleficarum*, quoting John Chrysostom, "but a foe to friendship, an unescapable punishment, a necessary evil, a natural temptation, a desirable calamity, a domestic danger, a delectable detriment, an evil of nature, painted with fair colors."[28] To Tertullian, Eve, from whom all feminine nature was derived, was "the devil's gateway . . . [who] softened up with [her] cajoling words the man against whom the devil could not prevail by force," while St. Ambrose fancifully explained that God chose Adam's *rib* as the body part from which Eve was made so that she could serve as Satan's bow in his hunt for men's souls. This metaphor was utilized in the

Middle Ages in one compendium of exempla where the narrator speaks of a man possessing a concubine as possessing a "rib" that will lead him to damnation as Eve—Adam's rib—provoked his Fall.[29]

As a repository for the projections of male sexual conflict, woman as the demon temptress was a useful construct both for individual males and for the policies of a celibate clergy, and anecdotes informed by this conception of woman abound in early hagiography and exempla of the eastern monks. In the celebrated fourth-century biography of St. Anthony, the sexual temptations of demonic women and female demons were so enduringly depicted that they have resonated through western art and literature to this day. Several of our exempla turn on this theme. For instance, in our two exempla from the apocryphal history of Saints Barlaam and Joasaph, "The Temptations of Woman as Devils" (W23 a and b), the identities of women and devils are explicitly conflated. Here, when the prince asks his father about the persons he observes—women, whom he has never seen before—the father replies that "they are devils who beguile men." The devil took particular delight in corrupting monks, priests, and other men sworn to celibacy by utilizing the guise of a beautiful female or by instigating a woman to offer them carnal temptations. The exemplum "A Bishop Tempted by a Demonic Beauty is Saved by St. Andrew (W27), one of the medieval homilist's favorites, shows how the devil's disguise as a lovely, wise, and innocent woman tempted even the highest of clerics.

The association of the devil with female sexuality also took the form of the devil's possession and seduction of women. In "St. Bernard Delivers a Woman from a Fiend" (W20), a devil possessing a woman causes her to experience lustful desires, while in "The Devil Seduces a Priest's Daughter" (W21) a demon is successful in his seduction because of the woman's lack of self-discipline. In another exemplum, "The Arrows of Lust," the association between demons and male sexual arousal stimulated by women is quite explicit. Here we meet Eros/Cupid in the demonic form of a "little black fellow like a man of India" shooting burning arrows into an old monk "who then became so excited by sensual desires that he stole out of his cell and went into the world to live," presumably destroying his spiritual health in satisfying his lust.[30]

Behind the medieval homiletic demonization of women was a belief in both devils and women as creatures defective in the male mode of reason and given over to the destructive passions. In privileging the perceived male mode of reason over the perceived female mode of feelings, negatively construed as the sources of sin, Christian theology cast women as "nature[s] out of control" that were incapabable of the self-discipline and mastery over desire that were essential to achieving salvation.[31] Until and unless women could master their sexuality and associated feminine passions such as vanity, anger, querulousness, and rumormongering, they would continue to disrupt society and foreclose their own possibilities for salvation. The Knight of Tour Landry, for example, castigated a wife who loved her husband so much that she was excessively jealous of him. Her jealousy brought her into a fistfight with one of his woman acquaintances, and after a hairpulling tussle, the accused woman broke the wife's nose with a staff, spoiling the wife's face forever, on which account her husband could never love her as before. It would have been far better, counselled the narrator, if the wife had controlled her passion and dealt with her errant husband as an aunt of his had done: lighting a candle in the window for him to find his way home after his amorous nights out![32]

Homiletic attribution of jealousy, spite, backbiting, and anger to women both lay and religious—as in our exemplum of "A Lustful Abbess" (W36)—may have had some foundation in the social realities of the Middle Ages, with its limited outlets for female intelligence and energy. Nevertheless, the severe punishments homilists recorded for these breaches of self-discipline, such as those in the exempla of "A Woman Damned for Dying in Anger"(W6) and "An Abbess' Severed Corpse" (W8), suggest a more deepseated concern about the ungovernability of female impulses than social conditions warrant. Such traits appear to have functioned unconsciously as metaphors for women's uncontrolled sexuality, or lust, an explosion of passion whose consequences were socially and spiritually fatal to men. Female gossip or tale-telling, in particular, as a metonym for female untrustworthiness and treachery in general, appears to have fueled the homilist's ire.[33] And in fact, as Chaucer's Wife of Bath recognized, gossip and the sharing of intimate secrets with one's female friends were a source of female empowerment.[34] Such gender solidarity magnified the threat of female power and suggested a community of complicity in sin reminiscent of the homiletic portrayal of the Jew.

Popular Christian homiletics both explicitly and implicitly promoted a defensive stance for men vis-à-vis women. Exempla from the early Christian period, addressed to the monks and the hermit saints of the desert, advocated complete isolation from women as the only real safeguard against sexual desire. As with Jews, the mere physical presence of women was perceived as dangerous, not only because of the sexual desire it aroused, but further, because proximity or intimacy with women might cause one to lose his self-discipline and become unrestrained, as women characteristically were. Even the strongest and holiest of saints was not immune to the loss of control in the polluting presence of women. As one medieval preacher told his audience, the great St. Jerome himself had to flee to the desert "for dreade of synne and foly gret." So threatening were women to the saint's purity and spiritual strength that flight was his only means of security, lest he "falle or fayle." Nor could the contemporary celibate insure his immunity to the wiles of women, continued this preacher; therefore, those priests "that dwelle at hom" (do not live in a monastic setting) were advised to heed St. Jerome's fear and flee women's company to avoid occasions of sin.[35]

Total avoidance was hardly practical, however, for the many types of religious males populating the medieval landscape whose duties as confessors, spiritual advisors, parish workers, pilgrims, and the like brought them into intimate rather than merely casual acquaintance with women. The celibacy of these men, so central to their calling, was thus at continual risk, and exemplum after exemplum turns on cases of church officials low and high who succumbed to temptation. In addition, as pulpit narrative was increasingly directed to lay audiences, female predatoriness and lechery involving secular males became a frequent theme. To discipline these daughters of Eve, the popular preacher duly exhorted women to spiritual conversion through the salvatory process of contrition, confession, and penance, rituals lauded for their efficacy. The Knight of Tour Landry, for example, relating a tale of a knight who sought to learn how his dead wife was faring, states that he was told that she would have to abide in the burning fires of purgatory for a hundred years in order to cleanse herself of the sin of adultry, which she had committed with a certain squire perhaps "ten or twelve times." The monk reporting the wife's punishment to her husband added that had she not taken confession so often, she would surely have been *eternally* damned for her sin. Several of our exempla conclude in a similar manner.[36]

But the salvatory rituals were seen as only a partial solution to the unreliability of women and their propensity for backsliding into a sinful state that entangled and injured men as well. Confession could only decrease the punishment for sexual sins, not eliminate it altogether. As the Knight of Tour Landry himself reflects about the wife in the exemplum above, had she committed her adultery with a married man; committed it with a priest, a monk, or a friar; or conceived a child in adultery, she would have had greater pain than she did. At a minimum, he warns his readers, for each occasion of the sin the couple spends seven years in the burning fires of purgatory.

Both the stick of damnation and eternal punishment and the carrot of salvation were modes operating after the fact, however. More desirable was a socioreligious idealization of female virginity and chastity and its presentation as an attractive alternative to the secular, that is, sexual life of ordinary women.[37] In the institution of the nunnery and in the cults of the virgin martyrs and the Virgin Mary, both of which denied women their natural identity until they had undergone a desexualizing transformation, the medieval church found this viable alternative. Nunneries, in which women were immured against the temptations of the world and disciplined to master their passions, were promoted through homiletic narrative as retreats appropriate for the reformed sinner as much as for the virgin maid. Just as the guilt of male desire could be assuaged only through the penalty of physical deprivation including sexual abstinence, the stain of female sexuality could also truly be extirpated only through enforced chastity behind nunnery walls. Many exempla, including those of Jewish female converts, conclude with the repentant sinner becoming a "holy woman" safely immured in a nunnery for the rest of her life. The removal of women from the secular, that is, sexual landscape also provided, of course, a means of protecting men from their depredations, an unstated but clearly evident subtext of clerical misogynistic narrative. To rationalize this self-interested means of social control the notion was advanced that chaste women needed the protection of the nunnery against the assaults of men, a theme informing several of our sermon narratives.

The power of female virginity as a mediating category between the inferiorized sexual female and the privileged celibate male, and its usefulness in limiting the contamination of men by women's "dirt," is evident in the vigorous and imaginative promotion of this ideal by the church almost from its inception. Virginity and chastity were long honored and powerful weapons in the armory of Chrisianity and served as touchstones of its difference from its pagan and Jewish enemies. In regard to the Jew in particular, Christian hermeneutics rested on a perceived opposition between the carnality of the older religion and the sexual self-discipline of the new. Jewish acceptance of polygamy and Jewish divorce, the Jewish stance against the ideals of both male celibacy and female virginity, and especially the Jewish refusal to admit the virginity of Christ's mother formed the basis of the Christian imputation that Jewish beliefs were odiously worldy and sensual in contrast to the virtuous salvatory dynamic of Christianity.[38]

To promote the clerical ideal of virginity and chastity among women and to offer them models of imitation, the creation and dissemination of hagiographies of virgin female martyrs and saints became a salient aspect of popular religious teaching that lasted well through the fifteenth century. The Knight of Tour Landry, for example, urging his daughters to eschew the "lechery [that] stinkithe afore God," included a strenuous appeal to remember those virgins who would rather have been martyred than "do that foule synne"; the eleven thousand virgins; such virgin saints as Katherine, Margaret, and Lucy; and so many other virgins that it would take too long a list to enumerate them.[39] Such hagiographical narratives as he refers to, often set in the context of a woman's resistance to a pagan husband or her rejection of marriage in order to become a "bride of Christ," were frequently imbued with an antimatrimonial bias, implicitly casting the female saint in a "manly," that is, spiritually validated role, by her rejection of what was the ordinary woman's destiny.[40] This transformation was, indeed, often made explicit, as the female saint donned men's clothing and took on a male persona in her effort to escape the sexual involvements the world was attempting to foist on her.[41] Our exemplum of St. Theodora (W32) is a prototype of such homiletic illustrations.

In dismissing earthly marriage as impoverished by comparision to the celestial union that the virgin saints would enjoy in heaven, and in degrading the ordinary human sexuality that was the lot of most women, the church promoted the notion that women in their natural, sexual status were outsiders to the salvatory process. Only by suppressing their natural selves and entering the state of *physical* purity could they achieve the spiritual purity required for eschatological reward. In the popular didactic literature of orthodox Christianity, martyrdom and even suicide were put forth as reasonable alternatives to sexual assault or even legal marriage. Admittedly, St. Augustine took a guarded view of the extent to which suicide was justified to avoid the loss of virginity. While he asserted that virgins who drowned themselves to prevent rape merited forgiveness and may even have had divine authority for their action, he explicitly warned others against following their example.[42] Yet, as the tale "Of a Woman Who Would Rather Drown than Lose Her Chastity" (W30) indicates, such suicidal actions were considered relevant and exemplary one thousand years later.

The virgin martyrs for the faith were under no such shadow of controversy as the suicides, however. Medieval hagiography and exempla trumpeted their tortures and subsequent miracles as illustrations of what women could accomplish (or withstand) if they were willing to stand apart from ordinary (read sexual) members of their sex and commit themselves to the ascetic ideal of a celibate male clergy. To support women in this transformation from Other to "us" by a reversal of their sinful sexuality, medieval homiletics offered the dramas not only of the virgin martyrs but of reformed seductresses and prostitutes such as St. Thais (W31). In these exemplary scenarios, female otherness was shown to be not unlike that of Jews: both women and Jews, having rejected spiritual purity by their own will and conduct, could, if they dissolved their former sinful natures by the revivifying waters of tears and baptism, become transformed from scorned and marginalized outsiders to insiders in the kingdom of heaven.

The apogee of clerical devotion to the ideal of female virginity was, of course, the veneration of the physically uncorrupted figure of Mary, the virgin mother of Christ, whose legend was created from a welter of biblical, apocryphal, and traditional popular sources.[43] In constructing this artifact of transcendant womanhood, male theologians, monks, and clerics developed not precisely an image, which reproduces what is real, but a *model*, which reproduces a prescribed ideal of behavior. The model of the Virgin Mary offered celibate churchmen a unique figure that could help reconcile their ambivalence about women and neutralize their fear of female sexuality, permitting them to retain their belief in a "good mother."[44] Required of this "good mother" was that she be forgiving of masculine appetites and sins and be a willing and capable protector of her errant sons, capable of defeating her archenemy Satan and his demonic tempters in the neverending combat for human souls, especially on the battlefield of carnality.[45]

To fulfill these conditions, Mary's own *physical* purity as a symbol of her *spiritual* purity was mandatory. Christianity, while disassociating its "mother goddess" from the pagan patronesses of sexuality and fertility, nevertheless inherited the classical notion that virginity conferred magical strength. Medieval clerical faith in Mary's inevitable triumph over the devil was grounded in the belief that despite her motherhood she was physically, that is sexually, uncorrupted and thus free of feminine "dirt." As a correlative to her virgin motherhood, the medieval church also promoted the notion of Mary's *bodily* Assumption into heaven, in defiance of the decay of the flesh that assailed all other mortals. Absolutely invulnerable to the constraints of the flesh that governed ordinary women, either in life or in death, Mary was thus the diametrical opposite of the carnal devil, woman, and Jew, and therein resided her power against their potential destructiveness.

The obverse figure to Marian veneration, and the female against whose sexuality and mortality Mary's physical intactness shone even brighter, was Eve, acknowledged in both theology and popular religion as the "bad mother," the first sinner who transmitted her transgression to the rest of the human race. Through the psychological mechanism of splitting the female sex into Eve, the despised emblem of human carnality and mortality, and the Virgin Mary, the ideal of physical purity and the donor of redemptive grace, celibate clerical authority was simultaneously able to rationalize its antifeminism, justify its asceticism, and present women with a model that supported the church's misogynistic agenda.[46] For while women could pray to Mary, repent of their sins because of her, and model their behavior on hers, they could never achieve her unique perfection as both mother and maid. Sacrificing the sexuality that defined them might bring women closer to the Marian ideal, but her paradoxical perfection, her singularity as mother and virgin that had enabled her to move from the margin to the center, was a miracle beyond even the purest imitator, and "fallen" women, albiet reformed and forgiven their sexual transgressions, could hardly have had their virginity restored. (In "A Lustful Abbess" [W36], however, this very thing does occur through Mary's sleight of hand.)

The Virgin Mary's "masculine" authority and intercessory power with Christ combined with her "feminine" maternal compassion made her the intercessor of choice for sinners of both sexes. In her personae as both the "good mother" and the virgin "bride" of celibate monks devoted to her cult, she was indulgent and protective so long as the male's supreme loyalty remained hers. Lust, despair, ambition, greed, pride, or blasphemy—such preeminently male sins Mary would forgive if it were Christ or God who had been abjured, but not herself. A despairing monk who never forgot to say his "Ave Maria" was turned from his loss of faith; the bishop Theophilous, who would not forswear the Virgin, was relieved of his contract with the devil through Mary's intercession; a knight who sought to increase his riches through a demonic bargin was brought to spiritual safety by his veneration of a statue of Mary; a pilgrim to St. James guilty of fornication and self-castration had his case successfully pleaded by Mary against Christ and the saints.[47]

While the cult of the Virgin flourished on the sublimated sexual longings of a celibate clergy, homiletic narrative frequently depicted her as the rescuer and redeemer of the female sexual sinner as well. A staple figure in popular religious literature was that of the errant female who, by remaining faithful to the Virgin throughout a variety of troubles, received the beneficence of Mary's intercessory and redemptive powers. To the unempowered female, that weak, guileless, or wanton Other rejected by clerical sentiment and controlled through ridicule, marginalization, immuration, and consignment to hell, the Virgin proved not only an ally but even an accomplice. On behalf of her devotees, Mary deceived and subverted male authority, both clerical and secular, covering up women's transgressions and taking practical steps to resolve the dilemmas provoked by their lust.[48] In "The Virgin Puts Devils in the Stocks" (W37), for example, Mary deceives a knight about his wife's infidelity; in a "A Lustful Abbess" (W36) she deceives a bishop by refuting the evidence of an abbess' pregnancy and securing a hiding place for her newborn; in "The Virgin Defends a Matron against the Devil" (W35), she confounds the true accusations of a devil against a mother who has committed both incest and infanticide.

Moreover, the homiletic theme of the Virgin's rescue of abandoned, despairing women influenced, and thus had its parallels in, popular secular literature as well. Throughout the Middle Ages, exempla, Marian miracles, the hagiographies of female saints, vernacular romances, and folk tales, cross-fertilizing each other and blurring the boundaries among them, shared one motif, however—that of a supernatural female rescuer of a slandered or denigrated heroine.

The "Cinderella/Catskin" tale group, for example, includes motifs such as the temporary obscurity or low estate of a beautiful, worthy woman; her despisal by false accusations against her loyalty (often by female kin); her abandonment, mutilation, or deathlike sleep; the heroine's miraculous rescue and the eventual restoration of her reputation (or sometimes a mutilated limb) by a supernatural female rescuer. These episodes may be seen employed in a religious context in exempla such as "The Trials of St. Theodora" (W32), in episodes from the Lives of various female saints, or in regional "histories" of holy but secular women.[49] In early secular forms of such stories, the supernatural female rescuer may be some milk-giving domestic animal—a sheep, a cow, or a goat—but by the medieval period, this role, and the related one of provider of a child to childless women, was largely occupied by the figure of the Virgin. (In later, less religiously oriented societies, this figure of the Virgin was itself transmogrified into a "fairy godmother" or a "wise old woman," depending on the literary or folkloric nature of the tale.)

The supernatural female rescuer and the victimized heroine were not the only representations of women that crossed from homiletic to secular romance or *marchen*, however. Clerical splitting of the female into saints or sinners, Eves or Marys, also surfaced in the secular storytelling idiom that developed throughout the Middle Ages. If the female saint tested by adversity or the wanton redeemed by penitence was attenuated into the falsely maligned or badly treated but ultimately rescued heroine of the "fairy tale"—a Cinderella or Snow White—the treacherous carnal daughter of Eve depicted in the exempla also found her place: as the envious stepsister, cruel stepmother, manipulative mother-in-law, or wicked, often cannabalistic witch. The exemplum's sexual transgressor setting her snare for Christian males traveling earnestly if haltingly towards salvation is an adumbration of these storybook villainnesses who, consumed by the sins of jealousy, vanity, worldliness, and avarice threaten the happiness of the *marchen* heroine and present stumbling blocks to her union with her handsome prince.

Secular popular storytelling genres were, like homiletic narrative, didactic and cautionary; hence, they similarly required the redemption of the worthy and the punishment of the wicked. In the grotesquely fitting punishments meted out to these latter females—being rolled downhill in a barrel stuck with nails, being thrown into ovens, or having their heels cut off to no purpose—we may discern their ancestors from the *exemplum terrible*: adulteresses tortured by burning and hacking, witches removed to hell by devils, fornicating women having toads drop from their mouths, and the like. The lesson of both the "fairy tale" and the exemplum was that the "happy ending" of both sexes was imperilled by women.

Medieval clerical misogyny, then, with its inability to consider women as human beings in the round but only as emblems of virginal innocence or carnal sin, overwhelmed the narrative voice of women as it did of Jews. Whether, as the exempla relate, women were employed by Satan to destroy men's souls or, as romance and *marchen* suggest, they were (with the exception of the heroine) motivated by the vices of envy, greed, or lust for power with no reference to demonic instigation, women by their nature symbolized the potential for loss. From the medieval clerical perspective that dominated western Christendom for over a thousand years, the mere proximity of women, like that of the devil and the Jew, was an occasion for sin or the potential loss of virtue, faith, and hope of eternal salvation. For many centuries clerical piety asserted that women, conjoined in their otherness with Jews and the devil, polluted the spiritual atmosphere and challenged the perfection of God's plan for the faithful.

Yet the inescapable presence of nefarious females in a universe created by God demanded their incorporation into the Christian worldview and made requisite such explanations about them as would support Christianity's redemptive scheme. Exempla literature clearly reveals the intersection of these three embodiments of wickedness. The devil was the instigator of evil through his pride and subversion of God's will. Women, marginalized by their assumed inferiority to men and stigmatized for their role in original sin, were demonized as obstacles to a man's spiritual progress. And the Jew was both demonized for his intractable subversiveness and feminized to highlight his inferiority. Medieval homiletic narrative, as an important intervention between abstruse theology and popular religious belief concerning the devil and women, played a similarly crucial role in moving its audiences from antifeminism to anti-Judaism.

Exempla about Women

Tales W1 through W4 are typical of the medieval homilist's fulminations against fashionable and extravagant female attire. The Knight of Tour Landry, in advising his daughters against vanity of dress, quotes a preacher who properly rebuked those ladies who nag their husbands for the new clothes they see on others and take no heed of their husbands' inability to pay for their finery. He also cites a bishop who ridiculed one of his parishoners who appeared at a feast "so strangely attired and quaintly arrayed that all who saw her ran to stare as if at a wild beast," and mocked the excessively high hairpins she wore, "like the post of a gibbet" that made her look as though she "bore a gallows on her head." Clerical disgust with vanity of dress linked it to the sin of pride, which thrust the angels into hell, to the lechery it kindled in women and men, and to lack of charity, as the cost of a fashionable dress might be better used to clothe the poor.

W1. A Gown with a Train of Devils

Caesar of Heisterbach relates that once there was a priest named Catus who saw an odd sight on a woman coming from church. This woman was gaily adorned with scarves, and trailing behind her was a long train upon which danced a multitude of fiends, little black men of India, as thick as fish in a net; they were making funny faces and clapping their hands. The priest stopped the woman at the church door and commanded the fiends on her train to remain where they were in the sight of all the congregants. Now when this woman saw that these fiends had great power over her because of her pride in her attire, and when she saw the appalled looks on the faces of those observing her, she ran home immediately and changed her clothes and never wore long trains again.

W2. The Lady Who Took Too Long to Get Dressed

I want you to know the story of the lady who would always take a quarter of a day to get herself dressed.

There was a lady that dwelled nearby the church, who took so long to get dressed everyday that it wearied and angered the clerics of the church and its parishioners to wait for her. Now one Sunday, she took so long at home to ready herself that it took nearly the whole day, and everyone said to each other, "Today we shall not wait til this lady is combed and arrayed," and some of them cursed her and said, "The devil should array her once and hold her mirror, for she makes us wait every day this way and delays us." And as God wanted to make her an example, at the moment and hour that she looked in her mirror, instead of the mirror, the devil turned his buttocks to her, which was such a frightening sight that she became mad with fear and went out of her mind and remained ill for a long time. Finally, God gave her back her wits and she was chastised, and no more would she make folks wait for her but was dressed and in church earlier than anyone else. And she thanked God that he had chastised her so that she might mend her ways; and therefore, this is an example that nobody should take so long to get dressed that they miss the mass and God's service and make others miss it as well.

W3. A Knight's Two Wives

a. Fair daughters, I want you to hear the example of a good knight who had three wives. This knight was a good man, and he had an uncle who was a hermit, a holy man in his way of life. And as for this knight's first wife, she was a fair and gentle lady whom the knight loved very much. It happened one day that death, which takes us all, took the wife from her husband. The poor man almost died himself from grief. His only comfort was to go to his uncle, the hermit, and see if that pious man could tell him the state of his dear wife's soul, and whether it was saved or not. The holy man, taking pity on his nephew, went sorrowfully into his chapel and prayed that God might show him where the lady was. After praying a long time, the hermit fell asleep; and in a vision, it appeared to him that St. Michael and the devil had this lady on a scale, with all her good deeds on one balance and all her evil deeds on the other. The things that told most against her were her fancy clothes and her furs of grey squirrel and fox. The devil cried out, "St. Michael! This woman has ten different gowns and as many coats, and you know well that less might have sufficed her. The value of one of her coats or gowns might have clothed fifty poor men and kept them from wearing cold complexions of white or red. And with what was wasted on her clothes, she might have kept two or three men from dying of the cold." Therefore, the devil gathered up the woman's clothes and cast them in the balance with her evil deeds, and then he added the rings and jewels, which had been given her by gallants seeking her favors, and he added, also, all the false words with which she had slandered others in order to make her own good name shine brighter by contrast. Every little wicked deed which she had ever done was brought in and added to the scale. Her good deeds were put on the opposite balance along with herself. And on account of her clothes, gowns, jewelery, and rings, the balance with her evil deeds pulled down the scale and overcame her good deeds. The devil took the woman and bore her away. He put her clothes and all her array into the burning fires of hell and then put them on her and cast her down into the pit of hell, where her poor soul cried and moaned, but to no avail.

Here the hermit awoke from his vision and then he told his nephew, the knight, this woman's husband, what he had seen. The hermit bade the knight immediately sell all of his wife's clothing and with the silver gained, buy clothes for the poor and distribute it among them.

b. Afterwards, this same knight took another wife, his third, and they lived a long time together. When she died, the knight became so sorrowful that it was scarcely thought that he would live. Again, he went to his uncle, the hermit, to find out how this dead wife's soul was faring.

The holy man lay down in prayer and fell asleep, and while sleeping he had a vision in which an angel showed him the pain and torment the the knight's wife was suffering. The hermit saw clearly that the devil held the woman by the tresses of her head, as a lion holds his prey, in such a way that the woman could not free herself, and the devil thrust hot burning awls and needles into her brows, temples, forehead, and brain. At every thrust of the burning implements, the woman cried out piteously. The hermit asked an angel why the fiend was making the woman suffer these particular torments, and the angel replied that as the woman had, while she lived, daily plucked her eyebrows and forehead of hair to make herself prettier in world's eyes, therefore, daily, into every root from which a hair was plucked, the devil thrust a burning awl or needle.

After this devil had made the woman suffer these pains a long time, a second devil, with great sharp teeth and claws, foul and hideous to behold, came in. He burned the lady's face with boiling pitch and tormented her so horribly that the hermit trembled and almost lost his mind for fear. But the angel comforted him and told him not to be afraid, for the woman had well deserved this punishment, and more. When the hermit wondered why this was so, the angel replied that when this woman was alive she plucked and painted and adorned her face to please the world, a sin that displeases God the most, for that is the sin of pride which draws after it the sin of lechery, for which reason Noah's Flood came and destroyed the world. For of all things, it is the most displeasing that a creature give himself a beauty other than that which nature has provided. Why does it not suffice that God formed men and women after His own shape, in which the angels take so much delight, to see God in this creation? If God had wanted, He did not need to have made them men and woman, but beasts and serpents. Alas! Why do women not take heed of the great love that God has given them to create them in His likeness? And why do they pick at and paint and pluck their faces to change what God has ordained for them? And therefore, the angel said, it was hardly a miracle that this lady, for her pickings and painting, should suffer this pain. And the angel bade the hermit to view her dead body and he would see that it was hideous and dreadful. The hermit asked the angel if the woman would be in torment for a long time, and the angel answered that she would be there for a thousand years or more, he would not say exactly, during which time the fiend would continually smear her face with burning pitch, grease, oil, lead, and tar. And the poor soul cried and cursed the time that she had been born.

In great fear, the hermit awoke out of his vision and went to his nephew, the knight, to tell him what he had seen. The knight, shaken, went to see his wife's body, as yet unburied, and when he saw that her face had turned black, horrible, and hideous, he was convinced of the truth of the hermit's words. He became repelled and fearful at this report, and wore a hairshirt Tuesdays and Fridays, and gave away the third part of his goods for God's sake. Henceforth he lived a holy life and shunned the vanity of the world on account of the sight of his wife, whom he saw in such a horrible state from her picking, plucking, and painting of her face. And also he recalled what his uncle, the hermit, had told him of his other wives.

W4. A Priest's Vision of His Mother

Once there was a woman who had a legitimate son who grew up to be a priest and two other children, born out of wedlock. When the two children born of her adultery were grown up, this woman died. One day, the woman's first son, the priest, who had continually said prayers for the salvation of his mother's soul, asked God to show him how his mother was faring. As he prayed, there appeared to him the form of a woman from whose head a dark flame arose; on her lips and tongue a horrible toad was gnawing, and from her breasts two serpents hung, sucking fiercely at her paps. The skin of her back was flayed off her and hung down to her thighs, trailing after her in a mass of flame. The priest cried, "What in the name of God are you?" and the apparition answered, "I am your mother. Look at me and see the everlasting pain to which my sins condemned me." Then the priest asked her what she had done to suffer these particular pains. She replied, "I am tormented with this blue flame on my head for my luxurious adornment of my hair and my concern for fancy clothes; my lips and tongue suffer with this toad for my vain and wicked talk and lecherous kissing; I have serpents sucking at my breasts, draining my heart's blood, because of the two children I bore in adultery; and my burning skin is drawn off me and trailing behind because while I lived on earth I wore dresses with excessively long trains. "Oh mother," grieved the priest, "may you not be saved?" "No," she said, and disappeared from sight.

Tales W5 through W9 exemplify a variety of "failures in governance" that were associated with women: gluttony, quarrelsomeness,
disobedience, and gossip. The pulpit exempla, tales W6 and W8,
attribute the sins of anger and gossip to the devil, and the women who
committed them are eternally condemned to appropriate tortures in
hell. In tales W5, W7, and W9, of folkloric origin, the chastisements of
the erring females—argument, shame, and beatings—are milder, but
the antiwoman bias is clearly evident.

W5. A Woman Who Ate Her Husband's Eel

There was a woman who had a magpie in a cage that spoke and told
tales of all the woman did. Now it happened that this woman's husband kept a large eel in a little pond in his garden, with the intention
of serving it to a friend who was coming to visit him. But the wife,
when her husband was out, said to her maid, "Let us eat this large eel
and I will say to my husband that an otter has eaten him." And so it
was done. And when the good man came home, the magpie began to
tell him how her mistress, his wife, had eaten the eel. So the man went
right to the pond but did not find the eel. He asked his wife what had
become of the eel, and she tried to find excuses for herself, but the man
said to her, "Do not excuse yourself, for I know well that you have
eaten it; for the magpie told me so." And so there was great argument
between the man and his wife about her eating of the eel. But when the
good man was gone, the mistress and the maid came up to the magpie
and plucked out all of the feathers in its head, saying, "You told tales
of us eating the eel," and thus was the poor magpie plucked. And ever
afterwards, when the magpie saw a hairless or balding man, or a
woman with a high forehead, it said to them, "You, too, gossipped
about the eel." Thus, here is an example that no woman should eat lus-
cious morsels in the absence of and without the knowledge of her husband, for this woman was afterwards ridiculed on account of the magpie and the eel.

W6. A Woman Damned for Dying in Anger

Once there was a rich woman who appeared to be very charitable and virtuous. After a time she became ill, and, feeling close to death, she asked the parson of her church, a good and pious man, to hear her confession and shrive her. When this woman came to the point of confessing sins of anger, the priest charged her to be generous in forgiving those who had offended her, and likewise, to ask forgiveness of those whom she had offended. Here the woman balked, telling the priest that she had a neighbor who had done her so great an injury that she could never forgive her. Although the priest advised the woman against such demon-inspired wrath, nothing he could do or say would make her pardon this neighbor, and so she remained in the deadly sin of ire.

That same night, the good priest dreamed a vision that the devil bore away the soul of this angry lady, and he saw further that a great foul toad was sitting upon her heart. The next morning, when day had broken, he was told that the woman was dead. When the dead woman's relatives and friends assembled to bury her, they called for the priest to read the service over her body in church, but he refused, saying that she had died in the sin of wrath and should not be buried in sanctified ground. Moreover, he said, if they searched her body they would find within it, at her heart, a foul toad. The assembled company was astonished and indignant at the priest's words and thought them lies. But when at last they opened her body, they found that the priest had spoken the truth, for inside her a foul, horrible toad was clutching at her heart with its paws. The priest then commanded the awful creature to speak and say who he was. The toad answered that he was a devil from hell who, for twenty years, had tempted the woman into many sins, but especially the one to which she was most prone, the sin of wrath. "I made her so angry at her neighbor," the devil said, "that she could not stand the sight of this neighbor. The other day, when you heard her confession, I was sitting upon her heart, and I clutched it with my four paws and held it so tightly imprisoned that she could muster no will to forgive. For a moment I was afraid that you would take her from me and reform her with your preaching, but now I have the victory; she is mine and shall be damned forever."

W7. The Obedience of Wives

It happened once that there were three merchants that went homeward from a fair, and as they fell to talking, riding along the way, one of them said, "It is a noble thing for a man to have a good wife that obeys him and does his bidding at all times." "By my truth," said the other, "my wife obeys me truly." "By God," said the last, "I believe that my wife obeys her husband best." Then the man who had begun to speak first said, "Let us lay a wager of a *denier*, that whoever's wife obeys the worst, let her husband pay the *denier*"; and thus the wager was laid. And they decided among them what they should tell their wives. They decided that each man should bid his wife leap into a basin that they would set before her, and they swore that none of their wives would let them lose the wager; all they had to say was "Look, wife, I order you to do it."

Be that as it may, when one of the men bade his wife leap into the basin that he had set before her on the ground, she answered by asking "Why?" So he said, "Because it is my desire and I want you to do it." "By God," said she, "I will first know why you want me to leap into the basin." And not for anything could her husband make her do it. So her husband struck out with his fist and gave her two or three great blows, and then the three men went to the second merchant's house. He commanded that whatever he gave orders for should be done, but it was not long after that, when he bade his wife leap into the basin that was before her on the floor, she asked "Why?" and said she would not do it for him. So then he took a staff and beat her badly, and then they all rode on to the third merchant's house.

At the third merchant's house they found dinner set out on the table and that husband brought in his fellows and said, "After dinner I will test my wife and bid her leap into the basin." And so they sat down to dinner. And when they were seated, the good man said to his wife, "Whatever I command, see that it is done, no matter what." And as she loved him and feared him, she listened to what he said and took heed of those words, although she did not know what they meant. Now it happened that they had had some eggs at dinner, but the salt was missing from the table. So the good man said, "Wife, *sele* [salt] *sus table*" but the wife misunderstood her husband to say, "Wife, *seyle*

[jump] *sus table*," which in French means, "Leap onto the table." And she, afraid to disobey, leapt upon the table and threw down the meat and drink and broke the glasses and spilled everything that was on the table. "What, wife!" said the good man, "don't you know any other form of amusing yourself?"

"By your leave, sir," said the wife, "I have to do your bidding, as much as is in my power, even if it brings injuries to both you and me, and I would rather the both of us came to harm than that I should disobey your command. For you said, "*Seyle* [jump] *sus table*." "Nay," said he, "I said, '*sele* [salt] *sus table*,' that is to say, 'salt is needed at the table.'" "By my troth," said she, "I thought that you had ordered me to jump on the table," and there was much mirth and laughter at this. And the other two merchants said there was no need to order her to leap in the basin, for she had obeyed enough, and they agreed that her husband had won the wager and they had both lost. Afterwards she was greatly praised for her obedience to her husband, and she was not beaten as were the other two wives that would not do their husbands' bidding.

W8. An Abbess' Severed Corpse

Once there was an abbess who was a chaste woman as regards lechery and bodily desire, but who was very loose with her tongue. When she died, she was buried in the church, but the night after her interment devils seized her body and beat it with burning scourges from the navel upward so that it was black as pitch, but from the navel downward they left it alone, and that part shone like the sun. As the fiends beat the corpse, it cried out so piteously that two of the nuns hearing it were very much afraid. Encouraging and supporting each other, the two sisters went to where the corpse lay to see what the fiends were doing to it. Then they heard the dead abbess saying to them, "You know very well that I was chaste in my body; therefore that part of my corpse is unharmed and shines as you see now. But because I spoke in a ribald and vulgar manner, that part of my body which was guilty is doing penance, as you see. So pray for me that I may be helped by your prayers, and be warned by my example."

W9. A Wife Reveals Her Husband's Secret

I would like to tell you the tale of a squire who had a young wife, and how he tested her discretion. "I will tell you a great secret," he said, "but do not reveal it for anything, for it holds my power, and therefore, for the love of God, do not reveal it. Such a strange occurrence has befallen me: I have laid two eggs." And the wife swore and assured her husband that she would never speak of it to anybody, but then she thought about it and went to see her friend. "I would like to tell you an important secret, but you must assure me that you will not reveal it," she said, and her friend promised her that she would not. "So help me, my dear friend, a marvelous thing has happend to my husband; he has laid three eggs."

"Oh, Saint Mary," said her friend, "this is a geat miracle. How can it be? It is a marvelous thing!" And when she had said this, they parted. And this friend, who heard the wife's secret, in all haste went to see another friend that she had, and told her every word of the secret, saying that such and such a squire had laid five eggs. And in this way it was reported, first by the wife, and after by her friends, and so the secret spread from one to the other, until the whole country spoke of it. Finally the squire heard the rumor that he had laid five eggs. So he called his wife before him, and in front of her friends and kin he said to her, "Dame, I told you in secret such things as you have revealed and spread about in such a manner that now the whole country is talking of it. I told you that I had laid two eggs, but thanks to God and your exaggerated report, you have increased them to five eggs. You did not do as I wished. I pretended that this thing happened and told you the secret only to test if you would keep it to yourself as you promised you would. So now I have discovered your fault and disloyalty to me." And thereupon the wife was so much ashamed that she did not know what she could do or say, for there was no excuse for her folly. And by this example, all good women ought to be aware and advised that they should not reveal the secrets of their husbands, but forever, as they are bound to, keep his secrets and obey his orders.

Tales W10 through W16 turn on the sins of lechery and lust in women, which, from the clerical perspective, were the chief means by which men were retarded in their spiritual progress towards salvation. Tale W10 is explicit in identifying women's sexuality with man's spiritual fall. It is prefaced in its homiletic context by a denunciation of men who fall under the spell of women and specifically the elderly man who does so, thereby losing his goods and his cattle, his respect and his reputation, his friends and comrades, and finally his reason, until he becomes "a mopish fool" who is mastered by his sweetheart.

W10. A Riddle of a King, Wine, and Women

I read, as the master storyteller relates, how King Darius questioned three of his chamberlains, asking them which was the strongest of the three: a king, wine, or a woman. Then one said, "A king, for he may command all men and their lives and limbs are in his hand." Then answered the second and said that "wine was stronger than a king, for wine often so overcomes a king, no matter how strong he is, that it makes him witless and without strength." Then said the third, that all that was nonsense, that a woman was stronger than a king or wine, for a woman brings up both a king and a man who makes and sells wine from childhood, and there is no man but who is afraid of losing his strength or his life for a woman. And then he told how he saw a king's mistress slap the king under his cheek with her hand and when she laughed, she made him laugh, and when she wept, she made him weep. Thus is a woman stronger than both a king and wine, and thus does the foul sin of lechery destroy a man, both in his life and in his death, and removes him from God's grace so that he fears neither God nor man.

Tales W11 through W15 exemplify aspects of female lust in the form of fornication and adultery. These sexual sins were perceived as threats to canon matrimonial law, in which the sexual intercourse of the couple was considered pivotal to the definition of marriage and a symbol of the indissoluble union between Christ and the church, buttressing the argument for marriage as a sacrament. Additionally, since fornication and adultery disrupted the civil peace, they were expressly forbidden in guild and town statutes upon pain of flogging, exile, fines, and, in case of men, being forbidden to practice one's trade. Moreover, where the fornication involved supposedly celibate clergy, as in tale

W14, and where children were born out of wedlock, the circumstances became more problematic. While male partners were supposedly held as guilty as females, in fact, as tales W13 and W15 suggest, it was the woman who was more likely to be blamed and punished for the sexual irregularity.

The concatenation of female lust with other sins, vices, and crimes was central to the clerical misogyny that informs these tales. In tale W11, a lustful wife is also shown as guilty of other sins, for her greed impels her husband to commit theft and murder. In tale W12, the adulterous wife not only betrays her husband by a sin of the flesh but, more viciously, denies and ridicules his saintliness, for which she is, in a ribald variation of a typical *marchen* motif, appropriately and humiliatingly punished.

Tales W13, W14, and W15, typical *exempla terrible*, dramatize their homiletic points as spectral visions in which females condemned for their lust are tortured eternally with the pains of hell. In tale W14 the folkloric elements of a magic circle and a hunter from hell flesh out the more routinely pious features of the *exemplum terrible*.

W11. A Woman Leads a Knight into Murder

I read that there was a knight who had no income of his own, but he had obtained much loot in the wars. And when he had spent all that, he went and married a lady of that country who was rich enough, for though he was poor, he was an attractive person. She had said to him thusly: "I know well that you are a man handsome in body; but because you are poor I can not, for the shame of it, marry you, unless you have much gold or income from an estate. Because you have no gold, do as I advise you and obtain it. Go to such a place where many rich merchants gather and obtain some gold and then you shall have me." So he went thither. It happened that a rich merchant came that way and the knight robbed him and took his gold and killed him and buried him, and then afterwards he came to the lady and said,"Lo, I have gotten a sum of gold from such a man and buried him there." So the lady said, "Go again tonight and watch that place."

The knight went that night and stood by the dead man's grave, and at midnight there came a light from heaven shining down on the grave, and then the grave opened and the corpse sat up and held up his hands to God and said, "Lord, you who are a righteous judge, revenge me upon this man who has treacherously slain me for my goods." And at once there came a voice from heaven and said, "This day, thirty winters from now, you shall have your vengeance." And the corpse thanked God and lay down in his grave again.

Then the knight was sorely afraid and went to this lady and told her everything and how the voice had said that on that day, thirty winters from then, the corpse should take vengeance on him. Then the lady said, "Yea," she said, "Much may happen thirty years from now. Let us go together and get married!" So they lived well for thirty years, in prosperity and health, but always this knight was fearful of this vengeance and he said to the lady: "Now twenty years have passed and the next ten will go by quickly. What is your best advice?" Then she said: "We will make our castle as secure and strong as we may, and on the appointed day we shall gather together all our friends and staff ourselves with plenty of men and so we shall escape well enough." And so they did. When the day came, they gathered together a great number of men into their castle and prepared a meal for them and made all the merriment they could. There was a harpist there, who played his harp throughout the meal, and no evil spirit could come near nor have power there as long as the harp was heard. But there came out of the kitchen a minion covered with grease who rubbed the harpist's strings with his filthy hands. Then the harpist was very angry and with his harp would have struck this kitchen hand, but the fellow hastened away too quickly. The harpist pursued him out of the castle, but when he came outside, the fellow had vanished away. Then this harpist turned around and saw the castle sink into the earth, all on fire.

W12. A Saint's Skeptical Wife

Once in France there lived a pious man named Genulphus who dug a well for himself, which, when he married and moved to Burgundy, miraculously sprung up again in the garden of his new home. Now one day, as Genulphus and his wife were walking through their garden he bade his wife sit down at the well, and there he reproved her for the adultery she had been committing, for, he said, the news that she had been lying with men other than he had reached his ears. His wife denied this, so Genulphus said, "Bare your arm and bring up a pebble from the bottom of this well, and if your arm comes up unhurt, then I will believe that you are innocent of this accusation." His wife thought there was no harm in going through this trial, so she put her arm in the well, but when she drew it out, the skin was scalded as if by fire. Then Genulphus said to her, "Lo! here is proof of your infidelity. Go away from me; from this time forth you shall not live with me." Then he divided his wealth in half, gave her her share, and sent her out to live alone.

Some time later, a clerk who regarded Genulphus as an enemy came to his house and slew that pious man as he lay sleeping in his bed. After Genulphus was buried, many miracles occurred at his grave. When his wife was told of this, she ridiculed the stories, saying, "It is as true that Genulphus performs miracles as it is that my anus sings." Just as she said those words, her anus began to emit ugly noises, which would not stop no matter what she did. And ever after, on Fridays, the day that Genulphus was slain, this woman's anus would sing and make ugly noises whenever she opened her mouth. And this continued for every Friday of her life.

W13. The Collier's Vision

It is told that an old knight who was wedded to a young lady did not please her in bed so she took as a lover a handsome young neighbor. After this couple had lived in adultery a long while, they both died suddenly. Soon after this, a charcoal burner who worked in a nearby estate was lying down by his great fire of coals when, just before midnight, he spied a woman running by him as fast as she could, looking like a ghost and crying in fear. Riding after her was a man clad all in black, mounted on a black horse, with a drawn sword in his hand. This man harried the screaming woman around the coal-fire and, at last, caught her and slew her to pieces, casting her limbs on the fire. Then he rode away. The next night the charcoal burner saw the same spectacle,

and night after night it was the same, until the collier was so frightened that he rode to his lord and said he could no longer continue to
work on his estate. When he told the lord the reason, the latter said,
"Go back now and I will come to you tonight and with the help of God
we shall discover what is going on."

The lord came later, as he promised, and after he saw the spectral
man hew the woman into pieces and throw them on the fire, he
grabbed the rider's bridle and commanded him to say who he was.
The rider replied, "I am a man who had this woman without her husband's knowledge, and thus night after night I slay her and burn her
in this fire, as she was the cause of my sin. I ride on a fiend in the guise
of a horse and this saddle burns hotter than any earthly fire, and thus
we shall continue until some good man helps us with his prayers and
almsdeeds."

W14. The Spectre of a Priest's Concubine

Once there was a priest's concubine who, realizing that she was about
to die, ordered those around her to get her a pair of boots and put them
on her legs, and this she needed done at once. So it was done as she
asked. That night the woman died, and some hours later, after the
moon had risen brightly, a knight and his servant riding in the fields
together, saw a woman ride up to them, crying and begging them to
help her. The knight, recognizing the recently deceased woman by the
chemise and the high boots she wore, dismounted quickly and drew a
circle around him with his sword, and into this circle he took the
woman. Soon he heard the fearsome blast of a horn blown loudly by a
hunter, and then he heard the frightful barking of hounds; at these noises the woman seemed terrified. When the knight asked her why she
was so afraid, she told him what was going to happen, that an effort
would be made to draw her out of the circle. So the knight took her long
hair and wrapped it tightly around his arm, and in his right hand he
held out a drawn sword. Up to them rode the hunter of hell; seeing him,
the woman begged the knight to let her go. The knight held fast to her,
however, even though the woman pulled away and tried to leave. At
last, she pulled so hard that her hair was torn off her head and she ran
away. The fiendish hunter followed her and caught her, then drew her

up on his horse, throwing her across his saddle so that her head and arms hung down on one side and her feet on the other. Then, when the demon had his prey, he rode away. As it was nearly day, the knight rode on into town, and told everyone he met what had happened. He showed them the woman's hair still wrapped around his arm, and sure enough, when they opened her grave, they found that the head of her corpse had had its hair plucked out by the roots.

W15. A Lecherous Woman Fails to Reform

I read of a woman who was the mistress of a man for many years. But it happened that one day when she was in church, she heard a sermon in which the preacher told of the horrible pains of hell ordained for those who refused to stop committing the sin of lechery, and she became contrite and stirred by the Holy Ghost. She went and shrove herself and did her penance, and was fully intent on never committing her sin ever again. But as she went homeward she met with her lover, who spoke with her amorously, as he was wont to do before. But she rejected him and said no, for she had heard the sermon about the horrible punishment ordained for all such as they in hell, and she was frightened on that account and had shriven herself and would sin no more. Then said he, "If all things were true that were told in sermons, no man or woman would ever be saved, and therefore, do not believe this, for it is not so. Let us again be of one mind on this, as we were before, and I pledge myself never to leave you but to love you always."

So the woman's heart was stirred and she committed the sin of lechery as she had done before. But it happened that a short time afterwards they both died suddenly. A holy man, who had known them both and the lives they led, prayed to God to know how they were faring. One day, as he walked by a stream praying for this, he saw a black dark mist on the water, and in the mist he heard the man and the woman speaking to each other, for he knew their voices well. The woman said to the man, "Cursed be you above all men and cursed be the time that you were born, for because of you I am dammed into everlasting pain." Then the man answered, "Cursed be you and the time that you were born, for you have made me damned forever! For had I once been contrite for my sins as you were, I would never have

weakened as you did, and if you had held firm to the promise you
made yourself, then you might have saved both of us. But I promised
that I would never leave you. Therefore, we are now both undergoing
the punishment of hell that has been ordained for us."

Tales W16 and W17, whose folk and fabliau elements portray
misogyny corresponding to that of more narrowly pious tales, both
involve the figures of the bawd, whose male counterpart, the pander-
er, is absent from exempla literature. Tale W16 combines with its
romance features such typical *exempla terrible* motifs as a dead sinner
appearing in a vision to warn a living person against misconduct, the
demonic punishment of sinners through tortures on their *bodies* appropriate to their sins of the flesh, and the emphasis on the efficacy of contrition and repentance in staving off eternal punishment in hell. In its
homiletic context, the allegorical interpretation appended to this tale
tells us that the stone is Christ, the hole is the blessed wound in his
side, and the skin shucked by the bawd is her sinful conduct amended
for Christ's sake.

W16. A Bawd's Warning to Her Husband

Once there was a woman who acted as the go-between for a husband
and another man's wife, and had frequently brought the couple
together for the purposes of adultery. The couple continued in their
adulterous relationship for a long time because of the help of this
bawd. At last, when this go-between fell ill and was near death, she
began to think of what a sinful wretch she was, and, feeling truly sorry
for her sins, she decided to reform. She sent for her curate, was shriv-
en, and resolved never to sin again. Thus, with much repentant weeping and praying, she passed out of this world. Soon after, the man and
woman she had brought together in adultery also died, but without
repenting their sins.

Now the husband of this bawd who died had always said prayers
for the salvation of his wife's soul, so one day he asked God to show
him how she was faring. That night, as he lay in bed, his wife appeared
to him and said, "Husband, don't be afraid, but rise up and go with me,
for you shall see marvels." So the man got up out of bed and followed

his wife until they came to a beautiful meadow, when she said, "Stand still and fear not, for you shall not be harmed, and look carefully at what happens." Then she walked a little way off from him until she came to a huge stone that had a hole in its middle. She stood in front of the stone and, shedding her own skin there on the ground, she suddenly changed into a long serpent who put its head in the hole in the stone and crept through. When she stood up on the other side, she had become a lovely lady.

Just then, two screaming devils came up carrying a cauldron full of hot, roiling brass, which they set down by the stone, and after them, there came another two devils, yelling and carrying a man. After them, still two more devils came, also making a fearful noise and carrying a woman. The last two pairs of devils each picked up the person they were carrying and cast them into the cauldron and held them there until the flesh had dropped off their bones. Then the devils took out their bones and laid them beside the cauldron, and the bones became a man and a woman again. The fiends again cast them into the cauldron and the same thing happened. This they did many times until finally the devils left as they had come. The woman who had been watching all this crept back through the stone and returned to her husband and asked, "Do you know these people?" "Yes," replied her husband, "they were our neighbors." "Did you see the punishment they suffered?" asked the woman. "Yes," answered her husband, "a hideous torment indeed." "This pain," his wife continued, "they shall have in hell forever, for they lived in adultery and did not repent. I was their go-between and had I not repented before I died, I would have been in the cauldron with them. But I was able to go back and forth through the hole in the stone, shedding my skin, by the grace of God." Then she advised her husband to go home and amend his life and give alms for the salvation of both their souls, for he would live but a little while longer. The husband went home and did as his wife advised, and within a short time he died and went to heaven.

W17. A Roper's False Wife

I would like you to know an example of a roper's wife who was not faithful in keeping her marriage vows to her husband. She had a friend who was a deceitful bawd who had taken a gift from a rich, lecherous prior to entice the roper's wife to lie with him, which the bawd entreated her to do. And thus, for the gifts and jewels that the prior gave to the wife, and with the enticing of the bawd, the wife allowed the prior to fulfil his foul lust with her. Here we see the truth of the saying that a woman who takes gifts from any man destroys herself. And so it happened one night that the prior came to lie with the wife when her husband was asleep, and when the prior had finished with his foul delight, he rose, and would have gone upon his way, when a fire suddenly lit up the chimney and the good husband saw him go out. So he started up and asked what it was, but his wife said she had no idea. But the good man was heavy with sorrow, for he feared that his wife had done wrong. And the wife, who was full of malice, went and spoke to the bawd, her friend, telling her all that had happened. And the bawd bade her to leave her alone with her husband and she would make a satisfactory explanation.

When the bawd spied the husband going to the pastures, spinning his wool, she came before him with a spindle under her belt, spinning black wool. And when he returned, she had on her spindle white wool, with the black wool hidden underneath. And each time he came to and fro, she changed the color of her wool. "What!" said the good man, "dear friend, I thought you just had a spindle of black wool in your belt." "Nay, not at all," said she, and afterwards, when he came again, she had changed the color on her spindle. "What, dear friend, I thought just now you had white wool." "Why, dear friend," said she, "What is the matter with you? I think there is something wrong with you. Last night was a night when folks believed they saw things which had not occurred. I believe," she said, "that you are ailing somewhat, that things are not right with you." And the good man thought that she had stated the matter truly, and said to her openly, "By my faith, dear friend, I thought I did see some black thing going out of my chamber last night, and I don't know what it was." "Ah, dear friend," said she, "it was nothing but the day and the night striving against each other and there was great lightning." And thus she appeased the good man by her falsehood.

Now another time it happened that the husband arose early, thinking that he would take a little bag that lay at the foot of his bed to the market three miles from his house and bring home some fish. So he picked up the prior's breeches (for that is what the bag was) and put them in his cloak. And when he had bought what he wanted at the market, he turned to take out his bag and put his fish in it, and found that it was a pair of breeches. When he saw this, he was full of anger and sorrow. And when the monk got up, from hiding between the bed and the wall, he missed his breeches and found nothing but a little bag. When the wife saw that, she was very anxious, for she guessed rightly that her husband had taken the monk's breeches instead of the little bag. So she told her friend the bawd what had happened and begged her to help her. The bawd said to her, "You shall put on breeches and I will do the same, and when your husband comes home, you will tell him that you and I are wearing breeches." So when the good man came home, full of sadness and sorrow, the treacherous friend welcomed him and asked him if he had lost some of his goods, for he seemed so cheerless. He said, "No, something else is bothering me." She made so much of him that he told her what was bothering him, that he had found a pair of breeches at the foot of his bed. And when she heard him, she began to laugh and said, "Dear friend, now you will see how you have been deceived and tempted to do my friend, your wife, shame and yourself as well, through this false suspicion. And let me tell you, there is not a truer wife to a husband in this town, nor one who keeps herself more chaste and faithful to her husband, for the truth is that she and I were wearing breeches because of the hooligans that grab women and grasp them by their private parts. And that you may see this is true, look for yourself." And she lifted up her clothes to show him how she was wearing breeches. Then he believed that she was speaking the truth.

Thus that deceitful bawd, the man's friend, rescued his wife twice, so that he might never learn of his wife's faithlessness, but in the end the devil wanted her horrible sins to be known. Now the good man thought that his wife was going too frequently to the priory without reason to be there, so he ordered, on pain of her life, that she should never go there again, no matter what the reason. A while later, to see what she would do, her husband said that he was going out of town, and he hid himself in a secret place to watch her. And she, full of sin and tempted with the devil, went out soon enough to the prior and her husband saw and went after her and brought her back again and said "Here, lady, you have disobeyed my orders." And then he went into the town and engaged a surgeon to heal two broken legs. When this was done, he came home and took a pestle and broke both his wife's legs and said to her, "At the very least, for a while, you will not go far and disobey my orders, quite the contrary," And he put her in bed.

Now the wife lay so long in bed that the devil tempted her, for when she was almost well, she made the prior come and lie with her where she was lying, even with her husband by her side in the bed. And the good man, thinking that there was a man there with his wife, pretended that he was sleeping and waited; and when the couple was right in the middle of their foul act of sin, the husband quickly took out a long knife and pierced them both through, fixing them to the bed. And thus he slew them both in the midst of their horrible sin. And when he had done this, he called his neighbors and the officers of the law and showed them what he had done, the which, they all said with one voice, was a proper way to punish them. And they all marvelled that she would take for a lover that great fat black foul prior and desert the good young man, wise and rich, who was her husband. But many women are like the female wolf, who chooses for her mate the foulest wolf of all that lives in the forest. And so did this lecherous woman, through temptation of the devil, choose this foul monk. And therefore take heed, the more abominable the sin, the more eager is the devil to tempt you, just as this was a man of religion and she a wedded woman. And thus it is with a woman, whether she sins with her kin or her friends, the closer the relationship, the greater the temptation, and the more horrible burning for the sin she shall have. For it is a true saying that "the pot may go only so long to the water; then it finally breaks."

Tales W18 and W19 both portray witches, although the first depicts a practictioner of "white magic," while the latter implies that its witch, punished in typical *exemplum terrible* fashion, engaged in demon-assisted sorcery. In the sixteenth century *Malleus maleficarum* (Hammer of Witches), attention is drawn to the contrast between earlier times, when women were the victims of the devil, and the current era, when witches consecrate themselves voluntarily to the devil's work and even fornicate with him. The presumed susceptibility of women to the sexual temptations of the devil and the opportunities for mothers and midwives to kill newborn, unbaptized babies and dedicate them to the devil supposedly accounted for the devil's preference for female accomplices.

W18. The Witch and the Cowsucking Bag

Lo, hear a tale of a witch
That lived no better than a bitch.
She was a witch who made a bag,
A belly of leather, with a great swag.
She so gathered up this bagbelly
That it could go and milk men's cows.
At evening and at morning tide,
In their pastures or beside them,
Long would it speed quickly about,
Until finally it was seen.
Then all the good men of the town
Summoned the witch before the bishop.
They ordered her to bring along the bag
To see what responses she would make.
It was shown before the bishop
That she performed the milkings,
Sucking men's cows dry in their pastures.
The bishop marvelled at this, and questioned
How she was able to do this.
"Dame," said the bishop, "do your trick
And let us see the results."
This witch began to say her charms:
The slops rose up and overflowed.
The bishop said, "Now we have seen this.
Make it go down again."
The witch did everything as he asked:
She made the slops lie still.
Then the bishop made a clerk write down
All that she had said, the great and small of it;
And every detail of what she did,
Then the bishop paid careful attention to it.
Then, said the bishop, "Now shall I
Do as you did, perform your magic."
The bishop began to read the charm,
And everything she had done, he did exactly.
He said and did every detail

Exactly as she had done, just right.
But the slop lay as still as it did before:
For him it did not rise a bit.
"Why," said he, "will it not rise?
I have done the same as you,
And said the words, no more, no less.
But when I say them, why will it not go?"
"Nay," said she, "And why should it?
You don't believe as I do.
If you believed the words as I do,
It would go and suck milk from the cows."
He said, "Then only belief is lacking?"
She said, "That helps me in everything.
It is so in our practice.
Belief does more than just words.
For you may say anything you like,
But unless you believe it, it is all wasted.
All that I say, I believe it well.
My belief has done these very deeds."
The bishop commanded that she should not
Believe nor work as she had done.
So here we learn that belief will make
Things happen that words cannot.
The bishop said the words, each one,
But belief in them he had none.
And no more will it avail thee
Who do not believe where belief should be.

W19. The Witch of Berkeley

Once upon a time an English sorceress who heard a crow caw and felt
the knife she held suddenly drop from her hand knew by these signs
that she was going to die. Sure enough, she fell ill, and when she was
close to death, she called her children, a nun and a priest, to her, and
commanded them that when she was dead they were to sew up her
body in a deerskin and enclose it in a tomb of stone whose lid must be
made fast with strong lead and iron, weighted down with a stone, and
then bound round with three strong chains. After that, they should say

masses for her and pray around her body for three days, and if the
tomb remained undisturbed, then they could bury her in the ground.

All was done as she asked. The first two nights, as prayers were
being said around the tomb, devils broke the gates of the church and
attacked the coffin. They broke two of the chains that bound it, but the
middle chain still remained firm. The third night, at cockcrow, the
fiends came again with such a din and cry that the church and the
whole of the earth quaked. Then the ugliest and most foul of the
fiends, who seemed to be the leader, came boldly up to the tomb and
called the sorceress by name. He bade her rise, but she answered from
within that she could not, for the tomb was bound. The devil then said,
"For your sins the chain shall break," and at once the chain broke and
the devil kicked away the tomb's lid. The sorceress rose up from the
coffin in the sight of all those at her wake and went roaring out of the
church door, where she was set upon a black, burning devil and borne
away to the pit of hell.

Tales W20 and W21 are explicit reminders of the devil's association
with the sexuality of women. In tale W20, St. Bernard's staff may be
viewed as functioning as an alternative, authorized phallus that drives
away the devil's phallic evil. In tale W21, the devil's seductiveness
suggests his later popular conception as suave and dapper in manner.
The futility of the priest's effort to save his daughter from the devil
may imply an admonition that in conceiving a daughter from an illicit union, the priest made himself and her vulnerable to the devil.

W20. St. Bernard Delivers a Woman from a Fiend

Once upon a time, when St. Bernard was in Normandy, a woman came
to see him, and complained that for the last six years she had been tormented by a fiend who stole into her bed and tempted her with lechery. The fiend always warned her not to tell St. Bernard about him, but
now she felt she must get the saint's help. St. Bernard gave the woman
his staff and told her that when she went to bed that night she should
put it next to her. She did so, and when the fiend came into the room,
he could not move close to her bed. Then he began to threaten her, saying that after St. Bernard was gone, the woman would feel his revenge.

The next morning the woman told St. Bernard what had happened. Then the saint called all the people together in the church and ordered that each one should carry a lit candle in his hands. With all these candles he cursed the fiend and interdicted him, commanding that he should never again visit this woman. And thus she was delivered from all the temptations of the fiend.

W21. The Devil Seduces a Priest's Daughter

Caesar tells us that once, in the town of Bonn, there was a priest whose married daughter had become a widow. As this girl was so beautiful, her father was afraid for her, and when he left his house he always locked her up in the loft. One day, the devil appeared to her in the likeness of a man and spoke words of love to tempt her. He was so persuasive that she consented to his advances and was seduced by him. Later, she realized that she had been seduced by a fiend and told her father what had happened. He was very grieved at her story and decided to move her across the sea to another country where she would be far away from this fiend and enjoy a better climate. After the girl was sent away, the devil returned and was very angry at finding her gone. He went to the priest and said, "Cursed priest, why have you taken my wife from me?" Then he struck the priest upon the chest so that the poor man was spitting blood for three days, and on the third day he died.

Tale W22 exemplifies the curious fact that while mother-son incest is, in reality, very rare, it carried specified penances in medieval ecclesiastic penitential literature, while father-daughter (or daughter-in-law) sexual relations, factually more common, did not. Similarly, exempla literature contains several other instances of mother-son incest, while references to incest by male parents or guardians are almost nonexistent.

W22. A Mother Forgiven for Incest

Caesar of Heisterbach relates that once there was a woman who committed incest with her son and became pregnant with his child. When the baby was born, she carried it to Rome in her arms. There, with much grieving and weeping, she confessed her sin in front of Pope Innocent and all his cardinals. The pope enjoined her to receive her penance the next morning, when she was to come back to him in the very clothes she had worn when she committed the incestuous act. On the next day, therefore, the woman left off all of her clothes except her shift and came before the pope ready to do whatever penance he would give her. When the pope saw her contrition, he said to her, "Your sin is forgiven." But one of the cardinals who heard this began to complain about the leniency of the pope's penance. The pope said to this man, "If I have judged this woman poorly, may the devil enter into me, but if I have judged well, may the same happen to you, since you have complained." And all at once, every one who was there saw the devil begin to possess the cardinal who had complained about the pope's leniency in forgiving this woman's sin.

Tales W23 through W27 deriving from the early period of Christianity, all suggest the influence of monkish asceticism on medieval clerical antifeminism. In tales W23 and W24, the otherness of women is evidenced clearly: they are devils, illusions, "secular" monks, and their very presence is spiritually harmful to the virtuous male. The theme of male separation from females is central: to be safe, men cannot be exposed to their presence. The motif of a prince locked in a tower to prevent harm from befalling him, recognizable as a *marchen* element, originated in Buddhist birth tales which have been Christianized here. The illusion of the devil as a woman and the temptations of demonic beauties, which pepper the biography of St. Anthony, a third-century saint of the Egyptian desert, became a staple of medieval homiletic narrative after the year 1000, when his cult developed in the west and anecdotes of his temptations appeared in the *Golden Legend's* Life.

W23. The Temptations of Devils as Women

A. We read in the story of Barlaam how there was a king who had a son, and when he was new born, wise doctors who saw him told that king that he must ensure that the child, until he was ten years old, saw nothing else but food and drink and clothes and a woman to take care of him, else he should die. And so the king did. At the end of the ten years the king began to bring before his son all manner of things which he had to see and know what they were. There was brought before him gold and silver, horses and cattle, and of every thing, as the boy asked what it was, he was told its name. And when young women and maidens came before him and he saw them, he asked eagerly what they were called and what they were. And those who were there answered and said, "These are devils that beguile men." And after the boy had seen all manner of things, they brought him to the king, his father, and he asked him, of all the things that he had seen, which he liked the best. The boy answered, "Father, truly nothing else but the devils that deceive men, for on them above all others is my heart set."

B. We read in "The History of Barlaam" how there was a king named Abennyr who had a son named Josaphat, who was baptized a Christian. Now this king, proposing to draw his son from his belief in Christianity and chastity, locked him in a chamber by himself, and he had brought into him fair young women, gorgeously arrayed, who sat down by him and embraced him and showed him their seductive beauty, trying to tempt him into lust and sensual desire. The boy had no one to whom he might complain nor ask advice of, nor take his meals with but these women, and they were all around him. So the devil had great power of temptation over him and he fell into lust and lechery. Yet notwithstanding this, his thoughts turned to God and he began to weep and beat his breast in remorse and prayed that God might help him. And thus he chased away all his wicked desires and despite all the efforts of these women, his temptation ceased so that he never fell into sin again.

W24. Women Called "Secular Monks"

The *Vitae patrum* tells us that once a certain monk raised his son in a monastery and never let him out into the world. Thus, the boy did not know what a woman was. When the boy was grown into a man, the devil appeared to him in the form and clothing of a woman. The young man described to his father what he had seen and asked the older man what it was, but he refused to say. Some time later, this young man accompanied his father into Egypt where, of course, he saw many women. He pointed out to his father that these were the same as the creature he saw in the wilderness, and his father realized that his son had been deceived by an illusion of the devil.

"Son," the father said, "these creatures are a type of secular monk that wear a different habit from other monks and hermits." And he took the young man home at once and would never after let him leave the monastery.

Tale W25 contextualizes the motif of the temptress in the conflict between Christianity and Islam, with the alterity of the female here being underscored by her belonging to a different faith. While the tale originated in the early eastern Christian church, it is embellished with such elements of medieval pulpit literature as the requirement that a Christian forsake his religion to gain some illicit end, the assurance that God forgives the sincerely repentant sinner, and the symbolic representation of the Holy Ghost in the form of a dove. The Saracen father's setting of three conditions before the monk can marry his daughter is a widespread folktale motif.

W25. A Monk and a Saracen's Daughter

If you have sinned greatly
You should ask for mercy with a sorrowful heart,
For God is always full of pity
And always ready to grant his compassion.
Do not be afraid to pray to him
For you shall receive his great mercy.
And that is well proved
By a tale told on good authority.
This tale was written in its entirety
In a book called *Vitae Patrum*.
There was a monk once who had a cell
In the wilderness where he did dwell.
This monk of religion
Had a great temptation:
He was so tempted by lechery

That he sped from his cell to seek amusement.
He took himself right to a city
In Egypt, that same country where he lived.
And as he came down a street
He met a woman
Who so aroused his flesh
That he coveted her at once.
He went swiftly to her father
And asked if he could have her.
Her father was a Saracen priest
Who followed the religion of Mohammed.
This priest said to the monk,
"As my God wills, so will I do,
She shall not be given to any
Without the permission of Mohammed."
The monk said he understood this well
And would follow that religion in every detail.
So the Saracen went to his God
And asked his advice about this matter,
If the monk should be given his reward
Or if this gift should be put off.
His holy spirit answered him,
"Give him your daughter on this condition:
That he forsake and entirely abandon
His God in heaven and his baptism,
And all the virtue of his monkish state.
He must forsake these three things.
And if he completely forsakes them,
Give him your daughter straight away."
So the priest went to the monk and told him
What had been said and how he would obey.
And if he would forsake these three things,
His daughter should be delivered to him.
This woman was so much in the monk's thought
That he regretted nothing if he could only have her there.
Alas, Jesus Christ he forsook,
And the Christian faith that he had devoted himself to,
And his religious orders,

And chose instead damnation.
Certainly, this was an outrageous thing,
To pay the devil so much homage.
And when he had granted all this folly,
Out of his mouth he saw fly
A dove into the firmament.
It was the Holy Ghost leaving him.
The Saracen went to his spirit
And told him how the monk had done these things.
"Those three things he will forsake.
Now shall I let him my daughter take?
Tell me truly in this matter,
Whether I shall give her to him or not?"
The spirit answered quickly,
"I warn you, however, for this reason,
That although the monk forsook his God,
His God will never forsake him,
For he is full of pity.
Men call him God of Christian mercy,
For if anyone will beg mercy of him,
Readily mercy shall he receive.
Though the monk departed from his God today,
Tomorrow his God will receive him again.
Therfore, I forbid his desire,
Do not deal with him ever again."
So the priest went to the monk
And said, "I have been ordered
Not to deal with you,
Nor give my daughter as a wife to you,
For your God is of such a kind
That although you forsook him just now,
Tomorrow you may come again
And make absolute peace with him.
No matter how evil a thing you have done,
He will grant you his mercy and good will.
My God has bade me that in no way
Should I deal with you or anything concerning you."
The monk repented and he thought,

"Alas" he said, "what have I wrought?
That I should ever have forsaken him
Who was so ready to receive me to him?
Your mercy, God, is spoken of by all.
When you see a spirit of hell
Who never loved you,
Even he speaks of your great pity,
Saying that you are so mild and meek,
So your great mercy I will seek.
Here I forsake my promised faith,
Yet I am praying to him whom I forsook."
Then he went to a hermit
And shrove himself of his earlier sin,
And told him what he had done,
Forsaking God and his religion.
The aforesaid hermit was very sorry
That the monk had committed such sin.
Nonetheless he bade him dwell
For three weeks with him in his cell.
For his sin he had to fast
And make sincere vows that would last.
This same monk who had been so wrong
Did just as the hermit bade.
They both prayed together for the first week
To God, who has such power
To grant the monk mercy;
This they prayed most especially.
At the end of the first seven nights,
The hermit said, "Brother, tell me,
Have you seen any grace
In the praying that you have done?"
"Yea," he said, "I saw a vision
In the likeness of a dove's flight
Above me in the firmament,
It was that dove that went from me.
The hermit thought then at once
That it was the same spirit
That had fled the monk when he first began

To forsake God for that woman.
The monk then did penance
For forsaking his Christian faith.
And still for a week he made a fast
Of his flesh, which had cast him down,
That never more through lechery
Would he abandon such great grace.
This hermit prayed night and day
That the monk's penance would be accepted.
When they had prayed day and night,
All that week in God's sight,
The hermit said, "Bless you,
Brother," he said, "What do you think now?"
"Well," he said, "through God's grace
The dove was in front of my face
And for a while stayed there by me,
That sight did me good."
"Then all is well with God's will.
Dwell with me yet another week still,
And continue your penance,
Your fasting and your prayers,
And I shall pray also with you
That God may hear both you and me.
Steadfastly, they prayed again,
Until that last week was ended.
At the week's end the hemit spoke
To the monk, asking about the spirit.
The monk said, "I have seen it,
And on my head it sat and rested.
I saw it was so mild and tame
That I might take it in my hand.
I thought it was the one that left me
And it would fly again into my mouth."
The hermit thanked God almighty
Who had given the monk the grace to see that sight.
"Now you are clean," he said, "of sin:
The Holy Ghost has entered into you.
Keep away from such situations

And do not trespass any more."
By this example you may see
How God is ever full of pity.

Tales W26 and W27 attach the motif of demonically inspired
temptresses to saints whose hagiographies were popularized through
the *Golden Legend*. Tale W28, of the saintly Abbot Macarius (ca. 300–90),
is set in the context of the devil's ongoing battle to overcome that
saint's piety. However, both the devil and the fornicating woman who
falsely accuses Macarius of her child's paternity are thwarted by the
saint's charity and humility. In tale W29, the demonic female's temptation of a bishop resides not only in her beauty but in her seeming
wisdom, whose speciousness is uncovered through the intervention of
St. Andrew.

W26. A False Accusation against St. Macarius

Another hermit was called Macarius,
Of him the fiend was greatly envious,
And one day the fiend met him
And would entrap him,
And said,"You do me great despite.
There's no way for me to hurt you
With all the penance that you do,
I do the same but it does not help me.
You fast much, and I fast also,
For I eat neither night nor day,
You waken much and so do I,
For I have never peace nor pity.
But you surpass me in one thing
That prevents me from getting at you.
"And what is that?" asked Macarius
"Of your humility," said he, "I speak.
In your meekness you surpass me,
That shames me when I see it."
For so meek was Macarius,
That his meekness was renowned.

In a hermitage long lived he,
In a cell, beside a great city.
Out of the city he had fled
And a hermit's life was such that he led,
That his meekness and his virtuous life,
Was soon known throughout the city.
Another hermit came to him
And served him with great good will.
Now it happened that this Macarius
Came into the city with the purpose
Of selling there his handiwork,
And so it happened that a clerk
Spoke with a burger's daughter there.
They both liked sinful play
So she became with child by and by.
Her father and mother asked about this,
Who had dallied with her,
And she answered, "The hermit Macarius."
Very angry then were all her friends
Against Macarius, that holy man.
They wanted to seize him and bring him to shame,
Since he had spoiled this woman's reputation.
About the marketplace they led him,
And beat him til his body bled,
And made him find the wherewithal
To feed and clothe this weak woman.
The other hermit that went with him
Was near him at this time,
And thought this situation shameful
And required his master do great penance.
Macarius begged him that he
Should in this case his surety be,
And he became his guarantor there,
Full of woe for him was this misery.
That man said to Macarius,
"You have a wife and thus
You must work faster and more
Both night and day, than you did before,

Or else, in this situation you cannot
Feed yourself and your loved one.
Both night worked Macarius and day,
And sent this [pregnant] woman a part of the money
Which he earned with his work,
So that she could buy some food.
This woman carried the child a long time
And then felt labor pains quite strong,
But she could not deliver the child.
Now she told everyone of this event,
She confessed the truth of who the man was
And absolved Saint Macarius of his blame.
When her friends heard of this,
They thought that they had indeed done wrong
In beating Saint Macarius,
For which they begged his mercy,
And when Saint Macarius heard it said
That they would come for this, he fled away.
For he was of great meekness,
Humble in speech and firm in devotion.
For love and happiness in this world,
Men should be meek, I believe.
Christ fled the attachment of men
When the Jews would make him king;
While the misery and poverty of the world
Keep many men meek,
The world's wealth tempts men,
Therefore, Macarius fled away from it.

W27. A Bishop Tempted by a Demonic Beauty is Saved by St. Andrew

Once it happened that there was a bishop who so adored St. Andrew, that everything he did, he commended to this saint. So the devil, because he could not sway the bishop from this veneration, came to the bishop in the likeness of a fair woman, who requested that she must speak with him for confession, and this was granted her. Then she began to speak thusly: "Sir," she said, "I am a king's daughter and have been raised with care, but because I see that this world is but a [fading] flower, I have sworn myself to chastity. And when my father would have married me to a great prince, because I would not break my vow, secretly in the night I stole forth in ragged dress, and when I heard of your great holiness, I came to you for help and advice and succor. Wherefore, sir, I pray you that you command me to do that which will help me so that the fiend cannot turn me from my purpose."

Then the bishop comforted her and bade that she should have trust in God, for she had set herself such a strong purpose in her heart that He would give her the grace to keep it. "But this day you shall dine with me and after our meal, we shall give you good counsel, so ordained for you that you shall be helped."

"Nay, Sir," she said, "Not so, lest men should suspect us of evil." "Of that you need not worry," said the bishop. "For we shall be so many in the company that there shall not be any suspicion of sin." So she gently thanked him and sat on a chair at the dining table. But whenever the bishop looked at her, he thought her so fair that he was quite tempted by her and almost forgot himself. Then unexpectedly there came a pilgrim to the bishop. Then the bishop said, "Lady, shall this man come in or not?" "Sir," said she, "first let him answer a question and then let him in." "Lady," said the bishop, "ask your question, for we know nothing of such things." Then she said, "Let us ask him: what is the greatest marvel God ever made in a foot of earth?" When the pilgrim was asked this he answered by saying, "A man's face; for that is earthly and only one foot long. Yet if all the men and women who were ever born were to stand in front of us, I should be able to tell one from another to some degree." And when he had made this answer, he was greatly commended for his wisdom. Then said she, "I see that he is wise. Bid him make another answer; ask him whether earth is more worthy than heaven?" When the pilgrim was asked this, then he said, "Christ took bodily form. Christ's body is of our kind, and our kind is earthly. Therefore, wherever Christ's body is, that place is higher than heaven." Then when he had given this answer he was allowed and bidden to come in. Then said the woman: "Let him try a third question, and then let him come in." Then she asked him: "How far is it from heaven to hell?" When he was posed this question, he answered and said to the questioner, "Go hence and bid her who is

sitting in the chair opposite the bishop to answer it, for she knows better than I. She is a fiend and has measured it, which I never have. She
fell down, with Lucifer, from heaven to hell; she is sitting here to tempt
the bishop and make him lose his soul."

When the messenger heard this, he was heavyhearted, but he
announced this answer so that all might hear. Immediately this fiend
vanished away with a horrible stench. The bishop thought of his temptation and was sorry in his heart and sent after this pilgrim. But by the
time the messenger came to the gate the pilgrim was gone and could
not be found. Then the bishop made all the company pray to God for
sending him this knowledge through the pilgrim who had helped him
in his need. Then came a voice which said he was St. Andrew, who had
come in order to succor him for the good life he had led and the worship he had done him. And he bade him always to be vigilant in the
future and preach to the people to help them.

Tales W28, W29, and W30 present ideals of femininity, which, if
achieved by ordinary women, would permit them to cross the bound-
ary from inferiorized Other to spiritually salvageable. Obviously, in
the everyday lives of medieval women, such perfect humility and obedience as the humble nun's in tale W30, and the preservation of chastity at the cost of mutilation or death as in tales W31 and W32, would
hardly be attainable or desired. Hence, homiletic literature promoted
isolation from society in a convent as the exemplary setting for realizing these feminine ideals.

Tale W28, beneath its homiletic guise, bears a remarkable affinity to
the "Cinderella" tale type of the "ill-treated heroine," subsuming the
related motif of "menial heroine" and "recognition by means of a
shoe," which is here transmogrified into recognition by means of spiritual qualities discernable only to the "rescuing male." Similarities
between the exemplum and its secular cousin include a dutiful,
unworldly heroine superior in character to her "sisters," who scorn
her and order her to perform menial tasks in the kitchen, where she
remains hidden from all eyes; a male visitor from the world outside the
heroine's residence, who calls together "all" in the house, only to insist
(through an unnamed but implicitly divine intuition) that one member
is missing; the "rescuing male's" contradiction of the envious "sisters' "
claim that the missing member is worthless and his command that she

be called up; and the "rescuing male's" vaunting of the heroine's merit and his insistence on those who formerly scorned her paying her the homage she merits.

W28. The Humble Nun

Heraclides relates that once upon a time there was in a monastery of nuns a maiden who, for her love of God, made herself as a fool, meek and obedient to everyone's orders. She made herself so vile and so great an underling that everyone was repelled by her to such an extent that they would not eat with her, but everyone struck her and scorned her, yet she always took it humbly. She never left the kitchen, but bade there and washed dishes and scoured pots and did all kinds of disgusting work. And she never sat down to meat, but held herself content with crumbs and crusts that were left at the table; and in this way she lived, and she was never properly shod or hose'd, and she had nothing on her head but torn and ragged clothes. And she was obedient to every creature, and would do no one a wrong, and whatever was done to her, no one ever heard her complain of it.

Now at this time, there was a holy man who lived in the wilderness who came to this very monastery and called before him all the nuns and all the sisters of the place that he might see them, but she did not come. And then he said, "You are not all here." And they said, "Yes, father, we are all here except for one who is but a simpleton." And he bade them call her, and as soon as he saw her he knew in his soul that she was more holy than he. And he fell down on his knees before her and said, "Spiritual mother. Give me thy blessings." And she fell down on her knees before him and said. "Nay, father, rather you should bless me." And with that the sisters of the house were greatly amazed, and said to him, "Father, don't permit this injury to you, for she is but a fool." And he said, "Nay, she is wise, and you are but fools, for she is better than either you or I." And then all the sisters fell on their knees before her and asked her forgiveness for the wrongs and injuries they had done to her, and she forgave them each with all her heart.

Tales W29 and W30, with their heroine's sacrifices to virginity, are typical of the hagiographical anecdotes that filled the lives of the female virgin saints whose strategems to maintain their chastity were disseminated through oral and written popular literature. The martydom of female Christians for their faith nearly always included the protection of their virginity as well as their endurance of physical torture. Tale W31, a Christianization of a motif from Hindu religious narrative, implies a "blame the victim" attitude to the modern reader, but the medieval clerical view that a woman's beauty was a danger to herself and to male observers provided a rationalization for women's seclusion in nunneries and the absence of punishment for the erring male that we find here.

W29. A Nun Tears Out Her Eyes to Preserve Her Chastity

Jacques de Vitry tells how once there was a mighty prince who was the founder of a nunnery, which stood not far from him, and he greatly desired that a fair nun of that place should become his lover. But notwithstanding his prayers nor his gifts, he could not persuade her, so at last he took her away by violence. And when his men came to take her away, she was very frightened and asked them why they were taking her, rather than any of the other sisters. They answered her back, saying, because she had such beautiful eyes. And as soon as she heard this she knew what she must do, and she put out her eyes at once, laying them in a dish, and brought them to the men and said, "Lo! here are the eyes that benefit neither his soul nor mine." And the men went to their master forthwith and told him, and he left the nun alone. So by this means she kept her chastity. And then, within three years, by the grace of God, she had her eyes back again as well as they had ever been.

W30. Of a Woman Who Would Rather Drown than Lose Her Chastity

We read how once upon a time when the city of Liège was being devastated by the Brabants, many women and maidens and other such put themselves in great bodily danger to preserve their chastity. Thus did one of them, to preserve her virtue, throw herself into the dangerous sea. Two of the enemy came up to her in a boat and drew her into the ship with the intent of taking away her virginity. But she would rather have gone again into the water and drowned than have them defile her, so she leaped out of the ship into the water. From the strength of her leaping, the boat overturned and these two men were both drowned, while she was saved by the grace of almighty God and came whole and sound to the shore.

Tale W31, the Thais motif of the reformed prostitute, has numerous analogues in folk and pious literature, in some of which the harlot makes a bonfire of her vanities in the public marketplace. The key element for the Christianized versions of the motif is the abbot's tag line (or its variations): "If you are ashamed to sin in the presence of men, I am more ashamed to sin in the presence of God." Early Christianized forms of the tale are related about two Mesopotamian saints, Ephraem and Alexis, and an unnamed saint, as well as this exemplum's Abbot Paphnutius (Pascuncius). The motif was also medievalized and attached to St. Padri, a local Italian saint, and to an unnamed Parisian clerk. Although scholarly opinion considers the legend of Thais no more than an invented moral story about a fictional woman whose historical ancestor may have been Alexander the Great's Egyptian mistress of that name, the church recognized her as St. Thais, whose feast day is October 8.

W31. Thais, the Harlot Who Reformed

We read in the *Vita patrum* that in the time of Valencian there was a lovely maiden named Thais whose mother put her out to be a prostitute at a young age. When her mother died, she became the most common strumpet in all the land, so that many men came to her privately. Now there was an abbot named Pascuncius, who, when he heard about her, disguised himself in secular garments, put a shilling in his purse and went to find her and gave her this shilling to let him have his will with her. She granted this and led him up into a room, and when she got there, where her bed was gaily arrayed and clean, she took off her clothes and went to the bed, and bade him come to her. Then he asked her if there was no place more private than that where he and she might lie together, and she said, "Yes." So he said, "Let us go there." So she led him there and said, "Sir, here you need not fear any man, be not afraid, for here no man comes and no man will see either you or me. And if your fear is of God, and you are afraid of him, doubt not that wherever we are, God will see us."

And then the old abbot asked her if she knew almighty God, and she answered that she did know Him and His kingdom that was to come, and also she said that she knew torments and pain were the reward of sin. Then he replied to her, saying, "If you know God almighty, why have you lost and bedeviled so many souls as you have? For you not only are damned in your own soul but you must also give account for the other souls that have been damned through you."

When she heard this, she fell down on her knees at the abbot's feet and wept sorely and made much sorrow, and even took all that she had ever gained through her sin and wickedness, and in front of all the people, she threw it in a great fire and burned it. Then, through the counsel of this abbot, not only for her wrongdoing, but also in order to worship God, she locked herself in a small cell for three years and great penance was enjoined upon her. As she did her penance, this was her prayer: "You, Lord, Who made me, have mercy on me." And when she had been there for three years, this abbot had a revelation that all her sins were forgiven her, so he took her out of her cell. Then she told him that she had made a great pack of all her sins and that she lay every day in sight of it, and gradually this pack grew less and less until there was nothing left of it. Then she knew that her sins were forgiven her after having done her three years of penance.

Tale W32 involves a cluster of motifs attached to the name of a holy woman, Theodora, who is not officially recognized as a saint of the church, despite the inclusion of her Life in the *Golden Legend*. In that hagiography and its direct imitators, Theodora actually engaged in the adultery of which she was accused, placing her in a Thais-like role as a reformed sinner. In the version in exemplum W32, however, the homilist wishes to make Theodora's virtue shine the more by having the accusation of adultery fabricated by a rejected lover and adds, too, the unique detail that her husband believed the slander and abused her because of it.

Central to all analogues of this exemplum is the cross-dressing motif, which, first, has Theodora entering a monastery as a monk and, second, has her accused of fornication and fathering a child by a maid

at an inn. The element of a woman entering a monastery disguised as
a man, fulfilling St. Jerome's dictum that a woman "who wishes to
serve Christ more than the world . . .will cease to be a woman and will
be called man," often in conjunction with the false "fathering"accusation, appears in hagiographies attached to several other female saints
such as Pelagius, Eugenia, and Anna. In this exemplum, the element
serves to underscore Theodora's traditional feminine virtues of
patience and humility, associating her with the "abandoned heroine"
of the "Cinderella/Catskin" tale type.

One pychoanalytic reading of this motif of a cross-dressed monk
accused of fornication and paternity and eventually being rehabilitat-
ed for her sanctity explains it as a monastic fantasy of celibate males
whose guilty desire to do that which the female monk has been
accused of, first has her punished as a surrogate for their sinful desires,
then overcompensates by having her turned into a saint.

W32. The Trials of St. Theodora

From the *Golden Legend*: A woman who was a devout lady, wife of a
great and rich man in Alexandria, was named Theodora. She was fair,
and a young man wished to lie with her, but she denied him his desire.
He, angry, slandered her falsely and said to the people that he could
have had his way with her if he had wanted. Her husband believed
him and gave his wife great distress on this account. She, in all that
tribulation, kept herself undisturbed and silent and suffered everything. She did not scorn nor chide the man who would have lain with
her, nor did she accuse him, but she shaved her head in secret and clad
herself in her husband's clothing and went then into an abbey, where
she was made a monk, saying that her name was Theodore.

A time came when, at the bidding of her abbot, she brought some
camels into a certain city and took them thither, to a particluar place.
And that night, a maid of the hostelry came to her bed to take her in
lust. This woman Theodore, who was a monk now, rejected her. The
maiden was angry with her and conceived a child by another man and
said that monk had begotten it and told the abbot that his monk had
defiled her against her will. The abbot reproved this monk named
Theodore, but she remained patient and suffered everything and did

not excuse herself, nor was she stirred by malice but kept it a secret from everyone that she was a woman. The abbot kicked her out of the convent gates, and there she lay for seven years in full view, outside of the abbey gates in the sight of all the people.

Now when the child was born, the mother brought it there and cast it into Theodore's lap and said, "Here is your child! Raise it yourself, for I never will!" Theodore received the child in a kind and patient manner and nurtured it on milk that she begged from the people. At the end of the seven years, because she had borne herself so tranquilly in word and deed, and so patiently, the abbot took her into the abbey again, and the child with her. Theodora kept her child in a cell with her and taught it to be devoted to God. And at the end of two years she died.

That night, as Theodora was dying, the monk saw angels and saints without number, and among them a woman full of joy, bright as the sun. A voice said to the abbot: "Abbot, this glorious woman is your monk Theodore. She was very falsely accused of conceiving this child, for she is no man, but a chaste maiden, a woman, and because she bore herself so calmly and patiently in all her tribulations, without giving in to the sin of wrath, she is and shall be in this joy without end." The abbot, with his monks, ran to the cell and found Theodora dead, and saw that she was a woman and not a man. The abbot called in the father of the daughter who had accused Theodora and said, "Lo! Was this woman the father of your daughter's child as your daughter said?" Then, all the onlookers were astonished. An angel said to the abbot, "Rise abbot, and go into the city and bring him hither whom you meet first." So the abbot went into the city and a man, running, brushed against him. The abbot asked him, "Where are you running?" and the man answered, "Where my wife is, for an angel bade me go and see her." The abbot took the man in and both together wept as they buried her. Her husband stayed in a cell there until he died. The child was so persevering in good works that he was made abbot when the other abbot died.

Tale W33, a debate between the Virgin Mary and the devil about possession of the soul of a female sinner, indicts her for gluttony, covetiseness, and lechery, a cluster of vices also commonly attributed to Jews. In this colloquy among God, the Virgin, and the devil, the Virgin uses "logic" to rebut the devil and legitimize her interventions to save the woman from the devil's grasp, a common theme in Marian narrative. The exemplum explicitly emphasizes the role of the penitential process in salvation, a major objective of the revitalization of preaching after the Fourth Lateran Council.

W33. An Argument between the Virgin and the Devil

It was shown to a holy person by revelation, that a saint spoke to God and said, "Why is the soul of this woman, whom you bought with your blood, so detested by the devil?" Anon the devil said, "Because rightfully, she is mine." Then God said, "By what right is she yours?" To whom the devil answered, "There are two ways, one that belongs to heavenly things, another that leads to hell. And when she beheld the both ways, in her conscience, reason said to her that she should rather take my way, and because she had a free will to turn to whatever way she wanted, she thought it was more profitable to turn her will to sin, and then she began to go my way. Afterwards I assailed her with three sins, which are gluttony, covetise of money, and lechery. Therefore now I am in her belly and in her nature, and I hold her with five hands. With one I hold her eyes, that they see no spiritual things; with the second hand I hold her hands, that they shall not do any good works; with the third hand I hold her feet that she can not go out to any good things; with the fourth I hold her understanding, so that she has no shame in sinning; and with the fifth hand I hold her heart, so that she cannot get away by contrition."

Then the Blessed Virgin Mary said to her son, "Son, compel him to say the truth of a thing that I will ask him." The son said, "You are my mother; you are queen of heaven; you are mother of mercy; you are the comfort of them that are in purgatory; you are the gladness of them that have gone on pilgrimage, heavenward in the world; you are the lady of angels; you are with God most excellent; you are also a princess above the devil. Therefore, mother, command the devil to say whatever you want and he shall obey you." Then the Blessed Virgin Mary asked of the devil, saying, "Say, devil, what intention had this woman before she entered the church!" To which the devil answered, "She had a desire to abstain from sin." The Blessed Virgin Mary said to him, "Since the desire that she had before stretches to hell, say now, wither this desire of abstaining from sin that she has now, leads to?" to which the devil answered, against his will, "This desire to abstain from sin leads her to heaven." Then said the Virgin Mary, "In justice, you have taken her to lead her away from holy church. Now devil, I ask furthermore, for her first desire was a rightful one, that she be brought again to holy church, and now devil, I ask of you furthermore, say you, what does she deserve on this point which is now in her conscience?" The devil answered, "She now has contrition in her mind for the sins that she has done and great weeping and determination never to do such sins again, but to reform herself as much as she can." Then the Blessed Virgin Mary asked of the devil, "Tell me whether these three sins—lechery, covetise, and gluttony—can be together in one heart with these virtues: contrition, weeping, and intention to amend?" To which the devil answered and said, "No." And then the Blessed Virgin said, "Tell me therefore, which of these ought to go and flee away, whether these virtues or these three vices, since you say they can not dwell together in one place?" The devil said, "I say that the sins must flee." Then the Blessed Virgin answered and said, "Therefore, the way to hell is shut to her and the way to heaven is open to her." Then asked, furthermore, the Blessed Virgin of the devil, "Tell me, if a thief lies before the door of a housewife and would defoul her, what should the husband do?" The devil answered, "If the husband is powerful and good, he ought to defend her and risk his life for hers." Then said the Blessed Virgin, "You, devil, are a most wicked thief; the soul that is the spouse of my son, the most mighty husband, who bought her with his own blood, you have corrupted and violently taken away. Therefore my son is husband of the soul, and is lord above you; therefore it is appropriate that you flee before him."

Tales W34 through W37 foster the medieval cult of the Virgin by illustrating how devotion to Mary is repaid by her intervention on the sinner's behalf, whatever the nature of the sin. In tale W35, despite the heinousness of the crime of mother-son incest and infanticide, the protagonist's prayers to Mary produce better results against the devil than the penitential ritual alone. This privileging of Mary as an intercessor in the salvatory process attracted many adherents, especially women, to her cult and retained them in the church when heresy was spreading, but it also became a source of controversy and skepticism that drove others away from orthodoxy.

W34. The Virgin Helps a Deceived Anchoress

Once there was a woman who, seeing the wretchedness, sinfulness, and unhappiness in the world, decided to leave it and go into the desert. There she lived for many years in solitude, eating only such roots, grass, and fruit as she might get and drinking only well water. One day, after she had lived a long time in the desert, the devil, in the shape of a woman, came to her hut and knocked on her door. The holy woman opened it and asked the stranger what she wanted. The caller replied, "I pray you, madam, will you harbor me tonight, for I am afraid the wild beasts will eat me." The good woman bid her come in saying, "For God's love you are welcome to me; you may have whatever he sends us." Then they sat down together and the holy woman read aloud the saints' lives and other edifying tales. When she came to the line, "Every tree that brings not forth good fruit shall be cast down and burnt in hell," the fiend interrupted her.

"Is it not true," the fiend in disguise asked, "that we who live a solitary life profit no one but ourselves and therefore can expect little heavenly reward? It would be better for us, I think, to go dwell among the folk and give good examples to ordinary men and women. Then we would gather many blessings." Having finished these remarks, the two women went to bed.

But the holy anchoress could not sleep or rest all night thinking of the other's words. So she rose finally and went to the fiend disguised as a woman and said to her: "Tonight I could not sleep at all for thinking about what you said last night. I cannot decide what is best to do." The devil said to her, "It is best to go out in the world and help others; they will be glad we have come, and it is much worthier than that we live in solitude."

"Then," said the holy woman, "let us be on our way now, for it does not seem evil to try out your suggestion." Just before she went out, however, the anchoress prayed to the Virgin Mary to bless her venture and keep her fom sin. As soon as she finished her prayer, the Virgin appeared and laid her hand on the anchoress' breast and gently pushed her back inside the door, telling her to stay where she was and not be misled by the lies of the enemy. At once the fiend disappeared and the good woman never saw her again.

W35. The Virgin Defends a Matron against the Devil

In the *Miracles* of the Virgin we read that once there was a respectable matron who committed incest with her son, whom she loved dearly. She had brought him up with great love, and when he was a young man she would kiss him and embrace him and let him lie with her as if he were a baby. One time, when her husband was gone on pilgrimage into a far land, she and her son, lying next to each other, had intercourse, and soon she was pregnant. Then she became despondent and contrite, and fell to praying to God and the Virgin Mary as she used to do. When the baby was about to be born, this matron left home, and after she gave birth to the child, sin upon sin, she killed it and cast its body into a sewer.

At this point the fiend thought he had a good chance to destroy this woman and win her soul. He dressed himself in the habit of a clerk and went before the judges and men of law, asking for a hearing at which he would relate an important secret and cruel deed. "A certain woman," he said, "whom you deem devout, is really very wicked and cruel and full of sin. She conceived a child with her own son and when it was born, she killed it and cast it into a sewer." At this tale, everyone was surprised, and the good men of the court said they did not believe it. The devil bade the judges fetch the woman and examine her, and if it was not as he said he would burn himself at the stake, but if he spoke the truth, then the woman should be burned. The woman was brought to the court of law and told by the judges: "We have a prophet in Rome, and he, although we can scarcely credit it, has accused you of a great sin. Therefore, you must either acknowledge this sin or else offer some explanation."

The matron asked for a delay in the proceedings, which was granted to her, and then she went home and confessed to a priest, telling him the whole story. The priest, believing in the sincerity of her repentance, comforted her and gave her as penance only the saying of one Pater

Noster. Then he told her to pray to the Virgin for help, which she did most devoutly. When the day of her trial came, she was sent for again, and appeared in the court with all her friends and household servants. She stood in the middle of the court where everyone could see her, and the judge, after silencing the spectators, said to the clerk who had accused her, "Lo! Here is the woman whom you have accused. Tell her everything you told us." The fiend looked at the matron and, seeming greatly surprised to see her, said: "This is not the sinner or murderer whom I accused. This is a holy woman whom Mary, the mother of Christ, is supporting and protecting." Everyone in the court was astonished and waved their hands in the air in joy. The fiend could not endure this and vanished with a great reek and stink, and this matron was delivered from his power.

Tale W36 involves a concatenation of female sins—envy, lust, deception, disloyalty, scandalmongering—all amended through Mary's intervention and her undermining of clerical authority and religious rule. That the errant abbess had provoked the passionate hatred of some of her nuns by the strictness of her rule perhaps may be read as a metaphor for an embattled church feeling itself under attack by heretic sects. The folk motif of the betrayal of a female protagonist by female kin (in romance literature usually a stepmother or a mother-in-law) and the punishment by death such action merited is transmogrified here by the specifically Christian setting. Similarly, while the abbess is, in fact, guilty of the accusation against her, she restores her innocence by her confession just as her physical purity is restored by her devotion to Mary, whose virginity was also doubted by the faithless.

W36. A Lustful Abbess

> There was an abbess of a nunnery
> Who, as she went about the duties of her abbey,
> In rags by the gate she found
> A young girl child weeping.
> She had pity at this sight,
> And ordered her to be brought to her nunnery

And well taken care of,
And provided her with instruction
And made her a nun in that nunnery
And loved her dearly,
As she loved all her nuns, the good woman,
Her spiritual daughters every one.
And so well did she love them
That there was no sin they might commit
That she would not chastise them for,
And command them to leave off their folly.
And these good women loved her for this
But fools hated her passionately.
Now the Fiend was sent to her
To harass her continually.
Both night and day he was busy
Kindling lust in her body,
And finally, in lechery,
He brought her to fall full sinfully,
And he knew her carnally
And her womb waxed great in her,
But she bore herself well neverthless
As women can who do such folly.
She pondered night and day
With whom she might take counsel,
And she thought that the best one to see,
Until her wicked deed undid her, was she
Whom she had found and fed.
So she went to that fair nun,
Who was most beholden to her
To be loyal and steadfast.
She told this nun privately,
And said to her, "Merciful daughter,
I have a terrible secret
To share between you and me,
But I would rather be dead
Than that you should hate me for this deed,
That you should be troubled because of me,
I have certain bold words to say."

This nun answered and said, "Lady,
Not for all this world's gold would I
Do anything against you;
Therefore, lady do tell me
Your secret without anxiety.
Then you will see proof of my devotion;
Confide your thoughts openly to me
For you may be secure with me."
This abbess truly believed her so,
And her sin she began to reveal,
And said, "Daughter, woe is me,
For great with child I am right now."
This nun answered and said, "Lady,
Do not be troubled by this thing,
For well I shall advise you,
And take care of the matter with your other
    devoted daughters,
For when the child is born, I shall
Kill it so secretly
That no one shall hear the squealing,
And bury it within our garden."
This abbess trusted her completely,
And believed that she was true as steel.
But things one does from wickedness,
Theft, or unrighteousness
Bring neither happiness nor reward,
Nor succor when one needs it.
So then full disclosure
Of this case occurred, for the nun
Went to the bishop immediately
And told him all that the abbess had done.
And who could be angrier than that bishop,
For he had believed that this abbess
Was a good woman.
And when he knew that she had sinned,
Her nuns all heard of her trespass,
And some were glad and some angry;
For some were very displeased

That they had chosen her their leader,
And in letters they requested
That the bishop should set a day
To prove their abbess had committed this sin,
So that she might not gainsay it.
The day was set, the time drew nigh
When this abbess should have labor pains,
And be delivered of her child.
And she prayed mightily to Mary mild.
At night in her chapel she awoke,
That next morning would she be examined,
For the bishop had arranged that in the morning
The midwife would come before him
And tell him the truth,
Whether this abbess was mother or maiden,
And thus was the abbess very frightened,
When she heard of this.
She prayed mightily to Our Lady,
And asked for her help and mercy.
When she was weary from her praying,
She fell asleep before the altar,
And to her at once came Our Lady,
And comforted her in her trouble,
And on her womb she laid her hand,
While this abbess was sleeping,
And delivered her of a fair boy child,
Who would be a good and mild man.
Our Lady took this child so warm
And laid it in an angel's arm,
And bade him bear this child at once
On her behalf, to a hermit
Who lived many miles away,
And she never gave away the child's parentage,
And bid him have the child baptized,
And bring it up as a good foster parent.
When this was said, she vanished away,
And the abbess awoke to the day,
And on her bare knees she kneeled

And greeted Our Lady sweetly,
And said, "Lady, I thank you for this,
Well have you delivered me."
And in the chapel all that night
She adored Our Lady until daylight.
The bishop came with his clergy
Upon the morn to the nunnery,
To give his righteous lawful judgement
Of this abbess who had been accused;
But he first had the midwives
Look over her whole body,
And ordered them to swear to say truthfully
Whether they found her wife or virgin;
And when they had her body examined,
She seemed an untouched virgin to them,
And then the bishop was quite angry
At those slandering nuns,
And at that nun who had told him this tale,
And ordered she should be burned to death
As a wicked woman who wickedly
Had lied so about her abbess.
This abbess had great pity
That the nun should be damned on her account,
And told the bishop in secret
The truth, how Our Lady
Delivered her and made her clean,
And sent her son to a hermit
To be brought up and properly raised.
The bishop immediately on the spot
Absolved her, and showed his compassion,
And thanked Mary greatly,
For helping those sinners who repent.
To this hermit he sent his messenger
And there he found the child in the cradle,
And when it was several years older
The bishop made the child a good scholar;
And when the bishop was dead,
This clerk became bishop in his stead.

By this tale we see a spiritual lesson,
That no one should despair,
No matter what shameful sin there is,
No matter what folly they have done,
If they will only call on Our Lady,
When they fall into sin.
I advise that upon her we call,
So that she can obtain grace for us,
And afterwards we should live in her service
Evermore to our lives' end,
And secure may we go
Unto that court where she is queen,
Where she will bring us all to bliss.

Tale W37 is essentially a fabliau to which the figure of the Virgin has been added as a *deus ex machina*. As in the previous tale, it is the female protagonist's devotion to Mary that permits her to avoid a merited punishment through the Virgin's deception of a male authority, here the husband.

W37. The Virgin Puts Devils in the Stocks

Once in Lombardy, nearby an abbey of monks, there lived a knight who loved religious men. This knight's wife was a good woman, devoted to the Virgin. Now in this abbey, there was a certain monk held to be an especially holy man, and this was the man chosen by the knight's wife to be her confessor. As he came often to see her and hear her confession, give her counsel and teach her many prayers, she had great affection for him. So the fiend, who is an enemy to every man and woman who tries to be virtuous, busied himself tempting these two people to sin with each other.

One day, when the monk came to shrive the lady, the fiend was there, ready to bring them into sin. He succeeded in making them agree to go away with each other. The woman said, "I shall go and pack some provisions for us," and the monk agreed to do the same. When all was ready, they proceeded upon their way. They had gained about four miles when the knight, who had been out, came home and asked after his wife. But no one could tell him where she was. Astonished at this, the knight went into his chamber and found his coffers had been broken into, and his treasure was all gone. He inquired among his household as to what had happened, and at last one man told him, "I saw your wife and her confessor go out of the gate today." "I believe," said the knight, "that they have not gotten far," and he bade his men take the horses and go look for them, some in one direction and some in another. The knight took his own horse and some few men with him and rode off in the direction he had been told.

The knight and his men rode on until they came to a town, where they made inquiries after the monk and the lady. When the knight was told that such a couple as he sought were at an ale house eating and drinking, the knight spurred after them and caught them by surprise at their dinner. He took both of them to an abandoned farmhouse where he set them up in a pair of stocks. Then he rode off to inform the monk's abbot.

While the knight was gone, the couple sat in the stocks weeping and moaning. Then the woman said to the monk, "You taught me once a prayer to the Virgin and told me that on each day I said it, I would not fall into deadly sin." "That is true," said the monk, "as it has been often proved." "But did you say it today?" "Yes," the lady replied, "for I always say it in the evening when I go to bed and in the morning when I arise." "Thank God," said the monk, "for indeed we have been kept from deadly sin, although we had wicked intentions." Then the lady said, "Let us now say this prayer very sincerely with weeping eyes, that Our Lady may help us and save us from shame." So they prayed, and when they were done, the Virgin appeared to them and said, "The fiend has deceived you both; beware from now on. But because you prayed to me for help and called me empress over hell, I will show you the power I have over hell. I shall set two devils in the stocks in your place and return you home again without slander and shame." The couple thanked the Virgin with all their hearts and immediately the monk was back in his cloister and the woman in her chamber.

Meanwhile, the knight rode over to the abbot, his neighbor, and told him the story. "Your monk has taken away my wife, and made me a cuckold," he said. "No," said the abbot, "that cannot be, for my monk is not so lustful as to do such a deed." "Sir," said the knight, "I and my men followed them and found them in a town, drinking, and I put them in a pair of stocks." The abbot replied firmly, "It is not so, for I just saw this monk sitting in the cloister." "How can that be," wondered the knight. So the abbot sent for this monk and he came at once. "Lo," said the abbot, "Here is the proof that you are not speaking the truth. Let us go to your house and see whether your wife is there." When they came into the knight's chamber, they found his wife sitting, reading, and they observed that his coffers were whole and his treasure intact. "There, sir," said the abbot, "either you are dreaming or you have become faint with too much fasting, for you slander both my monk and your wife." Then the knight said to the abbot, "Let us ride to the grange and see whether they are in the stocks or not, for I did set them there."

When they came to the barn where the stocks were, they found two demons sitting in the stocks, one looking like the monk, the other like the knight's wife. And everyone who looked on the scene was afraid. The abbot went over to the devils in the stocks and said a prayer over them; at this the fiends rose up and bore away the roof of the farmhouse and disappeared. "See, sir," said the abbot, "the wickedness of devils, who would instigate strife between you and your wife and slander my monk. But now we have the truth, that such slander was false and based on illusion. Therefore, sir, go shrive yourself of this folly, and let us be warned by this example."

Source Notes to Exempla about Women

1. *AT* no. 595. Original in *DM* 5.7; *IE* no. 1660 erroneously cites 5.27.

2. *KTL* 31, 45. See also Herbert *Cat. of Rom.* 3.55 no. 101.

3. a and b. *KTL* 49.65–68. *IE* does not include these precise motifs but lists many variants under Vanity.

4. *GR* 67 (Addit. MS 9066) 383–84. *IE* no. 63 records only one version of this motif without identifying its characters as a priest and his mother. A longer, versified analogue, "Trentalle Sancti Gregorii" in *Political, Religious, and Love Poems* 83–91, purports to be the story of the mother of Pope Gregory I. In this version, the saint's mother appears to him in the shining guise of a heavenly queen whose soul has been saved by her son's recitation of thirty masses for her.

5. *KTL* 16.22. *IE* no. 3147 records the motif of a magpie revealing a wife's adultery, but it is not precisely this tale.

6. *KTL* 104.138. *IE* nos. 4877, 4880, 4882, and 4888–90 refer to various tales with motifs of a toad fastening upon an unrepentant sinner's corpse, but omits this precise one.

7. *KTL* 19.26–28.

8. *Festial* 96. Original in Gregory's *Dial.* 4.53. A medievalized analogue of a merchant's daughter is told in *DM* 4.22. Both exempla are told in *AT* nos. 405 and 446, respectively; a retelling of no. 405 following *AN* is in *JW* 95. *IE* no. 723 omits *Festial*.

9. *KTL* 74, 96–97. *IE* no. 1359 records analogues of a wife who revealed her husband's secret that a crow flew out of his body.

10. *Festial* 287. *IE* 3868. The elements of the riddle are found in Proverbs 31:3–4: "Give not thy strength unto women, nor thy ways to that which destroyeth kings."

11. *Festial* 88–89. *IE* no. 2939.

12. *AT* no. 35. *IE* no. 2271 referring to St. Genulphus omits this tale but cites it under no. 295, "Anus, singing."

13. *JW* 53. Its direct source in the *AN* (*AT* no. 613) cites Helinandus of Froidmont (d. after 1229), a well-known preacher who had been a trouvere at the court of Phillip Augustus before entering the religious life. Over a dozen of Helinandus's homiletic exempla, including this one, were incorporated into Vincent de Beauvais's *Speculum historiale* as "Flores Helinandi" (PL 212; this tale is col. 734), which was probably the *AN*'s direct source for them. *IE* no. 4696 lists several analogues but omits the two versions told in the *Festial* 105, 291. Elasser "Exempla of Mirk's *Festial*" suggests a MS of Holcot's *Moralities* as a likely source of Mirk's tales, for which see Herbert *Cat. of Rom.* 1.134, no. 129. For a discussion of this tale and (W14) see Sinicropi "Chastity and Love" 109–13.

14. *AT* no. 456. The analogue in *JW* p. 166, follows the *AN*. Original in *DM* 12. 20. *IE* no. 2452.

15. *Festial* 287. I cannot locate analogues or a citation in *IE*.

16. *GR* 67 (Addit. MS 9066) 384. I cannot locate a citation in *IE*.

17. *KTL* 62. 79–82. I cannot locate a citation in *IE*.

18. *HS* lines 499–562. *IE* no. 5327. The editor offers the following source note: "This tale is from St. Gregory's *Dial.*, Bk IV, ch. ii, says Gaston Paris, *Hist. Litt. de la France* 28.193." According to Herbert *Cat of Rom.* 3. 311, no. 2, this tale is not found in William of Waddington's *Manual dés Péchés*.

19. *JW* 186 erroneously cites "Caesarius" (Caesar of Heisterbach), from an error in its direct source, *AN* (*AT* no. 728). The original in William of Malmesbury's *Chronicle of the Kings of England* bk. 2, chap. 11, is set in the year 1065 and identifies the woman as a resident of Berkeley (230–33). Vincent de Beauvais copied the tale into his *Speculum historiale*, bk. 26, chap. 26, which was

probably the *AN*'s source. *IE* no. 2461. Variants of this tale such as that in Herbert *Cat. of Rom.* 3.311, no. 42 (from William of Waddington's *Manual dés Péchés*) do not localize the anecdote and attribute the events to "a priest's mistress seized by devils."

20. *JW* 63, from *AN* (*AT* no. 114). *IE* no. 606 omits reference to *JW* and anterior sources, *DM* 3.7 and *GL* St. Bernard 2. 104–05.

21. *AT* no. 256. Original in *DM* 3.8. *IE* no. 1449.

22. *AT* no. 206. Original in *DM* 2.11. *IE* no. 870 lists this tale; nos. 2730, 2733–36, and 2738 list other exempla of mother-son incest.

23. a. *AT* no. 170. b. *AT* no. 749. Originals in the *GL* Sts. Barlaam and Josaphat 2.364–65. Historically there were no such saints as the Christian monk Barlaam and the royal prince Josaphat (Joasaph), a figure based on the Buddha. Their legend began when a Buddhist birth tale was combined with a Christian tract in the seventh or eighth century, probably by a Christian dwelling in the Near East. The legend spread to Europe and was entered into the church calendar with a feast date of November 27. *IE* no. 5365 notes de Vitry's use of the tale, which initiated its popularity and led to its incorporation into Boccaccio's *Decameron* (introduction to Day 4).

24. *AT* no. 747. Original in *VP* col. 878, no. 21.

25. *HS* lines 170–330. Original in *VP* col. 884. *IE* no. 1760. See source notes to exempla about devils, n. 17.

26. *English Metrical Homilies* 70–73. Original *VP* cols. 778 and 958. *IE* no. 3117.

27. *Festial* 9. Original in the Life of St. Andrew the Apostle in *GL* 2.18–20 was probably Mirk's source as well as that of the *AN* (*AT* no. 67). See also the Life of St. Bartholomew, in the *GL* 2.114. *IE* no. 214 refers to Grimm for the riddle motif, but no specific citation is given.

28. *JW* 81, from the *AN* (*AT* no. 322). *JW* Salisbury Cathedral MS 103, chap. 74, p. 172, col. 2, includes the same tale about a *monk* who made himself a fool for God, with all the motif elements of the earlier tale. The original of the "humble nun" is found in two places in the *VP*: the *Verba seniorum*, where it cites St. Basil (PL 73, col. 984, no. 19) and Heraclides' *Paradis* (PL 74, col. 299). Heraclides' version, which is the source of our exemplum, appears to have been based on a narrative in the *Historia lausiaca* (chaps. 41–42), a fifth-century collection of examples of virtuous Christian hermits written by Palladius, a bishop in Asia Minor, who dedicated it to one Lausus, an imperial official. Palladius may have derived the "Cinderella" motif at the core of his story from some Vedic source, for he is also cited as the author of a "Letter on the Races of India and the Brahmins," a treatise on the ascetic principles of the Hindu gymnosophists whose original may have included a variant of this motif. Praise of the scorned ascetic and the penetration of illusion by a spiritually

advanced person, motifs that inform this exemplum in all its variants, are Hindu philosophic themes that would have been equally consonant with the views of Christian ascetics. See *IE* no. 3504.

29. *AT* no. 136. The *AN*'s exemplum was also the direct source of that in *JW* Salisbury Cathedral MS 103, chap. 62, p. 133, col. 2). The version in JdeV (Crane) 57 may have been the *AN*'s source, although it does omit the element of the restoration of the nun's sight. JdeV (Crane) 158 notes this motif in a well-known life of St. Bridget and cites its prototype in the Indian collection of tales, *Ocean of the Streams of Narrative* (Katha Sarit Sagara). *IE* no. 4744.

30. *AT* no. 137; also *JW* 54 from the *AN*. Original in Jacques de Vitry's Life of St. Mary of Oignies (feast day June 5). *IE* no. 5160.

31. *AT* no. 3. *AN*'s probable source was *Speculum historiale* bk. 15, chap. 77. Original in *VP* cols. 323, 661–62, 916. *IE* no. 2440 omits reference to *JW* 22.

32. *JW* 101, from *AN* (*AT* no. 599), probably from the Life in *GL* 2.234. *IE* no. 4764 omits reference to *JW*. For a psychoanalytic approach to the motif of crossdressed female "monks," see Anson "Transvestite in Monasticism."

33. *GR* 93 (Addit. MS 9066) 422. *IE* no. 1587.

34. *GR 89* (Addit. MS 9066) 411–12. *IE* no. 207.

35. *AT* no. 320. The earliest known version is in a twelfth-century *Mariale* from the monastery of St. Victor in Paris; other medieval versions are those of Jacques deVitry (JdeV [Crane] 62), Etienne de Bourbon, and the Franciscan compilation *Liber Exemplorum*, ed. Andrew Little, no. 100. Its fullest form is in *Speculum historiale* bk. 8, chap. 93, which was probably the direct source of our tale and that in *JW* 66. *IE* no. 2730.

36. *English Metrical Homilies* 164–71. *IE* nos. 2,4.

37. *GR* 92 (Addit. MS 9066) 419–21. The editor of that volume notes that the central motif is told as a fabliau in several medieval French collections, some references to which appear in JdeV (Crane) 257.

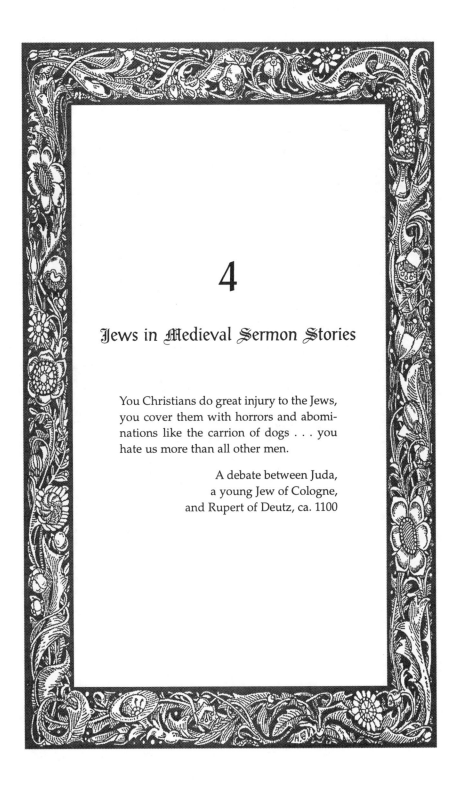

4

Jews in Medieval Sermon Stories

You Christians do great injury to the Jews,
you cover them with horrors and abominations like the carrion of dogs . . . you
hate us more than all other men.

A debate between Juda,
a young Jew of Cologne,
and Rupert of Deutz, ca. 1100

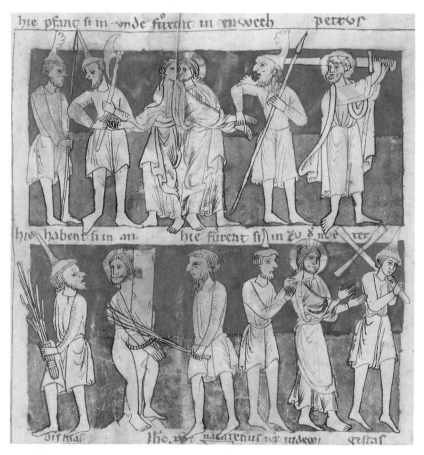

Illustration from a Moravian Hours of the Virgin belonging to a Premonstratensian nun ca. 1215, distorts the crucifixion scene by showing medieval Jews,
in their pointed hats and with exaggerated noses, betraying and flagellating
Christ. (Courtesy The Pierpont Morgan Library, New York. M.739, f.22v-23)

In his encapsulation of the medieval Christian perspective on Judaism through the metaphor of the dead flesh of a lowly beast, the Jewish interlocuter who spoke the words above justly, if elliptically, indicted Christianity for its virulent propaganda against his people. And indeed, it is true that in medieval Christendom's visual arts, its drama, and its homiletics, in the work of its most illustrious members as well as its anonymous sermoners and artists, there appears a systematic vilification of the Jew that has had repercussions even to modern times. The patristic and medieval church created its own reality of the Jew, a subjective perception that served its own theological ends. Furthermore, since medieval Christendom did not distinguish between the religious and social realms as we do today, its theology became law and social policy. Hence, the Jew came to be seen not only as a religious Other but as a socially and economically disruptive figure as well.

The attitudes most medieval Christians held about Jews derived, as most such human beliefs do, not from the reasoned observation of actual individuals or the understanding of Jewish communities neighboring one's own, but rather from a socioreligious inheritance that had been inimical to Jews for over a millennium. Medieval Christians "saw" the Jew with what the narrator of Ralph Ellison's *Invisible Man* called "a peculiar disposition of the eyes . . . A matter of the construction of their inner eyes, those eyes with which they look through their physical eyes upon reality."[1]

The primary agency for this "disposition" in medieval Christendom, the institution that most influentially articulated the moral and spiritual "facts" concerning the Jews was the church. Admittedly, the church itself was a multiplicity of units, agents, and individuals that did not speak with a single voice or represent the views of every individual in the Christian community. Increasingly through the Middle Ages, with the rise of strong princes and more centralized monarchial power, the church found itself in competition or disagreement with economic and political forces whose self-interest dictated policies about the Jews that differed from its own. Within the church as well, and in the growing number of heretical Christian sects, there were divergencies of opinion regarding the Jews. At certain times and places, for example, while the populace and local clergy were accusing the Jews of blood libels or ritual murders, a pope or bishop might contradict this canard or offer protection to the Jewish community targeted for persecution or massacre.[2] Yet, for the most part, for close to a thousand years, orthodox Christianity mobilized a vast and powerful array of resources with near totality to stifle the voice of the Jew and to deny, reshape or explain away those actualities of Jewish-Christian experience which did not fit the template of stereotypes that the church had created. Still less was any effort made to comprehend Judaism in its own historical context.

The susceptibility of the medieval masses to the church's theologically engineered image of the Jews was all the more heightened because of the marginalized status of the Jew since the fourth century, when Christianity became the official imperial religion. The negative myths of the Jew which developed in the patristic era ultimately led to their legal inferiorization. Then, dispersed from their homeland by the Romans, and economically and socially disadvantaged by Christianity, Jews were left as liminal figures in the Christian landscape. Like tribal youth gathered at the threshold of a distant encampment awaiting the rite of passage that would make them men and allow them full adult participation in their society, Jews in medieval Christian Europe were excluded from meaningful engagement with their society unless or until they would convert and be baptized in the Christian faith. As a liminal creature, an "empty vessel," as the Jewish traveller in the exemplum of "The Jew at the Devils' Council" (J3a and b) is designated until he makes the sign of the cross which fills him with grace, the Jew, not unlike women, could be infused with any symbolic values required by the dominant mentality.

The filling of the "empty vessel" of Judaism by Christian invention was facilitated by the absence of a public Jewish voice. This became especially true from the twelfth century onward, when popular hatred against the Jews, fueled by the fanatic crusading spirit, exploded into physical violence against Jewish communities, and shortly afterward, when the Fourth Lateran Council of 1214 formally codified anti-Jewish legislation.[3] An apt metaphor for Jewish powerlessness and Christianity's suppression of a Jewish voice that would raise itself in its own defense appears in a popular exemplum of the period, "The Canon and the Jew's Daughter" (J11), in which an outraged Jewish community, entering a church to protest its canon's seduction of one of their women, is miraculously struck dumb. Though there was a Jewish lyrical voice in the Middle Ages that mourned its innocent victims; a

Jewish reportorial voice that recorded its journeys to the Holy Land; and the voice of Jewish *responsa*, rabbinical interpretations of the Law as it applied to the problems of everyday life, such voices were heard almost entirely in a Hebrew literature intended for the consumption of the Jewish community alone.[4]

Where the Jewish voice articulated in talmudic commentary *was* "heard" by Christian theologians who had studied Hebrew, it was usually expropriated to hold Judaism up to derision or to "prove" the Jewish hatred of Christians. Another Jewish voice, that raised in officially sanctioned public debates with Christians, was scarcely ever one of real dialogue. Increasingly, Jewish leaders correctly learned to fear such public disputations, for their very appearance at such forums was an incitement to mob violence; and it was futile for them to reasonably promote their case since no Christian opponent would ever grant their point of view. The church administration shortly came to a similar position, if by different logic, and eventually forbid religious disputations between Christians and Jews altogether on both a private and public level. Thus we cannot take too literally the disputation mode that contextualizes several of our exempla such as "A Jew Debates the Virginity of Mary" (J17). However, it is also true that the repeated necessity for church statutes prohibiting Christian-Jewish religious discourse suggests that some informal dialogue may have continued sporadically.

Not only was the Jew's voice suppressed throughout the kingdoms of medieval Christendom, but, as has ben noted, the Jews themselves were sporadically physically absent.[5] From the thirteenth through the fifteenth centuries, in England and parts of France, in various communities of Germany, eventually in Spain and Portugal, and even in certain areas of Italy, Jewish inhabitants were alternately expelled and only sometimes partially reinstated, so that many medieval folk "knew" only the Jew created by church art; by the liturgy, sermon, and exemplum; by such secular literature or folk narrative as included Jewish characters; or by rumors of sorcery, blood libel, or ritual murder. Even where scattered Jews or small Jewish communities were resident in medieval towns, or larger Jewish communities existed in cities, these were segregated, in greater or lesser degree depending on local circumstances, from the mainstream of the Christian life around them.

With the venomous cast given to Judaism generating hostility to
Jews among the majority of ordinary people, and bereft of power to
refute the horrid images that Christianity disseminated about them,
Jewish survival dictated that each Jewish community or individual
Jew cope with this precarious situation as circumstances permitted.
The following account of a fifteenth-century Jewish traveller is instructive. Meshullam Ben R. Menahem, returning from Jerusalem on a fish-
ing smack full of Christian pilgrims, disclosed in his diary that the cap-
tain "concealed from the pilgrims that I and my companions were
Jews, and they all believed that we were Gentile merchants, God forbid! I knew that they were all wicked Germans and Frenchmen, but
strong nobles and lords, and I showed them many favours so that they
might not presume to injure me, even if they did know afterwards that
I was a Jew. As I thought so it was, for after they heard that I was a Jew,
they were much astounded, but still, because of their former love for
me they could not change their attitude."[6]

The roots of such anti-Judaism as Menahem records were inextricably intertwined with the preemptive salvatory vision of Christianity,
and to diverge from this view of Judaism promulgated by the church
was to literally risk one's eternal soul. According to one manual of
instruction for priests, among those persons who were to be cursed in
the announcements of excommunication that should take place two or
three times a year were "all that helpen with strength, or with vitayles,
or succouren Jews or Sarzons agen christendom."[7] Just as the Christian
belief in free will posited a devil whose temptations the individual
must withstand, and Christian scripture and exegesis colored the
medieval view of women, so too, Christian eschatology created in the
Jew a symbolic entity viewed as inimical to the triumph of the
Christian faith. To buttress its theology, orthodox Christianity manipulated the Jewish scriptures and interpreted the events of Jewish history to tell the Jewish story as Christianity wished it to be told. That
Judaism was the matrix of Christianity could not be gainsaid. But
Christianity accommodated this fact by erecting an adversarial and
antagonistic construct which pitted the older religion against the
younger. Jewish monotheism, its patriarchs and prophets, and select-
ed verses of Hebrew scripture were simultaneously accepted and
rejected by Christianity by misrepresenting them as merely an antici-
pation of the newer religion.

Christian hermeneutics, whose central mystery was that of the redemptive power of the crucified Jesus and the celebration of the Mass which memorialized this event, cast the Jew in the role of unbeliever whose *perfidia*, or lack of faith, was not only responsible for his own damnation but threatened the whole Christian community. The Jew's disbelief in the church's dogmatic linchpins of the crucifixion, the messiahship of Christ, the virginity of Mary, the transubstantiation of the communion wine and wafer into Christ's blood and body, and the redeeming quality of the sacraments became the fundaments of Christian anti-Judaism and the cornerstones of the church's anti-Judaic architecture. Historical events impinging on the church such as the Moslem threat to Christian Europe, the Crusades, the development of capitalism through money lending at interest, the rise of heretical sects within Christianity, the growth of literacy and scientific curiosity: all became encrusted with the myth of the perfidious Jews as people of the "Old Law," incomplete and spiritually imperfect because they rejected the "New" Testament brought by Christ as the Messiah. Blind to the redemptive possibilities offered by Christ because of their superficial, external dependence on the "letter" rather than the spirit of the Law, the Jews were designated by Christianity as the archetypal Other, a people abandoned by God who justly merited the opprobrium of their fellow men.

Though the cluster of negative myths that were to stigmatize the Jew throughout the Middle Ages was born of a particular relationship between Christianity and Judaism, an anti-Judaic sentiment did not originate in Christian Europe. In ancient Greece, Rome, and Egypt, Jewish culture had incited hostility for its separatism and an alleged enmity it bore to its pagan hosts. In the Greek value system of harmonious social intercourse, Jewish *amixia*, or apartness, the voluntary separation of the Jews from social intercourse with the majority because of Jewish food restrictions, was viewed with suspicion and dislike. Inevitably associated with Jewish separatism was an accusation of impiety, for the Jew, by rejecting the gods and religious cults of pagan culture, was also seen as rejecting the official state religion and the law of the land.

Antique perceptions of the Jew as having voluntarily put himself outside the bonds of human society made possible the bestialization and demonization of the Jew as Other, so that Jews could then be accused of all manner of fantastical chimera which no actual human experience could authenticate. Greek writers declared Jews guilty of worshipping an ass's head, and of fattening up strangers for anthropophagic rites; the Egyptians linked the origin of the Jews to the community of lepers; the Roman author Martial attributed an unpleasant odor to Jews, blamed them for sharp trading in the marketplace and warned parents abandoning their children not to leave them with Jews.[8] Fabulous legends were spun to "document" these accusations, which issued from both learned and popular sources. Gnostic writings of the first to the fourth century, although certainly anti-Christian as well as anti-Jewish, were particularly denigrating of the Jews, presenting the Jewish God as a demiurge combining various bestial characteristics and linking him to sexual perversion. According to their mythology the evil thoughts of the Jewish God resulted in nocturnal emissions of sperm that generated this God's children, the Jews, and they coupled together Voluptuousness and Death as the creation of the Jewish God.[9]

Yet while several of these anti-Jewish themes struck by the ancients maintained a place in the image bank of Christian anti-Jewish polemics, Greek and Roman anti-Judaism was but "little drops of water lost in the sea of a vast production [of] medieval anti-Jewish literature."[10] It was the Christian theological rejection of Judaism "woven into the significant documents of the Christian religion and . . . closely . . . connected with the church's expression of its faith" that generated the anti-Judaic themes that dominate medieval homiletics.[11] First among these Christian documents were the Christian scriptures themselves, especially the Gospels, where we find the narratives accusing the Jews of the deicide of Christ. To fully comprehend the persistence of this charge and its extention in medieval accusations of Jewish ritual murder, we must note the synchronic nature of the Gospel accounts of the crucifixion, which, by collapsing time, identify the Jews of Christ's era with their future descendants. Thus, in Matthew (27:25), we find the Jew's complicity in the killing of Christ a stain not only on those present at that time but on Jews for all eternity, in the putative words of the Jews themselves: "His blood be on us and on our children." Further connections are made in the Gospel of Matthew (23:29–35) and elsewhere in the Christian bible between the deicide imputed to the

Jews and their intentions to kill the disciples of Jesus, and by implication, all Christian believers, both contemporary and future (1 Thess. 2:14–16).

This conflation of disparate time periods under the hegemony of God's divine plan was characteristic of the medieval homilist's imagination as well as the evangelist's. It was a habit of expression for the popular preacher to veer back and forth between citations from the bible and contemporary conditions, and medieval sermon audiences were conditioned to accept as applicable to their own lives the lessons of moral narratives borrowed from the experience of a thousand years or more prior to their own existence. This temporal mode permitted the theological otherness of the Jew to remain fresh and vivid in the popular mind. Thus, for example, in the variant of "The Canon and the Jew's Daughter" (J11) from the fifteenth-century English sermon tract *Jacob's Well*, the preacher explains the "bloody flux" suffered by contemporary Jews as a symbol of their killing of Christ, supporting this explanation with Matthew's text cited above. Similarly, with the collapse of time, allegations that Jews profaned the Host, assaulted crucifixes, and murdered Christian devotees could be and were viewed not merely as symbolic representations of Jewish enmity towards Christianity, but as continuing reenactments of the first deicide that had put the Jews beyond the pale of human fellowship. In the *Festial*'s exemplum "Jews Attack a Christian's Crucifix" (J5), for instance, Jews are depicted as "killing" a crucifix precisely because it is "an image of Jesus that our fathers killed; therefore, as they did to his body we will now do to his image." As the Jews recreated the crucifixion upon the statue of Christ, blood and water ran out of its side, reminding the Christian listener that while the Jews killed Christ's body centuries ago, Christ still lives in his crucifixion statues and the Jews continue to kill him.[12]

The Christian scriptures were the source of other depictions of Jewish alienation from humanity which also surfaced in medieval homiletics. From Pauline writings, and from the Gospel of John in particular, was derived the image of the carnal Jew, the embodiment of the "old Adamic nature of fallen humanity," in contrast to the new, spiritually advanced Christian, who could free himself from the oppression of fleshly desires by acceptance of the covenant with Christ. Several sermon exempla mark or associate Jews with physical corruption, disease, or disability, symbolic of their spiritual corruption; these conditions can only be cured by conversion and/or baptism.[13] Thus, in one narrative, a Jew is trapped in a stinking pit (J7); in another the Jews are said to "bleed from below" and they are made mute (J11); in a third, a blind Jew regains his sight only when blood from some dead monks is smeared over his eyes.[14] The inability to see, whether from physical blindness or being blindfolded, a condition emblematic of the Jewish inability to comprehend the Christian message, occurs frequently in medieval homily and art following such imagery in the Christian bible.[15]

Christianity's "New" Testament was but one source of the disparagement and revilement of the Jews as the Other, the obverse of decent Christians, which flourished in popular medieval sermon story. Like the sermon matter itself, the exemplum had additional anti-Judaic sources upon which to draw. The anti-Judaic motifs of sermon exempla about Jews had been powerfully articulated throughout the patristic period of Christianity, from the fourth through the eighth century, by some of the most revered and influential figures in the early church. In their biblical exegesis and sermons, Christian theologians, notably those of the eastern (or Byzantine) church, attributed all the negative sides of the salvation dichotomies to the Jews: they were the flesh against the spirit, darkness against light, muteness against the Word, falsehood against the truth, damnation in hell against eternal heavenly bliss, death against life and the beast against the human race. It was chiefly from this patristic invective that the identification of Jews with fallen women and with devils, which was to become a staple of medieval homiletics, derived.

Yet as the Jewish presence did not disappear with the invective hurled against it, as Judaism would not abrogate itself by substituting for its old covenant the one provided by Jesus in Christianity, its presence had to be theologically accounted for. This accommodation, developed as the theory of "the remnant," also originated in the patristic period and was to become the means by which the preponderance of sermon narrative resolved the ambiguity of the Jewish presence. According to the theory of "the remnant," the Jews had to continue to exist as witnesses to the truth of Christianity; theirs was a preordained role in which they would enact the last event in the scheme of salvation. In the time which would announce the Second Coming of Christ and the Last Judgment, the Jews would finally admit that it was not through their

Torah and their "Old Law" that they would be saved, but through faith in Christ. Until such time, the Jews would continue as a pariah out-group; then they must either be converted or be forever damned in hell.

It was St. Augustine who most clearly and influentially articulated this notion of the Jewish remnant and elaborated on the place of the alien Jew in God's divine plan. In scattered writings, but particularly in his "Reply to Faustus the Manichean," St. Augustine expounded this idea, likening the Jews to Cain, who must not be killed but rather must wander the earth in misery, "proof to believing Christians of the subjection merited by those who, in pride of their kingdom, put the Lord to death." Testifying to "their iniquity and our truth," Augustine declared, "[o]nly when a Jew comes over to Christ, he is no longer Cain, nor goes out from the presence of God."[16] It is this concept of the Jew that governs his presence in the medieval exemplum, where he functions not as the true subject of the narratives that depict him but rather as an object of conversion to Christianity.

St. Augustine's influential remnant theory, then, posited the Jew as a liminal figure occupying a temporary ordained borderline space between patriarchal Judaism—which foreshadowed and gave rise to Christ—and the period of the Second Coming, when all the Jews must convert. From the theological perspective, actual Jews inhabiting the space between, from the time of Christ throughout the Middle Ages, were to exist only as a metonym for disbelievers. Again, St. Augustine was quite explicit about this ambiguous position of the Jews. On the one hand, they were a valuable "people . . . trained to become responsible for guarding the whole mystery [of eternal life]." In their diaspora they carried to many nations the knowledge of the scriptures in which eternal salvation in Christ was foretold by the prophets and foreshadowed by the patriarchs. "Everywhere," St. Augustine wrote, "the Jews bear witness to us through their Scriptures that we have not falsified the prophecies about the Christ. Yet [t]he Jews . . . refused to believe in [Christ] and killed Him."[17] Thus, just as the Jews had no choice about the uses to which Christianity would put the Hebrew Bible, and later on, the Talmud, so too it was not within their power to reject the manipulation of their very presence as a subtext for Christian eschatology.

This doubling of the Jews as both the disbelievers and the witnesses of Christ's message was a preeminent motif of Christian exempla in sermons of both the patristic and medieval period. In the exempla of

the earlier Christian centuries, when there was, perhaps, still a linger-
ing hope that a demonstration of Christianity's spiritual superiority
might suffice to convert the Jews, some Jews are depicted as relatively
neutral personalities engaged in relatively amicable relationships with
Christians. In one exemplum from the literature of the eastern church
(sixth to eighth century), for example, it is a Jew who lends money to
a Christian merchant when all his coreligionists refuse him; and in our
exemplum of St. Basil (J1), a Jewish doctor willingly and effectively
administers to the dying Christian saint.[18] In hagiographical anecdotes
of this earlier period whole Jewish communities, neutrally presented,
are shown as converting through the miracles or sermons of Christian
saints or by manifestations of the efficacy of Christian rites, although
certain of these tales also depict hostile Jews trying to prevent such
conversions.[19] By medieval times, however, Christian expectations of
voluntary Jewish conversions had clearly been disappointed. Exempla
of medieval origin treat Jews more vituperatively, portraying them in
violent assaults on the artifacts of Christianity and its worshippers that
were less apparent in earlier pulpit tales.

The preacher *ad populum* on the cusp of the High Middle Ages, then,
was the recipient of a double inheritance of theological dicta marginal-
izing and disparaging the Jew. On the one hand, the Jew was stigmatized as an icon of disbelief—a carnal, legalistic creature heedless of the
Christian message of salvation that could redeem him, and an impedi-
ment to the salvation of others. His very presence mocked Christian
belief and justified whatever vilification or even physical harm the
Christian community exerted against him. On the other hand, the
eschatological focus and missionary fervor of the thirteenth and fourteenth centuries supported the theological notion of the Jewish remnant, so that while it dictated a miserable, pariah status for Jews, it also
rationalized their continued existence as potential converts and testi-
fiers at Christ's Second Coming.

The homiletic exemplum, playing its part in the resurgence of
Christian homiletics after the Fourth Lateran Council, manipulated
these two seemingly contradictory ideas regarding the Jew to gratify
the historical and psychological demands of its time and place. Its anti-
Judaic themes were not arbitrarily or accidentally invented, but were
the legacies of earlier Christian homiletics, fine-tuned to the spiritual
concerns of the medieval European church and consistent with the

imagery of other popular religious media. Though conventional and repetitive, the anti-Judaic motifs of the exempla were made vivid and engaging by their setting in a narrative frame, their dramatization of conflict between clearly opposed villains and heroes (or heroines, particularly the Virgin Mary), and their transformation of theological argument into colloquial, accessible dialogue. They also permitted the individual preacher to dilate on the invidiousness of the Jews as he saw fit, adding "instruction" to entertainment. Thus, for instance, in one version of a patristic anecdote in which St. Macarius converses with a pagan skull, the medieval preacher departed from his Latin original to have the pagan inform the audience that "the Jews' souls are deeper in hell [than pagan souls], for God had chosen them as his people, and was born among them, and was of their nation. And they, as traitors, slew him and we did not. Therefore we have less pain in hell [than the Jews]."[20]

Pagans, Saracens, heretics, and Jews: all were disbelievers consigned to hell, but it was the Jew who was consigned to the "deepest part of hell." Sociological and psychoanalytic theories adduced to account for this unique otherizing of the Jew have, correctly, attributed it to the irrational urges of the unconscious and subconscious regions of the medieval mentality: it is a displacement of repressed hostility towards the stringent morality enjoined by a puritanical church; it is a hidden desire to "kill the father," that is, the parent religion, Judaism; it is a projection of the suppressed spiritual doubts of Christians themselves. It is an aspect of xenophobia; it is scapegoating for a variety of unresolved economic and social ills; it is a reflection of sexual anxieties in a culture idealizing celibacy.[21] And indeed, it *is* all of these things, which do illuminate the relationship between the two religions. But first, if briefly, an historical context for the operation of these psychological phenomena must be established.

The medieval period has been called the "age of faith." More accurately, it might be called the age of the crisis of faith. For while on the one hand, the church's religious authority was supreme throughout Europe, on the other, its spiritual hegemony was fractured and fissured by skepticism of many of its tenets. Transubstantiation—the actual rather than the symbolic transformation of the communion wine and wafer into the blood and body of Christ at the celebration of the Mass—though insisted on by the church, became one such point of controversy. The divine nature of Christ became another, and to quell doubts about this point, which is not explicitly confirmed in the Gospels, the church moved the crucifix into a more central place in popular worship. Another concern was the privileging of the Virgin Mary in her role as intercessor with Christ for the disposition of souls. Indeed, since the Virgin is hardly mentioned in the Gospels, issues such as her Immaculate Conception and her Assumption were raised by sectarians opposed to her cult. Another area of skeptical scrutiny was the penitential process, which had led to abuses such as the sale of indulgences. And it is obvious from the church's continued exhortation against the practice of sorcery, magic, and other illicit arts that these continued to be the recourse of people from every station of life.

Where did the Jew fit into this landscape of Christian doubt and disbelief? How did the church manipulate his image to suit its own agenda of suppressing doubt and erasing skepticism among its own? What role did the Jew come to play in relieving the intense spiritual anxiety generated by the obsessive homiletic concern for personal salvation? As we examine medieval religious anecdotes involving the Jew, it becomes apparent that these reflect, even as they reinforce, the unresolved psychic conflicts and spiritual discomfort specific to the circumstances of medieval Christianity.

The Jew, like the devil, was conceptualized in the Christian Middle Ages as a mysterious, amorphous entity, recognizably human on the one hand, yet strange and alien in beliefs and behaviors, a natural screen upon which to project the alienating emotions stirring the Christian unconscious. Like a servo—a mechanism which starts a motor from a remote distance—the Jew had the power to unleash in Christians projective fantasies by which the Christian could assuage his own anxieties and justify his persecution of the Jew on theological grounds issuing from the highest levels of the church and state. Popular anti-Judaic sermon story projected the same social norms that were reflected in all manner of medieval documents, both religious and secular, and not only instructed the Christian to hate and condemn the Jew, but offered him precisely the grounds on which he should do so.

One overarching theme that informed anti-Judaic sermon exempla was that of Jewish separateness from the mainstream of ordinary life. The subtext for this theme was the metaphor of contamination and impurity, which underlay much of the legislation against Jews. Christian spiritual anxiety, fueling feelings of vulnerability, projected the Jew as a perilous influence in the lives of Christian folk, and thus required their spatial separation from the larger community. Yet the causes for Jewish isolation, which actually derived from the Christian community, were projected upon the Jews, who were regarded as requiring secret space for the performance of their nefarious plots and rituals.

It was true, as noted, that Jewish communities, even before their first compulsory ghettoization in sixteenth-century Venice, were often voluntarily gathered together in certain neighborhoods for the convenience of their worship and religiously organized social life.[22] Throughout the Middle Ages it was typical that Jewish families lived on contiguous streets which also contained their slaughterhouse, bakehouse, ritual bath, synagogue, and even cemetery. In the early Middle Ages, it was not unusual for Christian homes and even ecclesiastic institutions to be interspersed in these Jewish quarters. Increasingly, however, church authorities perceived a spiritual threat in the contiguity of Jewish and Christian residence, "for great injury and inconvenience results from the constant society of Jews . . . being intermixed with Christians," as one Spanish churchman wrote.[23] To counteract the perceived menace of contagion of Jewish disbelief and heresy—Jews were continually accused of fostering heretical beliefs and protecting dissident sectarians—numerous laws were drawn up that regulated the mobility of Jews and the interpenetration of Jewish and Christian space. Jews were excluded from Christian neighborhoods, forbidden to administer medically to Christians, to employ Christian servants, to engage in certain business transactions with Christians, and to serve in the public offices of their towns and cities.

The religious angst behind such segregation is clearly revealed by one of the most curious of the Fourth Lateran Council's decrees concerning the Jews, that which confined them to their houses during Passion Sunday and Holy (Easter) Week.[24] This decree, and similar localized regulations forbidding them even to look out their windows at the processions of certain saints' days, was ostensibly motivated by the alleged Jewish practice of converting Christians on these sacred occasions. Such concern was manifestly projective, however, as historically such occasions were frequently utilized by Christian communities to convert or otherwise persecute their Jews, and apart from the so-called Judaizing heresy of fifteenth-century Poland, there were almost no medieval occurrences of Jewish proselytizing, certainly not on a wholesale scale. Such Christian legislation must be read for its latent content, as must those exempla that describe this inverted situation. In our variant of "The Canon and the Jew's Daughter" (J11), for example, the Jewish father's seclusion on Good Friday is attributed to his body flux, a Jewish infirmity that supposedly kept all Jews indoors at this sacred time, when in reality Christian legislation was its cause.

The absent presence of the Jew, hidden behind his windows on Christian holy days supposedly plotting the desecration of Christian artifacts or assaults on the body or soul of Christian worshippers, has its corollary in the medieval homilist's situating of the Jew, physically or metaphorically, in liminal or marginal spaces. It is useful here to glance at the loci of Judaism that were articulated in a popular sermon by the fourth-century saint John Chrysostom: "[The synagogue is] a brothel and theatre . . . a cave of pirates and the lair of wild beasts."[25] The brothel, where forbidden sexual practices took place; the theater where impious recreations and re-presentations of a world and its characters mocked God's unique creative powers; the lair, an abode of beasts, not human beings; the pirate's cave, from which light was excluded and in which society's outcasts and predators emerged to injure decent folk: these covert Jewish places with their unsavory connotations found an echo in medieval religious narrative as well as in legislation segregating and eventually ghettoizing the Jews.

In the tale "Jews Expecting the Messiah Are Deceived by a Clerk" (J10), for instance, the clerk "came by night to the wall where [his Jewish lover's] mother and father lay within," and the newborn daughter that defeats the Jews' expectation of their Messiah is killed by being thrown "against the wall" that encloses this quarter of Jewish false hopes. Another exemplum attributing the immuring of the Jews behind a wall by Alexander the Great suggests the same theme of separation, the punishment here presumably fitting the Jewish crime of perfidiousness.[26] This theme is also sounded in "The Canon and the Jew's Daughter (J11) mentioned above, where the clerk's Jewish lover is supposed to be confined within her Jewish space, "kept so strictly guarded by her father and mother" that it is difficult for them to meet. Yet meet they do: Christian lust penetrates Jewish space to the detriment of the *Christian*'s soul, but the Jewish penetration of the Christian space—when the Jews enter the canon's church to publicly accuse him—is converted through the miracle of the canon's repentance into Jewish acceptance of Christ. Other exempla also link Jews to secret places perilous to Christians. In "A Jew in Church" (J12) the Jew who knifed the crucifix "hid [the crucifix] in a secret place"; it was nevertheless recovered, leading to a miracle and Jewish conversion. In a second tale, "The Virgin Rescues a Jewish Merchant" (J18), a Jewish traveller is held by a band of thieves in "an old abandoned house," where his dreams of hell are specifically contrasted to "a high hill," an open Christian "place of great joy and bliss" shown to him by the Virgin. From the exemplum's perspective, the conversion of polluted, isolated Jewish space into free and healthy Christian ground was always, but only, possible with the conversion of the Jew. This theme is expressed symbolically in the tale of the Jew who remained trapped in a cesspit because he refused the proffered aid of a passing Christian (J17).

The fears of Jewish contamination that had assailed Christian authorities for a thousand years could not be easily assuaged, however, even by strict residential and other spatial legislation. The phantasmagoria of Jews erupting from their quarters or peering from their windows at passing Christian parades with maleficent intent required a measure that would finally resolve the ambivalence with which Christianity perceived its parent religion, a stricture that would unambiguously identify the feared and hated Other. Thus, Pope Innocent III, at the Fourth Lateran Council, decreed that Jews must wear a badge of identification—a yellow wheel—to distinguish them from Christians. The argument advanced by the pope (and in other councils adopting this and similar measures throughout the thirteenth century) was that such marking was "imperative to prevent intermarriage or concubinage between Christians and Jews."[27] Thus, just as the Christian scriptures had stigmatized all the descendants of biblical Jews as deicides, and the patristic "remnant theory" had marked the Jew as a fratricide of Christianity analogous to Cain, the Jewish badge would become an explicit marker of the Jew as a sexual enemy, a gleaner of Christian souls through sexual trespass.

To locate the source of this conflation of religious and sexual themes marking the Jew as trespasser on the sexual as well as spiritual space of the Christian, we must turn again to the homilies of the church fathers, where the metaphors of Judaism's carnality and associated traits originated. We have already noted that a staple of Christian Anti-Judaism was to oppose the higher spirituality of the younger faith to the earth-bound physicality of the elder. Grossness, gluttony, and sexual appetites were a cluster of sins characteristic of the Jew according to the influential homiletic invective of St. John Chrysostom: "Living for their belly, mouth forever gaping, the Jews behave no better than hogs and goats in their lewd grossness and the excesses of their gluttony."[28] The goat was a motif allied to sexual promiscuity and the devil, while the rooting and wallowing of hogs—an animal often associated with the devil as well as the Jew—suggested unbridled lust and willingness to swill all manner of impure food, hinting at taint and corruption.

In addition to Chrysostom's metaphor of the synagogue as a broth-el, other sexual anti-Judaic imagery peppered the homiletics of doctors of the eastern church. The Syrian churchman Ephrem, for example, accused the synagogue of being cut off by God "because she was a wanton between the legs" and described Israel as being "divorced" from God because she was "polluted": [God] . . . doubled back and lift-ed up her covering . . . and as an adulteress and harlot He drove her out and sent her forth from His chamber . . . disgraced." In the "Demonstrations against the Jews" written by another Syrian authori-ty of the church, the prophet Hosea's reference to the Hebrews as "a licentious and adulterous woman" became the linchpin of a contrast between Israel, "[who] has played the whore and Judah [who] has committed adultery" and the faithful and holy Christian community.[29]

This encoding of the Jew as sexually licentious—whether as a wan-ton woman or a lecherous beast—persisted in various forms through-out the medieval period, especially in the plastic arts, which often con-trasted a beautiful triumphant Virgin representing the church with a sexually seductive female symbolizing the synagogue. The metaphor of the Jew as woman—femaleness implied wantonness, whether it was explicit or not—was perfectly consonant with the dominant spiritual anxiety of medieval Christianity over personal salvation, with clerical misogny, and with homiletic anti-Judaism, all of which fused in con-demning both women and Jews as seducers of the soul.[30] In their pas-sions and unholy appetites, women and Jews were inextricably joined as aliens in a shared community of values, as outcasts like Satan and his devils, whose enmity to the faith could be combatted only by con-stant vigilance. Hence the requirement of a badge to mark the Jew (like the stench and cloven hoof that marked the devil), who otherwise might penetrate unnoticed into Christian space, poaching on its practitioners, undermining by stealth a faith which he did not have the physical prowess to destroy in open battle.

The containment of the perceived Jewish sexual threat through the feminization of the Jewish male was a useful construct in Christian theology. Cross-gendering the Jewish male as lascivious but female defused the threat of his physical aggression while maintaining his image as a peril to Christian purity through illicit sexual activity, which a clericized medieval society had already designated a cardinal sin linked to devils and women in general. (This same phenomenon occurred in white plantation society in the nineteenth-century American South, where the black male was simultaneously fantasized as sexually rapacious and desexed by the appellation of "boy" and the punishment of castration.)[31] The motif of the impotent feminized Jewish male is struck several times in medieval pulpit narrative. For example, the myth of the menstruating Jewish male, which enjoyed widespread belief in the Middle Ages, finds an echo in the "bloody flux" and "bleeding from below" attributed to the Jewish father in "The Canon and the Jew's Daughter" (J11). Also central to both this exemplum, the tale "Jews Expecting the Messiah Are Deceived by a Clerk" (J10) and several proto-Shylock exempla is the theme of the symbolically castrated Jewish father unable to exert his male prerogative of control over his daughter, who then puts Jewish masculinity further into question by her cross-gendering as an active (for which read male) agent in her own seduction.[32]

Since medieval misogyny had already encoded *woman* as temptress and sexual, ergo spiritual, threat, the Jewish *female*, rather than the male, was, from the homilist's perspective, a more eligible candidate for the role of seducer, and indeed, our exempla uniformly portray their miscegenous couplings with a Jewish female and a Christian male.[33] As alluring and exotic females, Jewish women were presumed not bound by the constraints on sexual feeling that marked the virtuous Christian female. Projecting an image of both desire and interdiction, the glamor of the Jewish woman—never shown in any other role than that of a concupiscent young person— is especially perilous to celibate Christian clerics, who should disdain her as a Jew and avoid her as a female. The repression of guilty desire which fueled homiletic sexual fantasy could not do otherwise than project upon the Jewish female that seductive character which would rationalize or mitigate the Christian male's sin. In our sermon tales, hints of the perceived sexual appetite of Jewish women appear in their cunning strategems for meeting their lovers in defiance of their familial and religious loyalties. Afterwards, for the sinful Christian male, cleric or layman, the penitential process could remove the stain of his illicit sexual activity. For the Jewish woman, as for seductresses in general, "conversion," that is, a sincere turning towards Christ, ends her threat, simultaneously eradicating her Jewish belief and her carnality. Indeed, the Jewish female in sermon story, like her Christian counterpart, often becomes a nun. But the homiletic neutralizing, or neutering of the Jewish male, does not signal *his* end as a threat, for if his aggression in the sexual context has been subdued by its transferrence to his daughter, he nevertheless remains a menacing figure in another, equally crucial role, that of a Christ- and Christian-killer.

While Christ's crucifixion and resurrection are the pivotal events of Christianity, the adoration of the image of the crucifix did not play so large a role in the earlier centuries of the religion's development as it was to play in the Middle Ages. As images of the crucifixion multiplied in sculpture, painting, and manuscript illumination and became an increasingly larger focus of Christian worship, so too did the violent anti-Judaic depictions of the Jews. St. Augustine had used the Gospels' discrepancies about the events of the crucifixion to emphasize the Jews' complicity in this occurrence, and medieval artists, writers, and dramatists elaborated the Jewish role beyond the details provided in the Gospels. Artistic distortions of the Gospel accounts such as those showing the Jews nailing Christ to the cross and spearing his side, callously regarding the crucified Messiah, or even dancing around the crucifix, impressed upon the medieval mentality the image of the Jew, clearly identified by his red, conical hat and/or his yellow badge, as a felonious deicide. Depictions such as those of Abraham sacrificing Isaac (regarded as a type of Christ) and the circumcision of the infant Jesus became adumbrations of the crucifixion. Furthermore, as medieval popular art and homiletics averred, contemporary Jews, by their rejection of Christ's divinity and redemptive grace, by injury to images of Christ, by ridicule of the Virgin, by profanation of the

Eucharistic Host (the communion bread), and by the actual murder of devotees of Christianity, continued to kill Christ.

Psychoanalytic theory generally explains rabid enmity and chimerical accusations of one group against another as the unconscious projection of our aggressive impulses onto some external figure or group who is both different from us and yet intimately connected to us in some way. By imputing to demons or to the outsider those violent and sinful instincts that cause us intolerable psychic unease, we void ourselves of our anxieties and establish a "rational" basis for combatting and persecuting these Others. Paradoxically, we attribute to these reflections of our own worst selves great power to harm us, and at the same time despise them for their inferiority to our purged version of ourselves.

Read correctly, artifacts of popular culture such as the exemplum are revealing of the central psychic concerns of the society from which they emanate. Thus, in the cluster of our exempla depicting Jews (always male) in assaults on the paraphernalia of Christianity, we uncover a subject of Christian doubt and disbelief too painful for Christians to confront directly. Orthodox medieval Christianity could not permit inquiry about the divine nature of Christ that might undermine belief, so guilt repressed skepticism, which could emerge only in the guise of *Jewish* attacks on Christ reenacting their deicide. Clearly, in the exempla "Jews Attack a Christian's Crucifix" (J5), "A Jew in Church" (J12), "Parisian Jews Bloody the Host" (J13), and "An Easter Miracle of the Host Converts the Jews" (J14), the depictions of Jews stabbing, beating, eviscerating, and inflicting a variety of bloody wounds on Christ and the religious artifacts associated with him contain a latent psycho-religious content that requires some attention.

From the Christian perspective, the first "bloody assault" by Jewish males against Christ is perpetrated in the act of circumcision, that necessary but invisible marker distinguishing Jewish men from their pagan neighbors and, later, from Christians. For the Christian, circumcision became the mark of physical loss that symbolized the spiritual loss of Jewish disbelief in Christ. The wound of circumcision might heal, but the spiritual loss would remain, and both the wound and the loss were the more portentous because of their invisibility—hence the requirement of an external badge to mark the Jew and prevent his spiritual and sexual penetration of Christian space.

While in Christian scripture it is only the Gospel of Luke (2:21) that mentions Christ's circumcision, this ritual is not infrequently depicted in medieval art, where it offered an opportunity to suggest the antagonism of the Jews to Christ and an anachronistically Christianized Mary. In one manuscript illustration, for example, Christ's mother is shown recoiling from a grim faced, knife wielding *mohel* and his mocking aides with a gesture protective of the infant Jesus.[34] Through ingenious exegesis and ahistorical distortions, the circumcision of Christ was turned into a painful Jewish ritual that the holy family painfully endured, as they were to endure other sorrows at the hands of the Jews. For the medieval mind to have fully acknowledged the circumcision of Christ in its cultural context would have been to explicitly acknowledge Christ's Jewishness, an intolerable admission that would undercut the crucial distinctions between Jew and Christian that the church and secular society were going to such lengths to assert.

As the events of Christ's life unfold in the Gospels, it is foretold by Christ that his fellow Jews "will kill and crucify" some of their "prophets and wise men" (Matt. 23:34), and, indeed, Christ is eventually brought before the Jewish high priest, the chief priests, the elders, and the rulers of the council who condemn him for blasphemy as "deserving of death." We are told that "[the] chief priests and elders of the people plotted against Jesus to put Him to death," and towards that end they take him to Pontius Pilate, the Roman governor, who asks what shall be done with him. The Jews express their desire that Christ be "crucified" (Matt. 27:22), and Pilate literally washes his hands of the matter, stating that he is innocent of the blood of Christ. Saying to the Jews, "You see to it," Pilate makes them the perpetrators of the crucifixion, although it is Roman soldiers who actually carry out the deed.

In the evangelist Matthew's record of the Jews voluntarily accepting the blame for Christ's death, Jewish otherness, which had hitherto been defined by the wound of circumcision, was now defined by the deicide for which Jews through all their generations would bear the guilt. The invisible bloody stigma of circumcision, which Jewish males inflict on their own, was now replaced, or displaced upwards, by the visible bloody stigmata of the crucifixion which Jewish males inflicted on Jesus. The medieval exempla treatments of further bloody wounds inflicted on Christ through attacks on his images, his devotees, and particularly on his body were continual, emotionally compelling reminders of the crucifixion.

With the doctrine of transubstantiation, the transformation of the consecrated bread and wine of the Mass into the reality of Christ's body and blood acquired a powerful totemic valuation that was central to the medieval church's revitalization of Christianity for the masses. To question transubstantiation was to doubt the literal application of Christ's words to his disciples at the Last Supper, when he blessed the bread and wine and commanded them: "Take, eat; this is my body" and "This is my blood of the new covenant which is shed for many" (Mark 14:22–24; John 6:53–58); such doubt was the precursor of the most heinous sin of despair. Yet to ingest these substances as the body and blood of Christ was an act of primitive injury that on a conscious level was abhorrent. Denial and repression of this psychically insupportable material and its rechannelling through displacement, overcompensation, and projection were inevitable if the tenet of transubstantiation was to become persuasive to masses of Christians. The church actively supported this controversial doctrine by homiletic overcompensation, multiplying narratives that glorified the Host and the blood of Christ. Just as exempla had been composed to show that even the devils rendered homage to the Host, sermon narrative was written to illustrate the power of the Host in converting the Jewish disbelievers. The Host is anthropomorphized, as when a communion wafer stabbed by the Jews in "Parisian Jews Bloody the Host" (J13) runs with blood as a human body would, reminding the audience that it is truly Christ's body, spilling blood as it did at the crucifixion when a Roman soldier pierced Christ's side with a spear. Furthermore, the blood of the Host, like that of Christ and the saints, has miraculous powers. In exemplum J13, for instance, the blood refuses to stop running until the Host is consecrated by a priest; in "Jews Attack a Christian's Crucifix" (J5) blood mixed with water, the precise liquid described in the crucifixion scene (John 19:34), runs from the image the Jews have pierced in their crucifixion reenactment and proves efficacious in healing the sick. The sacralizing of the communion materials extended to the secular realm as well: Christians were forbidden to buy communion wine from Jewish merchants and communion bread from Jewish bakers, presumably to avoid the taint of these items even in their unconsecrated state that would carry over to their liturgical use.

The church's campaign for transubstantiation did not altogether resolve the doubts and anxieties associated with it, however. The repressed ambivalence and guilt suffered by the Christian committing the atavistic sacrifice of the Mass required the projection of this action onto some other figure, outside the group, who could absorb the blame. The communicant "eating" Christ's body and "drinking" his blood had to see in the mirror of this act, not himself, but the disbelieving Jewish Other, shedding Christ's blood once again, not as the Christian did to gain everlasting life, but to disprove Christ's redemptive powers. Conversion exempla built on projective fantasies of Jewish attacks on Christian liturgical objects not only permitted the Christian listener to relieve his burden of guilt by transferring blame to the Jews, but also acted as a goad to the faith of the Christian, for if the power of the Host, the crucifix and Christ's blood could convert even the disbelieving Jews, how could any Christian remain unconvinced?

From the Jewish perspective, no doctrine could have been less likely to serve as a conversion scenario than transubstantiation, for although Judaism held to various divinely ordained food taboos, they were in no way based on a divine immanence and thus were of an entirely different nature from the notions of "fit" and "unfit" food raised by the sacrament of communion. To the Christian, the Eucharist was the ingestion of an edible substance, or "food" that became "nonfood" by its consecration. Yet these liturgical elements were empowered by their metaphorical associations with real food, for just as edibles provide the body with the nutrients it requires for physical life, the sacramental bread and wine provide the Christian with the spiritual sustenance that brings everlasting life. It is essential to the belief in transubstantiation, however, that the communion wafer and wine not be viewed as mere "real" food, an insistence that is pivotal in the exempla of the Jew who tried to feed the Host to his neighbor's pigs (J16) and the Jew who sought to trick his dog into eating the Host (J15). These homiletic narratives decry the stubborn Jewish literalness that cannot distinguish between the Host as Christ's body, that is, nonfood, and the unconsecrated biscuits that are food, a distinction that even the dumb animals tested by the Jews can perceive, as is demonstrated by their refusal to consume the former.

The Jewish inability to comprehend the notion of "sacred food" from the Christian perspective is the motif of other conversion exempla as well. In J14, a Jew attacking a Christian cleric who has just received (consumed) the Host compels the man to reveal in which part of his body he "has put it"; this demand suggests a blurring of the boundaries between the consecrated wafer as "food" processed by the digestive organs and spiritual food nourishing the "soul." The miracle here is that the "food," that is, the Host, transforms itself into the Christ child, a literally impossible form of bodily nourishment to Jewish eyes, but one comprehensible to Christians. Related to this theme is a tale of a Jew who, attending Mass with a Christian friend, sees Christians "each eating a bloody child," a *literal* perception of the sacrament of the Eucharist which "proves" again the inferior spiritual capacity of the Jew when compared to the "higher" understanding of the Christian faithful.[35] In these narratives, Christian motifs of orality derived from the liturgical or theological realm are projected as instruments of Jewish conversion without regard to the incongruity they presented within a Jewish context.

For the Christian, it was the food taboos of Judaism, after circumcision, that chiefly demarcated the otherness of the parent religion. Jewish dietary laws of *kasruth* (kosher), with their minutely articulated prohibitions listed in the Hebrew scriptures, had been blamed since pagan times for the Jews' self-inflicted separation from the rest of mankind. Christian theologians viewed these scriptural injunctions as Hebrew "misunderstandings" of God's will, for since God made all animals, none could be "unclean." Rather, the Mosaic restrictions should be interpreted as restraints on the gluttonous ways of the Jews, with the so-called unclean forbidden animals merely symbolizing such swinish or brutish ways as men should avoid.[36] With the new covenant sealed through Christ's offering of his body and blood in the consecrated bread and wine, these old Jewish taboos should have become discarded relics of their more literal, lesser law. The cluster of sermon stories informed by orality motifs signalled that Jewish literalness here, as in other matters, led to a material, legalistic, and exclusionary faith that sustained physical life while neglecting the spiritual food—the Host—that would bring salvation. The image such anti-Judaic narrative left with its audience was that of a contentious deceitful Jew secretly spiriting the Host away from the altar, hiding it under his tongue in a parody of communion, and attempting—futilely, as it will appear—to disprove its efficacy as spiritual food by its consumption as real food by a hungry beast.

Jewish disbelief in Christ's divinity and the sacrament of the Eucharist struck at the liturgical heart of Christianity just when these tenets were still controversial among the faithful. This rejection was perceived as active antipathy to Christianity and a stratagem to undermine religious orthodoxy and support heresy. Through the sermon story, the popular preacher was instrumental in shaping this Jewish disbelief into a dramatic battle where the alien Jew played the role of a determined combatant against the central articles of the Christian faith.

In a parallel manner, homiletic narrative engaged the Jew as an assailant against the Virgin Mary, whose cult was also reaching a crucial point in the thirteenth century. Here, too, fact and logic had to give way to homiletic fantasy and wish fulfillment, for no aspect of Christian mythology could be less congenial to the Jew, with his notions of strict monotheism, social cohesiveness centered on the integrity of the family, and the devaluation of celibacy and asceticism, than the veneration of a virgin goddess.

The elaborate fictional strategies that projected the Jew as the special enemy of the virgin mother of Christ had a long history. Eastern apocalyptic literature from the fifth century onwards, originating the *Transitus*, a narrative attributed to St. John the Evangelist, depicted Jewish antagonism towards the Virgin in the following tale. The Jews, embittered against Christ and his disciples, plot to stone Mary to death, and Mary is terrified that the Jews will attack her bier. As her litter is borne to her tomb, Jews set upon it, and the chief priest tries to touch her bier. In some variants, his hand withers and sticks to her tomb; in others, an angel cuts off his hand, which sticks to her tomb, but in any case, the miracle converts the attending Jews.[37] Jacobus de Voragine incorporated this legend into his story of Mary's life in the *Golden Legend*, and it was widely disseminated through other homiletic and hagiographic tracts.

On both a personal and doctrinal level, historically and culturally, it seems inevitable that the Jew would become the scapegoat for Christian ambivalence concerning the figure of the Virgin. Jewish rejection of the paragon of Christian womanhood was viewed as but another instance of their earthbound, material perspective; yet, in fact, the virginity of Christ's mother, her intercessory role with Christ, her immaculate conception, and her bodily assumption into heaven after her death were becoming major issues of dissonance between orthodox and heretical Christians. To combat this disbelief, popular pious narrative portrayed

her as the confuser of heretics and, by extension, the primary convert-
er of Jews, for no group was as friendly to heresy as they. Jewish skepticism about the Virgin, such as presented in "A Jew Debates the
Virginity of Mary" (J17) rankled deeply; the orthodox homilist's,
dramatist's or hagiographer's response for the masses was the Marian
miracle in which the Virgin triumphs over Jewish enmity and/or converts the Jews through tender persuasion.

In an exemplum of a one-eyed knight who slapped a Jew for blaspheming the Virgin, for example, the Jew sues the knight in court for
assault, but when he describes his assailant as a one-eyed man, he
loses his case, for the knight has had his missing eye restored by
Mary.[38] In several exempla the enmity that existed between the devil
and Mary also comes into play in the antagonism between Mary and
the Jews because of the connection between devils and Jews that was
to become a staple of medieval anti-Judaism. In the variant of the bishop Theophilus's pact with the devil (J9) where the intermediary
between Theophilus and the devil is a Jewish magician, Theophilus's
release from his contract through the intercession of the Virgin
becomes a Marian victory over Satan and the Jews simultaneously.

The anti-Judaic Marian exempla, perhaps more than any other, presented the homilist with an opportunity to engage the Jew in opposition
to Christianity on a recognizably human scale, with scope not only for
dramatic conflict but emotional, usually pathetic, interest as well.
Several of these, including the exempla analogues of Chaucer's well-
known "Prioress's Tale," portray the Virgin's rescue and conversion of
Jewish women and children who have suffered at the hands of male
Jews, either as individuals or as a community.[39] One of the most notable
of these is "The Jew of Bourges" (J20), where a Jewish child is saved by
the Virgin from death at the hands of his father, who is punished for his
wickedness, while the child and his mother convert to Christianity. The
conversion of women and/or their children while Jewish men play out
the role of unrepentant disbelievers is typical of the "splitting" that
occurs in various anti-Judaic narratives, where some of the Jews are rendered as salvageable characters and others as irredeemably rooted in
their disbelief.[40] Some Marian conversion exempla do, however, depict
scenarios in which individual Jewish men, rather neutrally presented,
are converted through miraculous manifestations by the Virgin (J17 and
J18). In J19, where a Jewish merchant is converted by a painting of the

infant Christ being nursed by Mary, whose breast issued real milk, the orality motif fuses the image of Mary's maternal "nourishment" with that of the spiritual nourishment provided by the church.

While Christian ideology asserted that true conversion required sincere internal change, in fact, what Marian as well as Host and crucifix conversion scenarios portrayed was the instant "completion" of Jewish law by belief in Christianity brought about through miracle. The rituals of contrition, confession, and penance that the Fourth Lateran Council was proposing as the cornerstone of its revitalization of the faith on a popular level played no part in the Jewish conversion stories. This disjuncture was not scrutinized closely because of the church's agenda to promote the efficaciousness of the Host, the crucifix, and the figure of Mary as conversion instruments to Christians as well as Jews. The reality was that Jews were not converting; logical argument had proved futile; Jewish resistance to these specific aspects of medieval Christianity, for which the church was determined to gain popular assent, required the homilist to resort to fantasy and wish fulfillment. The depth of orthodox Christian frustration with the Jew for his adamant rejection of these pivots of the faith can be measured by the rise in social anti-Judaism during this period—accusations of ritual murder, well poisonings and the like—which accompanied the dissemination of these narratives.

Disparaging Jewish disbelief by linking it to the lust of women, the apostasy of heretics and the repudiation of the Saracen was not, however, sufficient to execrate the Jews, for while these categories were despised, they were still recognizably human. If the redemptive power of Christ and the Christian scheme of salvation represented the only rational belief system, then the stubborn resistance of the Jews to this theology presented an intolerable paradox which could, for some, be resolved only by questioning the rationality, hence the humanity, of the Jew.

Perhaps, then, as some theologians from the patristic period onward had suggested, Jews belonged more to the realm of beasts than to the world of men.[41] St. Augustine, among others, identified Jews with the serpent, a loaded charge that also associated them with the devil and with Eve, preeminent symbols of original sin. We have read St. John Chrysostom's characterization of the Jews as hogs and goats;

elsewhere he writes that they have become worse than wild beasts, murdering their own offspring, a charge that surfaced in several exempla from the early church. In one, a lonely Jewish shepherd boy in Persia is not permitted to eat with his Christian and Persian fellows until he agrees to be baptized. He finally accepts baptism and is given a gold earring as a symbol of his conversion to Christianity, since a free Jew will never pierce his ear. When the boy's parents observe this symbol of his apostasy, the father pursues him and, in spite of the pleadings of other Jews present, kills him by the pool in which he was baptized. Contemporary with this tale, from France, is another that tells of one Lucius, the son of a Jewish elder, who was converted at a sermon preached to the Jews. Lucius's enraged father knifes to death both the preacher and his own boy.[42] Later medieval exempla of attempted or successful infanticides include "The Jew of Bourges" (J20) and "Jews Expecting the Messiah Are Deceived by a Clerk" (J10), in which the callous murder of a newborn baby by the Jewish community is explicitly linked to its rejection of belief in Christ as the Messiah.

Charges of Jewish bloodshed were joined with images of the Jews as beasts to add yet another pejorative epithet to anti-Judaic sermon invective. John Chrysostom again, in his sixth sermon against the Jews, introduces an analogy between Jews and beasts in the arena who, once having tasted blood, long for it anew.[43] The ascription to the Jewish community of a bestial carnality, gluttony, lewdness, and rapaciousness has already been noted. The questioning of the humanity of the Jews by comparing them to animals is made explicit by the renowned monk, Peter the Venerable, in a treatise arguing for the divinity of Christ. For disbelieving this tenet, wrote Peter of the Jews, "I dare not declare that you are human lest perchance I lie, because I recognize that reason, that which distinguishes humans from . . . beasts, is extinct in you or in any case buried . . . Truly, why are you not called brute animals? Why not beasts? Why not beasts of burden? The ass hears but does not understand; the Jew hears but does not understand."[44] Indeed, as we have seen, two of our exempla, "A Jew's Dog Rejects the Host" (J15) and "A Jew Tests the Power of the Host with Pigs" (J16) take Peter's comparison one step further, suggesting that the Jew is even lower than his beasts, who apparently comprehend the divinity that the Host embodies. The bestiality of the Jews made all Jewish feasts unclean, John

Chrysostom had thundered, a notion that the clerical raconteur Caesar of Heisterbach dramatized in an exemplum of a toad appearing on the altar during the celebration of a Jewish feast day.[45]

But neither was the invective of Jewish otherness as bestial sufficient. Firmer *theological* grounds for *theological* despisal was sought. Jews, unlike beasts, were not ignorant of Christ's salvatory grace. Rather, like the devil, they knew God's will but rejected it and attempted to subvert it out of malice. This crux of identification between the disbelief of the Jews and that of devils has a long history which began in the Christian scriptures with Christ's rebuke to the Jews disdainful of his teachings as related in the Gospel of John (8:44): "You are of your father the devil, and the desires of your father you want to do. He was a murderer from the beginning and does not stand in the truth, because there is no truth in him. When he speaks a lie, he speaks from his own resources, for he is a liar and the father of it."[46] Like the devils, who foment spiritual murder and sometimes instigate people to actual homicide, the Jews, too, will continue to be accused of murder— not only the deicide of Christ but the murder of the Host and crucifix, and Christian children. We find explicit expression of this notion in an exemplum that includes the statement that "the devil has his murderers" and concludes with the assertion that "the devil does as the Jews, who at the place of Christ [church altar] crucify a wax image and sometimes [Christian] children."[47]

A typical example of the medieval identification of Jews and devils is also articulated by Peter the Venerable, this time in a letter to his monarch, in which the monk accuses the Jews of "fencing" sacred Christian objects stolen from churches because they bear the same irreconcilable enmity towards Christ as Satan does: "what [the thief] had stolen from holy churches he sells to synagogues of Satan . . . Christ now, through the insensible vessels consecrated to him, suffers directly the Jewish insults, since, as I have often heard from truthful men . . . they direct such wickedness against those celestial vessels as is horrifying to think and detestable to say."[48]

The popular homiletic exemplum exploited the established identification between the Jews as "companions of the devil" that had arisen in earlier Christian homiletics, and in our tales we see projected onto the Jew many of those anguished displacements of doubt, anxiety, and guilt that were projected onto the devil as well. The yoking together of

the devil "and his old friends, the Jews," was a commonplace that gave
rise to exempla of Jewish familiarity with demons and made them vulnerable to accusations of participation in sorcery.[49] For instance, in
some exempla analogues of Shakespeare's Shylock motifs, in which a
spendthrift servant of a Jew deflowers his master's daughter and steals
his treasure, we find the Jewish father questioning his familiar demons
to discover the name of his daughter's lover.[50] And in some versions of
the tale of the ambitious bishop Theophilus, not only is the intermediary between the bishop and the devil a Jew, but in certain variants this
Jewish magician is expressly accused of a de-Christianizing motive in
aiding Theophilus's illicit desires.[51]

    While anti-Judaic sermon story linked the Jews and the devil in a
variety of ways to expose the noxious subtleties of Jewish theology, it is
never as explicitly venomous in its depiction of the Jewish-Satanic
alliance as the medieval drama, especially in the events that played out
the Passion of Jesus. The chief work of exempla narrative lay elsewhere.
Its primary purpose was to offer the Christian the means by which he or
she could avoid sin and embrace virtue, and pulpit narrative was
shaped, ultimately, to glorify the power of the Host, the Virgin Mary,
and the acts of confession and contrition as a means of defeating the enemies of faith, be they Jew or devil. Thus, for instance, in some exempla
analogues to the Shylock subplot mentioned above, the Jewish father's
hoped-for revelation of his daughter's lover by the demons, is unfulfilled
because the young Christian servant, taken by remorse, had already
confessed and made restitution. In one version of this pulpit narrative,
the devil proffers a reminder that Christians can always escape him by
confession, but that "[the Saracens and the Jews] will never escape our
hand."[52] The power of confession is also vaunted in the tale of the canon
who lay with the Jew's daughter (J11), for despite the doubly heinous
nature of his sin, the young man escapes both social disapprobation and
spiritual punishment by his sincere confession. In still another sermon
story, which tells of a Jew who called up the devil, the Jew is impressed
by the devil's genuflecting on both knees and doffing his crown to a
priest carrying the Host to a sick man but bending only one knee and
retaining his crown when the priest returns without the Host.[53]

    Given the centrality of Christian theology in shaping the negative
image of the medieval Jew, it is perhaps surprising that homiletic narrative did not exploit the figure of the Jewish usurer to a greater extent

than it did, for usury, as all else in medieval life, was related to theology. Certainly the *Christian* usurer provided an egregious category of sinners upon which homiletic narrative dilated; and while Jews were not exclusively usurers, their role as moneylenders in both the private and institutional, secular and religious domains was highly visible.

Pulpit narrative, however, is not very forthcoming regarding the economic function of the Jew in medieval life, but where occupation is alluded to, the Jew is generally a merchant, as in our anecdotes from the Life of St. Nicholas (J2a and b) and "The Virgin Rescues a Jewish Merchant" (J18), whose protagonist is portrayed as travelling about on business to his coreligionists. In the proto-Shylock exemplum of the Jew betrayed by his daughter's Christian lover, the reference to the Jewish father's hidden treasures suggests a man of commerce, but it is only in the Marian miracle of the Jew who tried to defraud his Christian debtor by having him pay back the same loan twice that we receive any explicit image of the economically exploitative Jew.[54]

In all of these portrayals of the "economic" Jew, including the last mentioned, where the Jew is indeed depicted as a moneylender, imprecations against Jewish usury are absent. Real life, however, was less benign in assigning a connection between Christian theology and Jewish commerce. In England in 1275, for example, a concern over the debasement of the currency through coin clipping and the circulation of counterfeit bullion led to the establishment of tribunals to prosecute offenders, both Jewish and Christian. In short order, however, the investigation of the charges against the Jews changed their offense to blasphemy, and under this *theological* indictment many Jews were arrested, hanged, or burned, and Jewish property confiscated.[55] While Christian morality had from the first been antagonistic to mercantilism, and usury by Christians was condemned under the sin of avarice, Jewish moneylending at interest that involved Christian debtors, secular or religious, stirred deeper anxieties than just the commission of usury. It led to potential intimacies between lender and borrower and an asymmetrical vulnerability between Christians and Jews that generated the primal fears of contamination which were the subtext to anti-Judaism in the parallel domains of sexual behavior and religious belief.

The opprobrium attached to usury, a term that denoted all transactions carrying payment of interest, had biblical origins in the Mosaic law "Thou shalt not lend upon usury to thy brother" (Deut. 23:19).

However, while Jews read "thy brother" as referring only to their fellow Jews, which meant that they could lend money at interest to Christians, the Christian incorporation of this biblical injunction into canon law took it to mean the Christians could not lend money at interest at all. Yet Christian ecclesiastic and secular administrators, as well as impecunious Christian individuals of all strata required the usurer's services—where were they to turn?

Here was the Jew: the theological "remnant," whose undesirable but temporarily useful role could be transferred to the economic realm. He had already been assigned a distinct and inferior legal status based on his religion, and his soul was already damned, so it could not be further imperiled by usury, a rationalization that proved convenient for Christian authorities wishing to employ the Jewish moneylender's services. There was a satisfying psychological symmetry in conflating the impurity of Judaism with the impurity of money in the stereotype of the Jewish usurer, which permitted the medieval Christian to relieve his financial and spiritual anxiety simultaneously.

Scapegoating the Jew as an economic exploiter of innocent Christians was not only convenient for Christians engaging in economic activities considered morally reprehensible by their own ideology, but was also a good physiological fit with the image of the Jew as poacher, one that the church handily manipulated between the economic and spiritual realms. The subtext of the Jew requiring a Christian's repayment of a loan was that of his requiring the Christian's soul as well. Thus, Jewish disbelief, which was the cause of the Jew's damnation but also the basis for permitting Christians to borrow money from him, could conveniently serve as a suitable pretext for the cancellation of one's debts to him, and even as grounds for Jewish expulsions, another useful, religiously sanctioned means of Christians defaulting on outstanding loans to Jews.

The concept of the Jew as a spiritual remnant, condemned for his perfidy but "protected" from complete elimination because of the theological ends he served, laid a foundation for the concept of the Jew as an economic remnant, "protected" by ecclesiastic and secular authorities so long as they could exploit his financial capacities but disposable when deemed necessary for the "spiritual" safety of the Christian community. A *tertium quid*, a third category of person occupying an unstable space delimited like his religious space by Christian ambivalencies, the Jew was relegated to a distinctive but anomalous status outside the general life of society. One exemplum that testifies to the precarious-ness of Jewish economic space is the tale of a king's Jewish servant who, although carrying the royal safe-conduct, is waylaid and robbed by one of the king's men. When the Jew complains to the king, the thief is punished for having robbed one of the king's servants.[56] But what must be read in the king's protection is the possessive nature of the Jew's privilege, which was, in fact, bought, sold, or traded by various authorities.[57] Thus it rendered the Jew an object, like chattel, rather than endowing him with the same rights as other citizens. Moreover, it had the further disadvantage of distancing him from the mass of his Christian neighbors and exciting a hostility which had already been inflamed on religious grounds.

The unequivocally negative depiction of the exploitative economic Jew in the visual arts of the Middle Ages—the Jew with his moneybags, counting coins, and the like—raises the question of why the exemplum was so shy, in general, of promoting this image as well. The answer, again, lies in the primary purpose of pulpit narrative, whose strategy was to present the Jew as a potential convert in order to rekindle *Christian* enthusiasm for the sacraments and such newly important tenets as the cults of the Virgin and the veneration of the crucifix. Sermon stories involving Jewish subjects pushed their despised eco-nomic activities to the background in order to highlight the main point: the superiority of Christian salvatory procedures. With the end of the feudal Middle Ages and the development of individual and state capi-talism in the Renaissance, religion receded from the center of social and political life and the valuation of mercantile enterprise shifted to the center. Thus it would be left to the Renaissance stage to dramatize the old nexus of Jewish disbelief and Jewish usury from a new perspective, unforgettably embodied in the anti-Judaic creations of Barrabas the Jew and Shylock, and their morally ambiguous Christian debtors.

The exemplum, then, as a popular medieval genre, shared with the drama and the plastic arts of the period a purpose that, informed and shaped as it was by the single viewpoint of a proselytizing orthodox Christianity, could not help but be inimical to the Jew. Like these other genres of popular artistic expression, the exemplum embodied a social commentary and criticism cut on a theological bias that could not accommodate Jewish otherness. Medieval Christian ideology, as reflected so well in the sermon exemplum, did not permit the Jew to be viewed as an individual. Rather, it dictated that the Jewish human being be submerged in a type, a pattern that could easily be manipulated by the preacher or the dramatist or the manuscript illuminator. And because this pattern had its source in and derived its power from an explosive combination of unconscious phenomena buried deep in the mass unconscious of the medieval mentality and external historical circumstances interpreted through the lens of Christian theology, it could not be easily eradicated. Although alterations were made in the pattern, and the image of the Jew changed as times changed, the figure mirrored in the exemplum, which dominated European Christendom for so many centuries, has been retained in startlingly and regrettably distinct outline to our very day.

Exempla about Jews

Tales J1, J2, and J3, originating in the early centuries of Christianity when both eastern and western saints were influential figures in the effort to convert the Jews, reflect a milder attitude towards the Jews than obtained in the medieval period. Indeed, in tale J2a, it is the Christian who defrauds the Jew and Christians who alert the Jew to this deceit. From the eighth century onward, when it was evident that mass conversions of the Jews were not going to occur, most homiletic narrative involving Jews betrays a distinct antipathy absent from many earlier tales.

J1. A Jew Predicts St. Basil's Death

We read that when St. Basil was sick and drawing nigh onto his death-watch, he commanded to be fetched to him a man called Joseph, a Jew, who, it was revealed to the saint in a vision, would become a Christian. Now this Joseph had some fair skill in taking the pulses of the sick, and so he came and felt the saint's pulse. When St. Basil asked him what he thought, the man replied by saying, "Sir, you shall die before the sun sets." Then St. Basil said, "And what if I do not die before morning?" And this Jew replied, "Sir, that may not be, for you are practically a dead man now; your soul and your body will hardly bide together for an hour." Then St. Basil said, "What will you say if I live until tomorrow at 6:00?" So the Jew replied again and said, "If you live, I know well that I must die." And then the saint answered him again and said, "Indeed, you speak the truth, for you shall die from sin and live in Christ." So the Jew replied again, saying, "I understand what you mean and if you live, so shall I too."

Then the saint made his prayer to almighty God that his life might continue for a bit so that man could be saved. So this Jew went his way and came back again in the morning and found the holy man still alive. And he fell down on his knees and worshiped the Christian's God. And then the saint, even as ill as he was, rose up and went into the church and baptized [the Jew] with his own hands. And when he was done, he went home again and lay down and about noon of the same day he was delivered to God.

The Saint Nicholas of tales J2a and J2b is the fourth-century bishop of Myra in Asia Minor who is the popular patron saint of the children (as Santa Claus) and pawnbrokers among others. His emblem of three balls (probably arising from confused pictorial representations of three bags of gold with the heads of three young girls he saved from prostitution with this money) has become the pawnbroker's sign. Thus St. Nicholas's involvement with Jewish merchants has a kind of folkloric logic.

J2. Two Tales of St. Nicholas

a. St. Nicholas and a Jewish Moneylender

A certain man had borrowed some money from a Jew, giving him his oath on the altar of Saint Nicholas that he would repay it as soon as possible. As he was slow in paying, the Jew demanded his money; but the man declared that he had returned it. He was summoned before the judge, who ordered him to swear that he had repaid the money. In the meantime, the man had placed the money that he owed in a hollow staff, and before giving his oath, he asked the Jew to hold the staff for him. Whereupon he swore that he had returned the money and more besides. Then he took back his staff, the Jew handing it over all unaware of the trick. But on the way home the defrauder fell asleep on the roadside and was run over by a chariot, which also broke open the staff in which the gold was hidden. Learning this, the Jew ran to the spot; but although the bystanders pressed him to take his money, he said that he would do so only if, by the merits of Saint Nicholas, the dead man was restored to life. He added that if this came about even he himself would receive baptism and be converted to the faith of Christ. Immediately the dead man came back to life and the Jew was baptized.

b. A Jew and St. Nicholas

We read in the Miracles of St. Nicholas how once upon a time there was a Jew who had heard stories of the miracles done by the saint, so he contrived to make an image of him which he set up to protect all his goods. But one time, when this Jew was away from home, thieves came and stole away all his goods. When he came home and found them stolen, he began to reprimand his image of St. Nicholas and beat it severely. Then St. Nicholas appeared to the thieves and showed them how his body was beaten on account of the goods which they had stolen and threatened them that they should be hanged unless they took the stolen articles back and restored them. Then he told them that he was indeed St. Nicholas in whose keeping this Jew had put all his possessions. These thieves became afraid and brought all the stolen goods back, and told the Jew about this miracle. So the [Jew] was converted, and he and the thieves both became good men, and the Jew was baptized.

Exempla J3a and J3b are two of the many homiletic variants of this tale which originated in the *Dialogues* of a sixth-century pope, St. Gregory the Great. One of the more moderate churchmen of his times regarding the Jews, Pope Gregory believed that persuasion rather than force should be used for their conversion. In this tale Gregory presents the ideal conversion scenario, for the Jew converts solely through his personal experience of the virtue of the cross in defending him against demonic powers. In the rubric to variant J3a, from a popular medieval encyclopedia of exempla, the labelling of the Jew as an "infidel" suggests Judaism is a rectifiable religious error. Further, the Jew's action in helping the bishop avoid the sin of lust implies that Jews could act morally and even on behalf of Christians, a motive almost wholly absent from medieval conversion tales.

Nevertheless, this exemplum does assert the traditional Christian perspective on Judaism through its metaphor of the "empty vessel." The Jew is an "empty vessel" because Judaism was considered an incomplete, failed religion that could not offer the spiritual protection of Christianity. Once having made the sign of the cross, however, the Jew was "well filled" with Christ's redemptive grace, as the "New Testament" fulfilled the "Old."

The details of the devils' reports of their mischief making that appear in exemplum J2b are not found in Gregory's original or in any other medieval variants that include the Jew. An earlier patristic analogue of a devil's council, minus the Jew, is a spiritual warning in the narrative tradition of the ascetic desert-dwelling monks resisting the devil's temptations.

J3. The Jew at the Devils' Council

(*a*.) According to St. Gregory there was once a bishop in Italy who had a nun staying at his house, and through the instigation of the devil, the bishop began to feel the desires of the flesh for her. He was so tempted by her that he had reached the point of asking her to lie with him.

Now it happened one night that a Jew taking a journey found himself without any place to rest, so he went into an abandoned temple of Apollo and there he prepared to spend the night. He slept for a little while, but then, at midnight, he saw a company of fiends come in and set up a chair in their midst for their leader. Then they each came before him, and he examined them on their skill. When each of the fiends had talked about himself, one stepped up before the chief devil's chair and told how he had tempted the bishop of that vicinity with a nun staying in his house and had actually driven the prelate to give the holy woman an affectionate pat on the back. The chief devil complimented the fiend and charged him to continue the work as he had begun.

Then the chief devil ordered the devils to look around the temple and see who was hiding there. When the Jew heard this, he made the sign of the cross, so that when the devils finally found him and hauled him out of hiding, they cried, "Woe is us! What was an empty vessel is now well filled." And with this cry the fiends all vanished away. Then the Jew got up and went to the bishop of whom the devils had spoken and told him what he head heard. The bishop repented of his sin, sent the nun away, and converted the Jew.

(*b.*) St. Gregory tells as a warning to good men,
That once there was a Jew
Who travelled on a time about the country
To such places as he had to go.
At night he found himself in a desolate place
Where he saw no habitations,
No place where it seemed best
To lie down for the night and rest,
Except for an old temple which he saw standing,
Where formerly pagan folk
Had therein made their sacrifices
To their god called Apollo.
This Jew rested there that night
And took his ease the best he might.
As the Jew lay there alone,
To himself he made a moan
That his belief was in a Law
That could not help him with words of prayer.
Of Jesus Christ he had heard men speak,
How Jews had put him on the crossed stake.
Inspired with hope,
He thought so on Christ's passion
That our faith ran through his heart
Although he was not a Christian.
So partly in faith and partly in fear,
He made the sign of the cross all around him
And then laid himself down to sleep,
And thought no more about it.
Soon at midnight he began to wake
Because of a great noise and quake.
He looked up and saw sitting there
Many foul fiends who had gathered together.
He saw one sitting in a chair,
Who looked most foul, and foully conducted himself.
This one had the fiends yield their accounts
Of the deeds they had done, in what amount,
What they had done for many years,
And queried them in this regard.

On one he cast a great grimace:
"Say you, fellow, what have you done."
"At a wedding," he said, "I was,
And there I did great mischief.
I slew, through might of hand
Both the wife and the husband.
And I did further other harm,
All the others I brought into conflict,
And made each the foe of the other,
So that every man began to slay another."
The Master Fiend glared at him
And set at nought what he had said.
"For that, how long did it take you?"
"Twelve months," he said, "not more."
"For your deeds you got very little,
And therefore, you shall be beaten."
With him no longer would he argue,
Bur called another before him
And evilly, with a grim eye,
"Where have you been?" he asked.
"At sea I have been
And created much sorrow among men.
I have brought great destruction upon
Innumerable ships and men,
What with fighting and with storms,
Twenty thousand at least."
The Devil said, "That's not bad.
How long were you about this work?"
"Seven winters altogether
Have I been haunting thither."
Satan commanded for this service
That this devil's questioning be done.
A third devil was then bound over
And set before Satan.
Satan said, "Where were you?
How have you done? Tell me now."
I have harassed a bishop
To see if I could make him sin,

But he was of such goodness
That I could never turn him to you.
But one night, I thought
That after tempting him so much
I might make his desire a party to my will.
There had come to him for his guidance
A nun, a prioress I think,
To listen to him
That she might perhaps learn virtue.
So I brought it about
That while she was staying there
He patted her a bit on her back,
Playfully, when he conversed with her.
God knows what was in his mind
And in his heart, for I do not."
Satan asked how long a time
He had taken for this betrayal.
"Forty winters, and ever in fear
That I might never so quickly,
Or never at all, bring him to this sinful plight,
But indeed I did it, this very night."
Then was Satan fully gratified
Because the devil had brought the bishop down.
He clasped the devil to him in bliss
And gave him his mouth to kiss,
And said he was very worthy
To come and sit beside him.
Before all those who sat there,
He set the devil right by his side
And said, "Finish what you have begun.
For what you have done, you have earned my love."
This same Jew that lay there
In the temple was very afraid,
And truly, he slept very little
Because of overhearing this great council meeting.
After sleeping a bit, he came awake,
And when he awoke, he was quaking.
For Satan asked, from where he sat,

"Who is hiding here and who is that
Who is so bold
As to lie down here without my permission?
Go quickly now, one or two of you together,
And bring this man, whoever he is, hither."
The devils came to [the Jew's] bed,
But gave a start, they were so afraid,
For neither the bed nor [the Jew] dared they touch
For he had made the sign of the cross upon himself.
They turned again to Satan, their Lord,
And said that they dared not seize the man.
He asked the reason, what had happened;
They said it was an empty vessel:
"An empty vessel that was marked
For protection against you and yours, Lord Satan.
This vessel when it first came here
Belonged to us, it would appear.
But alas for us, while we began our meeting,
He covered himself with this sign."
The Jew, they had called an empty vessel,
And so in truth he was:
He had forsaken his Law,
Forsaken it in his great awe.
Empty, because he had not taken up our belief
After he forsook his own.
Thus it was with hope that [the devils] named
And called the Jew an empty vessel.
But they could do him no harm,
Nor lead or bring him to Satan,
Because he had blessed himself with the cross,
So they had to let him go.
The fiends and their Lord Satan
Then went away crying, "Alas!"
The Jew quickly arose.
It was no wonder he was filled with dread.
He quickly went to the bishop
And told him what he had seen and done.
And took on the faith of Christianity,

And forsook his false Law,
And believed every article of our faith,
And the bishop shrove him well.

Tale J4 is based on a narrative that became widespread after the conversion of the emperor Constantine to Christianity in the fourth century. Eusebius, the bishop of Rome, Constantine's contemporary and
the author of the emperor's Life, claimed to have heard from
Constantine himself the story of how Constantine's mother Helen had
journeyed to Jerusalem and there discovered the True Cross. In the
same period St. Ambrose described Helen's discovery of the True
Cross but attributed its identification to an inscription written upon it,
rather than to the miracles of resurrection narrated here. The dissemination of the story of Helen and the True Cross in early hagiography,
and the Iconoclastic controversy, which condemned the adoration of
other images, elevated the status of the cross as a Christian artifact,
and it was frequently depicted in medieval anti-Judaic exempla as an
object of assault by the Jews.

The eighth-century Anglo Saxon poet Cynewulf's poem "Elene,"
commemorating the legend of the True Coss, includes motifs such as
the gathering of the council of Jewish elders, their referral of Helen's
inquiries to a man named Judas, Helen's threats of torture unless Judas
revealed the location of the cross, and the identification of the True
Cross by its resurrection of a corpse that were later popularized
through the *Golden Legend*.

J4. St. Helen and the True Cross

On the advice of the pope, [the emperor Constantine] sent his mother
Helen, who was queen of Jerusalem, requesting that she seek out the
cross upon which Christ had been crucified. Now this Helen was the
daughter of a king of England who was called Ceolus, and when that
Constantine who was father of the emperor Constantine had come into
England and saw how beautiful Helen was, he had wedded her for her
beauty and so made her empress of Rome. But after her husband had
died, she had taken the kingdom of Jerusalem for her dowry, and
thereupon she had caused to be gathered all the Jews that might be

found, and told them that truly, they would all be burnt unless they showed her the cross of Christ. Then the Jews all agreed that there was one man, whom they called Judas, who knew where the cross was, and ordered him to bring it to her at once. Then she was very happy, and put this Judas into the misery of prison until he would tell her where this cross was. Then this man saw that he had to do this or he would die, and he bade them take him to the hill of Calvary. And when he had prayed there a long while, the earth shook where the cross lay, and smoke as sweet as spices came out of the earth, and when they dug there, they found three crosses. Then, in order to know which was Christ's cross, they each lay down, one after the other, upon a corpse, but when they came to Christ's cross, at once the body that was dead arose and thanked God.

Then Helen took a part of this cross and sent it to Rome to her son, and the rest she made into a shrine covered in silver and left it in Jerusalem with all the worship due it. Thus, good men, as holy church reminds you this day, the holy cross was found.

Tales J5 and J6 reaffirm the power of the crucifix to thwart Jewish insult to and attacks upon articles of Christian ritual. Tale 5 is a reenactment of the crucifixion, a motif circulated from patristic times. In one early variant the statue of Christ is said to have been particularly beautiful and carved by the Christian who had rented the Jew's house; in another, the carving is attributed to the Jews, who pretend to worship the cross when they really wished only to insult it.

J5. Jews Attack a Christian's Crucifix

Then, as I have read, I find that in a city called Beritus, a Christian man needing a house in which to live rented one from a Jew. Now this Christian man had a cross which Nicodemus had made out of devotion and regard for Christ, and he took this cross and set it in a secret place in the house out of sight of the Jews and worshiped it according to his belief. It happened afterward that this Christian man moved into another house and so took all his goods with him, except for the rood, which he forgot, as God ordained he would.

Then the Jew came back to live in this same house the Christian man had left, and to entertain himself, he invited his neighbors in to sup with him. And as they sat at supper and talked together of the Christian man who had previously been the tenant, one neighbor looked curiously about and became aware of the cross standing in a hidden niche. When he saw it, he began to grimace and gnash his teeth, and he berated the Jewish landlord, accusing him angrily of being a Christian and keeping the cross to worship it. Swear as the first Jew might that this was not so, and that he had never seen the cross before, his neighbor went throughout the vicinity telling all the folk that this Jewish man was secretly a Christian and kept a cross hidden in his home. Then they all became angry and beat this Jewish man in the worst manner they could. And finally, they said angrily, "Here is an image of that Jesus that our fathers killed." So they took the image and beat it and buffeted it and banged it about, and then flailed it with scourges, and crowned it with thorns and then put it on the cross, nailing its feet and hands to the struts. And at the last, they made the strongest among them take a spear and thrust it with all his might through the heart. As the man did so, blood and water ran out of the image's side. Then these men were very much astonished at that sight and said, "Let us take a pitcher and fill it full of this blood and take it to our temple where many people are lying ill with various maladies, and we will anoint them with this blood and see what happens." So they anointed these sick men with this blood and at once they become hale and sound.

Then the Jews went to the bishop of the city and told him what had happened. When he heard that, he fell to his knees and thanked God for this great miracle. He followed these Jews to the house, taking with him vials of crystal and amber glass in which to put the blood, and these he distributed among the different churches. And of this blood, as men tell and believe, were holy miracles done.

Exemplum J6 links the image of Christ's blood with the cross, not only recapitulating the Jews' involvement with the crucifixion but also referring obliquely to other negative associations of the Jews with blood: their circumcision of Christ as an infant, their bloody assaults on Christ's worshippers, their disbelief in transubstantiation (refusal to believe that the sacramental wine turned into blood at the Mass), and their alleged monthly bleeding, indicative of their inferiority. The central event of this tale, the inability of the Jews to rebuild their temple in Jerusalem, which had been destroyed by the Romans in A.D. 70, was a legend inherited from patristic times and was viewed as punishment of the Jews for the crucifixion.

J6. Jews Attempt to Rebuild Jerusalem

As Miletus tells in his chronicles, many years after Jerusalem was destroyed, the Jews wanted to build it again. When they strode into the city on the next day, they found many crosses on the ground, so they were afraid and returned homeward. The next morning they came again, but their clothes became spotted full of crosses of red blood, and when they saw that, they flew home in fear. Yet they would not be warned but came again the third day, when suddenly, in a moment, a fire rose up out of the earth and burnt them all to cold coals and ashes.

Exemplum J7 illustrates the type of anti-Judaic story in which the Jews are scorned for obeying the letter of the law rather than its spirit, as Christ taught, and in which Jewish custom, whether intentionally or from ignorance, is misinterpreted. The key verses for Jewish observance of the sabbath are Exodus 31:14–15: "Ye shall keep the Sabbath therefore, for it is holy unto you . . . for whosoever doeth any work therein . . . he shall surely be put to death." However, the keeping of the Sabbath, enjoined in the Torah as a symbol of the covenant with Jehovah, was intended to prohibit work for worldly gain and pursuits that necessitate the work or service of others, such as draft animals or servants. The Talmud and Jewish commentators such as the medieval philosopher Maimonides make it clear that saving life on the Sabbath does not defile the day. This flexibility regarding the Sabbath was known to Christian homilists; in fact, Luke's Gospel, in a verse which was quite likely the kernel of our exemplum, portrays Jesus rebuking the Pharisees for their hypocrisy by breaking the Sabbath to save an ass or an ox which had fallen into a pit (Luke 14:5). The fanaticism of the Jew in the pit keeping the Sabbath to his death is, therefore, a clear misconstrual of the Jewish commandment, fabricating a Jewish punctiliousness which did not exist. Further, the exemplum implies the damnation of the Jews by associating the pit into which the Jew fell with the stinking pit of hell.

Other variants highlight the supposed Jewish fanaticism even more strongly: in a fourteenth-century French satire the incident is reported to the sainted King Louis who orders his men to keep the Jew in the cesspit until the following Monday so that he will be forced to keep the Christian Sabbath as well, and in a Latin analogue from Germany with the same elaboration, the pope is substituted for the French King. Despite its false premise, that tale was put to legal use in a thirteenth-century French commentary on canon law (which from 1150 to the early fourteenth-century included teaching about the Jews), where it glosses a discussion of the Jews' observances of the Sabbath.

J7. A Jew Falls into a Stinking Pit

There are some men who are advised to turn from sin, but they say that they are yet too young, and they say that when they are older, they will stop their sinning. It will happen to them as it did to a Jew that I read of.

There was once a Jew that on their Sabbath day fell into a foul, stinking pit. And there came a man who saw him in this pit, and wanted to help him out. But the Jew said no, because it was his Sabbath day: "Therefore you shall not labor for me and I will not labor for you." And so this passerby let the Jew remain there. And within a little while the stench of this pit was so great that the Jew died there. Truly, I am sore afraid that these men will not turn from their sin until such time as they die of its stench.

Tales J8 and J9 present two motifs popular with medieval preachers: the intimacy between the devil and the Jew and the role played by the devil in the advancement of ambitious clerics. In the original of tale J8, the Jew is portrayed as being so enamored of his books that he kept them in a secret hiding place, underscoring the medieval belief that Jews hid their religious writings because they contained anti-Christian diatribes and prescriptions for sorcery. Another of the tale's elements, the devil sowing mischief in the guise of an angel, appears in both the Talmud and the Koran as well as throughout homiletic exempla.

Tale J9, familiar in secular form as the legend of Faust, enjoyed wide medieval popularity as the story of Theophilus. While not all variants of the tale invoke the Jew as Theophilus's intermediary with the devil, this anti-Judaic element does appear in medieval manuscripts from England, France, and Germany. One surprising Low German variant, written in an anticlerical spirit, actually draws a favorable picture of the Jews: here, Theophilus, sent by a magician to the Jews, enters their synagogue and offers to join them, but he is rejected as a faithless Christian who will make a faithless Jew. Finally, after trying to persuade Theophilus to abandon his mission, one Jew does introduce him to Satan's domain but leaves him on the brink, stating that he would not, for all the money in the world, become one of Satan's disciples. Typical analogues, however, are more critical of the Jew's role. In a French version the Jew poses as Theophilus's friend and ally while actually being the instrument of his delivery into Satan's clutches; an English narrative in a collection of virgin miracles dilates on the Jew as "a most wicked Hebrew soaked in all kinds of wickedness, who had already drowned many faithless men in the chasm of perdition." A cycle of popular tales attributing dominion over the demons to King Solomon, utilized in religious disputation as early as the sixth century, was undoubtedly instrumental in reinforcing the medieval view of a link between Jews and the devil.

J8. The Jew Who Would Be a Bishop

Once, in Cologne, there was a Jew who converted to Christianity and went to live in a monastery where he became a great student of the holy books. Then he began to write books of his own. But this the monks prohibited him from doing, nor would they let him study any more. When these restrictions were laid on him, the Jew stole away from the monastery and went out into the world, intending to continue his studies. There the devil appeared to the Jew in the form of an angel and bade him hasten his studies along, for he was soon going to be made a bishop.

Some time later, the devil appeared to the Jew again in the same angelic guise and said, "Tomorrow morning you will become bishop, for the bishop is dead. Therefore, hurry into the city, for God will make you the bishop there." So this wretched man went along his way and that night he lodged with a priest nearby the city; and because he wanted to come into the city in dignity, he awoke before dawn and stole the priest's cloak and horse to enhance his arrival. In the morning, the horse was missed by the priest, so men were sent to ride after the thief, and when they caught him, they brought him back to a trial in civil court. There he was convicted, and thus he ascended not as a bishop upon a throne but as a thief upon the gallows.

J9. Theophilus, a Jew, and the Devil

A miracle of the Virgin records that in the year A.D. 300 in Sicily there was a wise and gracious man named Theophilus who was chancellor to a bishop. After some time in office, he was dismissed, and on account of this, he fell into great sorrow and despair. [In order to recover his dignities, he sought the assistance of a certain Jewish sorcerer. The Jew therefore summoned the devil, who appeared with all speed.] When the devil came to speak with him, he told Theophilus that if he would forsake Christ and His Mother and renounce his faith, the devil would be bound to his service as long as he lived. Theophilus drew up a contract to this effect in his own hand and sealed it with his ring. When it was done, he delivered it to the devil. A short time after, through the efforts of the devil, Theophilus was restored to office. Then, however, he began to think back on what he had done, and he prayed to the Virgin for help. She appeared to him and blamed him greatly for the pact that he had made, but she promised to help him if he forsook the devil. This he did, and turned again to God and the Virgin, before whom, it seemed to him in a vision, he was put on trial. There the devil showed in evidence his handwritten contract, but the Virgin took it from him and laid it on Theophilus's chest as he lay sleeping. When he awoke and found the pact, he became so remorseful for what he had done that he went out in front of the bishop and all the people and openly confessed his sin. He did the penance that was enjoined on him, and, after living a short time longer in virtue and faith, he died.

Tale J10 incorporates one of the common medieval biases against the Jews, that they were not loath to kill their own children to serve the social or religious needs of their community. This exemplum also projects the Christian tenet of the virgin birth of Christ onto the Jews in regard to their expected Messiah, a notion that plays no role in Jewish belief. It is notable, too, that in this and most versions of the tale, the clerk, who should be condemned for lust, breaking clerical vows, prohibited sexual intercourse with a Jew, and the cunning deception of the girl's parents, escapes without discovery or punishment. In Caesar of Heisterbach's original, however, when Caesar's audience of monastic novices express astonishment that the clerk did not attempt to convert his Jewish lover to Christianity, the novice-master replies that perhaps he did not have the spiritual power in himself to do so, being too vainglorious about his deception of the Jews to consider the girl's welfare.

In a variant form, this exemplum circulated as a miracle of the Virgin, who intervenes to save the woman and her child and convert them to Christianity.

J10. Jews Expecting the Messiah Are Deceived by a Clerk

Caesar [of Heisterbach] tells how once there was in the city of London a clerk who got a Jew's daughter with child and became afraid of the complaint of her mother and father. So he got a long reed and came by night to the wall where her father and mother lay within, and he put the upper end of the reed in at a hole, and he spoke into the other end and said, "Oh you righteous folk, well-beloved of God!" and called out their names and bade them be merry, for their daughter had conceived the Messiah although she was a virgin. And with that, the man was astonished and asked his wife if she had heard this voice, and she said she had not, so they prayed that they might hear it again. And the clerk stood still and heard them, and as he had done before, he spoke again. And when they heard him, they were extremely pleased and believed that it was true. They waited for the day, and grasped their daughter's body, and found that she was with child. They asked her how she had conceived, and she answered as the clerk had bidden her and said, "I do not know whether I am with child or not, but I know well that I am a virgin and have never had to do with a man." And then her father and mother were so joyful that at once they spread through the city that their daughter was pregnant with the Messiah. So when the time came that she was to deliver, there came to her many Jews with great mirth and joy and waited until the birth. But instead of a son, she bore a daughter, who cried and wailed and made a great outcry. And when they saw this, they all were highly confounded, so much so that one of them in his anger took this child by the leg and threw it against the wall and killed it.

Tale J11 well illustrates the type of exemplum whose intention was to reinforce the sacraments essential to the scheme of salvation for Christians but which had anti-Judaism as its subtext. In its most common homiletic context, the story is told as an exempla of *sincere* contrition, which erases the most heinous sins. The young canon has committed multiple religious errors. He is guilty of lust, fornication, prohibited sexual intercourse with a Jewish woman, breaking his vows of celibacy—and on Good Friday, the holiest of Christian days no less— and saying the Mass without being confessed. In Caesar of Heisterbach's original version he is also found guilty of abandoning the girl he seduced and is admonished by the bishop to forgo ecclesiastical advancement and marry the Jew's daughter after converting her rather than letting her remain in "the sins of her father," that is, her Jewish religion. This ending reflects the focus on conversion of the Jews which issued from the policies of the Fourth Lateran Council.

The anti-Judaism of this exemplum is both explicit and covert. The notion that Jews "bleed from below," or are laid low by a "bloody flux," as a reminder of Jewish culpability for Christ's crucifixion; the use of this chimera as a rationalization for the reluctance of the Jews to venture out on Good Friday, when in fact they were prohibited by law from doing so; the implied seductiveness of the Jew's daughter by references to her "fairness" (in the original, her beauty "common to her race"); and her willingness to lie with the clerk all express derogatory popular beliefs regarding the Jews. There is in tale J11, as in Shakespeare's *Merchant of Venice* and Marlow's *Jew of Malta*, disparagement of the Jewish family in the daughter's easy betrayal of her father, a presumption of Jewish hostility towards Christians, and a suggestion of Jewish powerlessness in the fear of the Jewish father to retaliate against the canon because of the canon's relationship to the bishop. Furthermore, there is an indictment of the Jews as a despised *community* in the bishop's assumption that the appearance of the Jews as a group in his church portends disruption and in the punishment of muteness that is inflicted on the entire gathering of Jews.

J11. The Canon and the Jew's Daughter

Caesar tells how once there was a clerk in England who was a canon in Lincoln Minster and close cousin to the bishop. And there was a Jew living in the town who had a fair daughter, and this clerk pursued her so that she promised him that he could lie with her. But she said that her father loved her so well and kept her so protected that they could never come together except on Good Friday evening, for then the Jews have a bloody flux, and they do not go about their business or venture out. So when that night came, this canon, having no thought of the Passion of Christ that he had suffered that day, came to the girl and lay with her until the morning. When her father rose and came into the chamber where the girl lay and saw a man in bed with her, he wanted to kill him. But when he looked at him, he knew well enough that he was the bishop's cousin, and therefore he was afraid to slay him. But he cried out with a hideous voice and said: "Oh, you false Christian man! What are you doing in sin here today? Where is your faith? By the judgement of God, truly you have given yourself over into our hands, and were it not for dread of the bishop whose cousin you are, I would slay you at once." And thus with great vexation he showed him the door and the canon went home. That day, that is to say, Easter eve, the canon happened to be assigned to serve the bishop as his deacon at the Mass and to read the Epistle. The canon was afraid on such a day to commit his office to some other clerk, for fear of suspicion, and he was also afraid to come near the altar and the holy sacrament with so great a sin as he bore. And yet for shame, he could not find it in his heart to confess himself, so overcome with shame was he. So he put on his garments for the Mass and stood at the altar before the bishop.

And suddenly this Jew and a great many other Jews with him came in at the minster door with a huge commotion and noise, in order to make a complaint to the bishop about his cousin. And as soon as this young canon saw them, he waxed pale and was greatly afraid, and made his prayer to God in his heart, and said thus: "Lord, Jesus!

Deliver me and save me from shame at the hands of these Jews and I promise you heartily that I shall shrive myself of this sin and make a vow that from this time on I shall never offend you." Now the bishop saw these Jews and was greatly astonished at what they were doing in the church, and especially on such a day, and he commanded them to stand still and asked them what they intended. And just as soon as they would have accused this clerk, by the virtue of God, they were all dumb and could not speak. And when the bishop saw them opposite him, gasping with their mouths, he believed that they had come to disturb communion and with indignation he commanded them to be put out of the minster. Then this clerk felt that God had had mercy on him, and when the service was done, he went up to the bishop and shrove himself and afterwards made himself a monk in the Cistercian order. And they were able to convert the girl and made her a nun of the same order, and afterwards both lived good, holy lives.

Tales J12, J13, and J14 belong to the exemplum type that inculpates the Jews for the killing of Christ by portraying reenactments of the crucifixion and depicts the miraculous nature of Christ's blood shed by the Jews. Homiletic narratives such as these were a centerpiece of the effort of the medieval church to compel belief in the doctrine of transubstantiation, promote devotion to the crucifix, and proselytize the Jews. These tales share several anti-Judaic motifs: the subterfuge attributed to the Jews in their relentless assault on Christianity; the brutality with which the Jews attack their Christian targets, whether human beings or ritual objects; and the miraculous power of Christ's blood and flesh, consumed sacramentally at the Mass.

J12. A Jew in Church

I read in the *Golden Legend* how a Jew came to a church and because he did not see anyone within, he went up to a crucifix and, on account of the great resentment which he bore Christ, he cut the throat of the image with his sword. Thereupon, the blood spurted out, besmattering all his clothes. And when he saw himself so bloodied, he became terrified, so he took the crucifix and hid it in a secret place.

Later, as the Jew was riding homeward, a Christian man caught up with him and, seeing the Jew bloodied all over, said to him, "You manslaughterer, where have you hidden him whom you have slain?" Then the Jew disputed the man, and said it was not so. "It is so," said the Christian man, "and your clothes still bear the bloody traces of him." Then this Jew knelt down and said, "In truth, that God whom you Christian folk worship is of great might." And he told him all that he had done and begged for Christ's mercy with all his heart. The Jew was converted and later became a holy man.

J13. Parisian Jews Bloody the Host

There was in Paris a Jew living near the Church of the Blessed Virgin who pretended to become a Christian. One day at Easter he received the body of Christ but kept it in his mouth until he got home. Then he came together with some other Jews who assaulted the Host and finally, one of the Jews present pierced the Host with his knife. At that, the Host let out so much blood that the Jews were astounded. Then one of the Jews threw the sacrament into a bowl of boiling water, but the blood would not stop running, and it continued so abundantly that it ran out into the street. Among the crowd who gathered there was a Christian priest, who, when he arrived, consecrated the Host, and then the miracle stopped. That neighborhood is still called The Quarter of Blood.

J14. An Easter Miracle of the Host Converts the Jews

As I read, I learn that there was once a Christian clerk, holy and devout, who had sworn to him as a brother a man who belonged to the nation of Jews. And this Christian clerk, as the Chronicle tells us, would, during the holy period of Lent, part from his sworn brother, the Jew, and go to the temple of God to receive communion. Once a week, that is to say, the clerk shrove himself so that he might receive the blessed Sacrament on Easter Day and worship it as it should be.

Now one time, during this period, the Jew spied this Christian clerk going toward the church and inquired of him where he was bound.

The clerk replied, "I am going to God's house, there to purge and cleanse myself of my sins, so that I may be worthy to receive the holy sacrament on Easter Day for the salvation of my soul."

Then this Jew said, "Good brother, after you have been at God's house and received your Lord, come back to me and tell me how things stand with you." "Truly," said the clerk, "I will do that." Then this Christian clerk sped to the temple of God and found there his spiritual father ready with the holy Sacrament. and with great meekness and humility, the clerk received the Sacrament. Then, when the service was done, he took himself off to his sworn brother, the Jew, as they had agreed. As he went along his way, he saw a great company of Jews tarrying and loitering about where his sworn brother had set the meeting place. Because of this, the clerk was fearful and full of dread and besought God to come to his aid. And suddenly, at once there came down an angel from heaven and comforted him and bade him not to be afraid, for God would protect him. So he went boldly forth to his sworn brother, the Jew, who, as soon as he saw him, seized him and bound him hand and foot, and asked him where he had been. And the Christian answered him humbly, saying, "I have been at the temple of God and there I have received the Lord Jesus Christ, who made both you and me."

[Then the Jew said, "Tell us in what part of your body you have put him." [[The clerk replied, "He is in my soul." Then the Jew said, "Where is your soul?" The clerk said, "I believe that it is in my heart."]] So [the Jews] cut his body across the middle and took out the viscera and organs and pulled out his heart. But they could not hold it, for it threw itself upon the ground and broke in two, and in the middle was the body of Christ in the form of the Host shining like a bright spark. And the Jews were made blind and could not flee. When the Mass was finished, the Christians came out of the church and, seeing the crowd gathered, more people gathered around. They saw the dead Christian with his heart broken in two and the Host in its center. Then the Host transformed itself into a boy who rose from the heart and said, "I am the living Host who came from heaven. Who eats my flesh and drinks my blood lives in me and I in him. And that is why I return to my house from whence I was thrust out." And the heart returned to the body of the corpse, to the place from which it had been taken, and the viscera and organs were returned to the body, and the corpse returned to life. And everyone thanked God and the Jews were baptized. Thus were many thousands converted to the Christian faith by this glorious miracle.]

Tales J15 and J16 both turn on the anti-Judaic motif that Jews were lower than animals in their stubborn refusal to acknowledge the reality of Christ in the Host, an indictment that was generalized to show that Jews lacked the rationality which was the defining characteristic of humankind. Other versions of tale J15 do not specify a Jew as the disbeliever, indicating the concern of the church to compel belief in the Eucharist among skeptical Christians. The sterotype of Jews as cunning, especially in their schemes against Christian belief, surfaces again in these two tales as the Jew of tale J15 resorts to a deceptive strategem in order to win his wager and the Jew of tale J16 only pretends to respect the Host until his Christian friend has departed. Both tales are set in the context of disputation with Christian layfolk, a circumstance that had become expressly forbidden by the fourteenth century, when these tales were in circulation.

J15. A Jew's Dog Rejects the Host

In proof that this bread you are receiving today [at Communion] is truly God and man, I have found a story, a chronicle, where I read a marvelous thing. There was a good man, a baptized Christian, who happened to meet a Jew, and they began to dispute with each other about the Christian faith. The Jew said that it was nothing but falsehoods, and the Christian man contradicted him, saying that in token that Christian belief was true, Christ, the Second Person of the Trinity, came from heaven to teach Christian men that faith here on earth.

"Yes," said the Jew, "You believe that."

"It is true," said the Christian.

"You Christians," said the Jew, "believe that by virtue of the words the priest says at the Mass, the bread turns into God's flesh and blood." "Yes, it is true," said the Christian man," and in that faith I will live and die."

"Well, well," said the Jew, "That may be. But you and your fellows are foully deceived. For I will wager you twenty shillings that my hound that I have at home will eat that bread, and if it were really God, I am very sure that he would not allow himself to be eaten."

"So be it," said the Christian. "I will bet my twenty shillings against yours, and also I will stake my life against it. And if your dog eats the Host, then take me to your prison and kill me, or do with me as you will."

So they set a day for this wager, and when the day had come, the Christian man went into the church and prayed that the priest would shrive him well, for he was sick. And when the priest had given him God in the form of the Host, the man secretly took it out of his mouth and put it in his purse and took it to the Jew's house.

Now this Jew was cunning and had fed his dog all this time with communion wafers, and for three days before he had starved it of all food except a few of these. And on the day set for the wager, he had not given the dog a single thing to eat. Finally, the Christian came to the Jew, as they had agreed, and took out the Host that is and was God's body in the form of bread.

And then the Jew said, "Now, man, you say that this bread is God's body?"

"Indeed I do," said the Christian man.

"Now you shall see," said the Jew, "how you and other Christian men are deceived." And he whistled for his dog and threw four or five communion wafers in front of him. And the dog was so hungry that he ran up to them and devoured them at once. Then the Christian man drew the Host out of his purse and cast it in front of the dog. Immediately, the dog fled and would have run out of the house, but the Jew caught him and petted him and slowly drew him back. But the Jew saw that for all his petting, the dog would not take the Host, so then he beat the animal. And at once, the dog fell on all four knees and did such reverence as he was able to the Sacrament. Then the Jew was infuriated and took a staff and beat the dog and grabbed the dog in his arms and thrust him at the Host. And the dog felt that the man would force him to eat the Host, so he leapt up at his throat and tore him apart.

Then at once, the Christian man ran to the priest who had shriven him and told him what had happened with the dog, how such a beast without the power of reasoning worshipped God's body in the form of the Host.

So by this miracle you may be guided to believe in this, which even a dumb animal, untaught by the holy church, understands.

J16. A Jew Tests the Power of the Host with Pigs

An English Catholic frequently urged his Jewish friend to convert to Christ. The Jew told him to bring him the sacrament that is affirmed to be Christ from the altar and, he said, "I will adore it and believe in it and then I can be baptized." So the Host was carried to him and the Jew pretended to receive it with respect, but after the departure of his friend, he threw it in the trough for the pigs that belonged to a neighboring Christian. Now this man called his pigs to eat, but when they came to the trough they drew back and began squealing like they had gone mad. And they would not touch the trough. This happened for two days. Then the Jew became convinced that the behavior of the beasts was due to the power of the sacrament, so he pulled the Host out with reverence, washed it, and adored it sincerely. To all whom he met he related this incident, and later he was baptized. As for the pigs, they afterwards approached their trough as usual.

Tales J17 and J18 are typical conversion narratives whose didacticism suggests the strenuous efforts of the medieval church to foster the Marian cult and compel belief not only in the virginity of Christ's mother but in her Assumption, the rising of her physically uncorrupted body to heaven after her death. These beliefs were often challenged by Jewish debaters in the era when public religious disputation was possible, and as the Virgin remarks in tale J18, the Jews were her special enemies.

J17. A Jew Debates the Virginity of Mary

Good men, you have now heard me speak about the Annunciation. But there are some who ask why a wine pot and a lily stood between Our Lady and Gabriel at her Annunciation. This is the reason: because Our Lady at the Annunciation conceived [Jesus] at this sight. And that was the first miracle that was wrought as proof of the Christian faith.

Now it happened that a Christian man and a Jew were sitting together talking of the coming of Our Lady. And where they were, a winepot stood between them. Then said the Christian to the Jew, "We believe that just as the stalk of the lily grows and produces a green color and afterward puts forth a white flower without any aid of man or grafting of the stalk, just so did Our Lady conceive of the Holy Ghost and afterward brought forth her son from the womb of her body, which is the flower and chief fruit of womanhood."

Then said the Jew, "When I see a lily sprout of this wine pot, then I will believe such, but not before." At the moment that he spoke, the fairest lily ever seen sprang out of the wine pot. When the Jew saw that, he at once fell down on his knees and said, "Lady, now I believe that you conceived Jesus Christ, Son of Heaven through the Holy Ghost, and that you were a virgin both before and after." And so the Jew went and was Christened and became a holy man thereafter.

For this reason the pot and the lily are set between Mary and Gabriel. For just as this Jew disputed with this Christian man about the manner in which Mary conceived Jesus, just so did Our Lady dispute with the angel about how she could conceive and the manner of her conception so that she would remain a virgin then and after. And finally she affirmed it.

J18. The Virgin Rescues a Jewish Merchant

I read in the miracles of Our Lady how there was a Jew that was born in France and went to London for certain duties he had to carry out with others of his nation, and from there he went on to Gloucester and then to Bristol. Afterwards, as he was proceeding from Bristol to Wilton, he was set upon by thieves and cruelly treated by them, and then brought to an old abandoned house, where the thieves bound him to a post by his feet and tied his hands behind him and left him there all night. As he fell asleep, he saw a fair lady clothed all in white, more beautiful than any he had ever seen. This lady came to him and unbound him, and thus, when he awoke and looked around him, and found himself loose, he wondered greatly how that could have come about. Then he saw Our Lady so glowing that her brightness surpassed that of the sun. So he said to her, "What gentle lady are you who has so kindly helped me during the night?"

She answered, "I am Mary, whom you and all your nation despise, and dispute that I ever bore God's son from my body. But nevertheless I have come to bring you out of the error you are in. Thus, now, come with me and stand on yonder point before you and look downward."

And when he looked down, he saw such horrible pains of hell that he was nearly out of his mind with fear.

Then Our Lady said to him, "These pains are ordained to all those who will not live in Christ's faith. Now come forth and follow me." And she set him on a high hill and there showed him places of great joy and bliss, so that he could not have described one quarter of the joys he saw and the sweet smell that he breathed. Then Our Lady said to him: "This place is ordained for them that believe in the Incarnation, that God's son of heaven was born of me yet I was a virgin before and after that, and afterwards he shed his blood on the cross for mankind. But now I have showed you both the joy and the pain, choose whichever you prefer." And then she disappeared from him.

Then he walked through much of the night, never knowing where he was going, but on the morrow he came to Bath, and there had himself converted by the bishop and was renamed John and afterwards was a holy man, forever deeply devoted to Our Lady.

Now you should kneel down and pray to Our Lady. As she gave this Jew the choice whether he would go to joy or pain, so she keeps you from the pain of hell and brings you to that joy that shall last forever.

Tale J19, in other versions, identifies the monkish protagonist as John Damascene, the eighth-century saint and doctor of the eastern church who died in Jerusalem. Stories of the Virgin's intervention on behalf of Jerusalem's citizens under seige by the Moslems in 638 linked her to the life of John Damascene. Here that legend, joined to the popular tradition of Jewish enmity against the Virgin, transforms hagiography into a Jewish conversion scenario.

The tale's conclusion of the skeptical Jew converted by the miracle of the Virgin's portrait appears to be unique. There was a tradition of a portrait of the Virgin painted by the evangelist Luke; there was also a medieval narrative of a portrait of the Virgin and the Jews that is connected with John Damascene. In a letter to his emperor, Theophilus, the saint related that a painting of the Virgin in the church at Lydda, which had formerly been a synagogue, was the subject of complaint by the Jews. In response the emperor closed the church, but when the apostle Peter opened it forty days later, the portrait was still there. The Jews never reentered the church, and when they were later commanded to destroy it in the reign of Julian the Apostate, they were afraid to touch it.

J19. The Monk, the Virgin, and the Jew

There was once a holy monk who loved Our Lady with all his heart. This monk never wearied of praising her and telling wonderful miracles of Our Lady and marvelous stories of her night and day, and he was known, therefore, as the finest writer in all the world. Now the emperor of Rome had a dear cousin who was a young man, whom he sent to this monk, praying that he would teach the cousin to write as well as he did, to increase the merit of this cousin. And so the monk taught the young man to write as well as he did.

Then this young man became envious of his master and fain would see him dead, for then he would become the world's master of writing as the monk had been, and so he plotted how he might bring about the monk's death. The young man thought about it and wrote a letter to the sultan, stating therein that very shortly the emperor was going to order the sultan slain and all his lands destroyed. And therefore, the sultan should, with all the haste he could, come and destroy the emperor first. And when this letter was finished, the young man let it drop in the emperor's hall, where the letter was found and read and was brought to the emperor at once. The emperor marveled much at who could have written this letter, and then the young man came and looked at it and said at once that no man could have written such a letter but his master and himself, and, he said, "You may be well assured that it was not I." So the emperor immediately sent for this monk and apprised him of this letter, but the monk said that he knew nothing of it. Then the emperor showed him the letter and said that it was in his hand. But the monk declared that he never wrote it. Nevertheless, without any further debate, the emperor commanded that the monk's arm be cut off at the elbow. And so it was done and they sent him home to his abbey, along with the piece of his arm. His abbot was commanded to put him in prison and not allow any treatment to be permitted him, and so the abbot did.

Now as the monk lay in the prison, he cried continually to Our Lady for help because of the pain in his arm as it rotted away. And so, finally, Our Lady came to him one night and said, "How are you faring?" And the monk said, "Very poorly, for my arm is rotted away, that arm that was used to paint an image of you wherever I went."

And then she said, "Come to me and show me your arm."

"Lady," said the monk, "it is rotted away."

"Bring it hither to me," said she, "and show it to me." And so the monk went among the pile of stones where his arm lay and brought it to Our Lady and showed it to her. And she bade him place it again on his arm as it had been joined before. "Lady," said the monk, "but it is all fallen to pieces."

"Join it again," said she, "and it shall be made whole." And so the monk did as she bade him and it was as whole as ever it was before, and he wrote with it as well as he had ever done. And then the monk strode out and rung all the bells in the abbey so that the abbot and all the convent rose and saw this great miracle and thanked God and Our Lady. And then a steward came and told the emperor that it was the young man, his cousin, who had written that letter and not the monk, and the emperor, in the same manner that he had served the monk, then punished his cousin.

Now after this, the monk went forth to Jerusalem on pilgrimage and to many other good and holy places. And thus, one day, a Jew who was a great ruler of that country, met the monk and they spoke of Our Lady. And the Jew said that a virgin could never give birth to a child, and the monk said it was so, and they disputed vigorously about it. Finally, the monk praised Our Lady so highly and greatly that the Jew requested him to portray an image of her upon a canvas that he might see her picture. And so the monk drew a wondrously fair portrait of Our Lady with her child in her arms and a lovely little nipple on her breast. The Jew stared at the picture and thought the lady very beautiful, and asked the monk whether she was as fair as he had drawn her, and the monk said yes, and in truth she was twenty times fairer than any man could paint her. And then, as this Jew stood and looked upon her, the child that was in her arms moved his head out of the canvas and took his mother's breast in his hand and squeezed out some milk and sucked it. And when the Jew saw that, he kneeled down and thanked God and cried for Our Lady's mercy, for he said that he knew that it was less of a miracle that a virgin could bear a child than that a painted image on a canvas could move his head beyond the canvas and take milk from a painted breast. And so the Jew was converted and turned to the Christian faith and converted many others to Christianity as well.

Tale J20, "The Jew of Bourges," is better known in its variant of "The little chorister" (the Christian child singing the Virgin's praises who was killed by the Jews), because of its literary retelling as Chaucer's "Prioress's Tale." The two motifs are related in their anti-Judaic elements but different as to plot. Our exemplum J20 does not specify the location as Bourges, but this became traditional in homiletic and Marian analogues after the twelfth century, such as the *Golden Legend*'s version in its chapter on the Assumption of the Virgin. The *Golden Legend* dates the event as 527, and the story does appear to have originated in the eastern empire around that time; early versions are set in that area or in "the Orient." As the tale spread westward, however, it became associated with Bourges from its inclusion in the *Miracles* of Gregory of Tours, who localized another anti-Judaic exemplum in Bourges, one in which a blind archdeacon, having had his eyesight restored by the relics of St. Martin of Tours, became blind again after his distrust of the saint's cure led him to consult a Jewish doctor.

In most homiletic renderings of this tale the glassblowing furnace of the original has become a baker's oven, perhaps because in medieval Europe glassblowing was no longer a Jewish trade. (Interestingly, in manuscript illustration of the tale, the furnace appears as a boiling bath, possibly a representation of the Jewish ritual bath, which was a common establishment of every Jewish community.)

While the core motif of the burning of an innocent child in an oven may have had its distant antecedents in the biblical story of Shadrach, Meshach, and Abednego being thrown into Nebuchadnezzar's fiery furnace (Dan. chaps. 1–3), the dynamics of the medieval exempla lie in a different direction. Primarily they are associated with actual accusations of ritual murder against the Jews, which occurred throughout Europe during the Middle Ages. In both "the Jew of Bourges" and "the little chorister" variants, the life of a child devoted to the Virgin is threatened by the Jews and the Jewish precinct is the setting for the heinous act. In some versions of "the little chorister" analogues, the enmity between the Virgin and the Jews is made more explicit by noting that the child's hymn to the Virgin was the "*Gaude Maria*," which contains the phrase "Blush [for shame], unhappy Jews." Fourteenth-century inscriptions of this motif on the cathedral facades of Puy in France and Messina in Italy appear to be associated with the expulsion of the Jews from those locales.

J20. A Jewish Boy Is Saved from a Furnace (The Jew of Bourges)

We read how once upon a time there was a child that was a Jew's son, and he was so fair and gentle that Christian men and children loved him very much, so much that at a certain time they desired him to go into a church of Our Lady with them and then take the sacrament as they did. And he did so. And afterwards, when he came home, he told his father, who was heating up an oven; the man was so full of wrath at this that he took this child, his own son, and cast him into the hot oven. When the child's mother saw how he had put their son in the oven, and how the moans came out of his mouth at this, she became quite mad and ran out the door and wailed like a mad person. Christian folk were astonished at this sight and ran into the Jew's house and put out the fire in the oven, and found the child within it, sitting upon the hot coals just as if he were sitting upon fair flowers and showing no sign of ailment or anxiety. When they took him out, he told them everything that had happened. So at once they took this Jew, his father, and thrust him into the oven, and immediately the fire consumed him so that they could find neither bone nor stone of him. And then the child told them how that woman who was in the church where he had eaten the bread with his fellows, who had a little child wrapped in a cloth sitting on her knee, had covered him with her mantle so the fire should not burn him. And so this child and his mother and many other Jews were converted because of this fine miracle of the sacrament.

Source Notes to Exempla about Jews

1. *AT* no. 101. Original in *GL* St. Basil, Bishop 1.112. *IE* no. 2792 leaves the monk unnamed. Toldo *Archiv* 117.290, offers a brief note on intermediary patristic versions.

2. (a) *AT* no. 558. Original in *GL* St. Nicholas 1.25. *IE* no. 3471 lists this as Stith Thompson motif 333.1. *IE* no. 3469 refers to a similar motif where St. Nicholas offers himself as security for a Jew. (b) *GL* St. Nicholas 1.25. *IE* no. 3.

3. (a) *AT* no. 228. *AN* identifies the bishop as Andrew of Fundi; its rubric is "Sign of the cross is made by an infidel." Original in *Dial.* 3.7 includes the detail that the nun tempting the bishop was a demon in disguise. It appears in JdeV's exempla (Crane) 189–90. *IE* no. 2972. (b) *HS* lines 7725–880. The details of demonic wickedness reported to Satan are similar to those in *AT* no. 128, derived from the *VP*, col. 885, no. 9. In the *GL* Exaltation of the Holy Cross 2.172, the origin of the tale in Gregory's *Dialogues* is alluded to, but de Voragine notes Gregory's brevity, leading him to add the report of the devils' council, which "can be deduced from a moral tale that we read in the *Lives of the Fathers*" (*VP*).

4. *Festial* 144. *IE* no. 1339 omits this citation and that of Mirk's probable source, *GL* Finding of the Holy Cross 2.280–82. For a detailed history of this narrative, see Kennedy, *Early English Christian Poetry*, 173ff.

5. *Festial* 5. Mirk's direct source was probably *GL* Exaltation of the Holy Cross 1.171. A condensed version in *AT* no. 227 sets the anecdote in the time of Constantine IV, but omits the place name, "Beric(h)o (*GL*: Berith), a city in Syria." The *AN*'s vague citation, "*Ex. cronicis*," may refer to the version by Vincent de Beauvais who apparently copied the tale from Helinandus's *Chronicle*, a source frequently cited by de Beauvais and sometimes cited in the *AN*. For a discussion of medieval analogues, see Toldo *Archiv* 117.288–89; for some early eastern variants, see Parkes *Conflict* 292–93.

6. *Festial* 146. Mirk's probable direct source was *GL* St. James Apostle 1.276–77. *IE* no. 2776. For other legends of the Jews' inability to rebuild their temple, see Parkes *Conflict* 299.

7. *MES* 159. *IE* no. 2795 cites an English version that dates the event in 1258 and names the characters as Richard de Clare, Earl of Gloucester, and a Jew of Tewkesbury.

8. *AT* no. 251. Original in *DM* 5.16 locates the incident in the bishopric of Holberstadt and specifies the converted Jew's monastery as Cistercian. *IE* no. 2794.

9. *AT* no. 467. Bracketed material describing a Jewish magician as Theophilus's intermediary with the devil does not appear in this version; it is included in the *GL* Birth of the Blessed Virgin Mary 2.157, which was probably not the direct source of our exemplum. Toldo *Archiv* 118.76 notes the tale's occurrence in de Beauvais's *Speculum historiale*; it also appears in Caesar of Heisterbach's *Miracles of the Virgin* 8-3.76. *IE* no. 3572. Ward *Cat. of Rome.* 2.595, offers a history of the figure of Theophilus, supposedly a sixth-century cleric in Cilicia whose life was translated into Latin from the Greek original by Paul, a deacon of Naples (accounting, perhaps, for the confusion between Sicily and Cilicia [in Asia Minor] in later medieval exempla versions.

10. *AT* no. 406. Original in *DM* 2.24, where it is one of a sequence of tales with similar motifs, two of which were incorporated into the *AN*. LeGoff "Le Juif" 210 notes that the tale was well known through its incorporation into a collection of Virgin miracles of the late twelfth century, *Mariale magnum*, the probable source of de Beauvais's account in the *Speculum historiale*. For a discussion of this motif in fabliaux going back to Hindu and Greek sources and its variants in Arabic and later European literature, including Boccaccio's *Decameron*, see Toldo *Archiv* 117.291–99. *IE* no. 2807.

11. *AT* no. 207. Original in *DM* 2.23, where it is followed by a contrasting tale of a canon who was punished because his contrition was *not* sincere. Our tale appears in *JW* 177, for a discussion of which see Gregg "Exempla of Jacob's Well" 361. There are versions in *GR* 61 (addit. MS 9066) 377 and numerous other English collections. Toldo *Archiv* 117.229 discusses its sources. *IE* no. 2811.

12. *Festial* 252. Original in *GL* Exaltation of the Holy Cross 1.170–71. See Parkes *Conflict* 293n.4 for a suggestion of its earlier, eastern source. I cannot locate this precise motif in *IE*.

13. Cambridge Trinity College Library MS 262, B.11.23. fol. 105v, a preacher's manual including exempla. In the manuscript this tale follows a very brief version of our tale 14. *IE* no. 2689 b.1.

14. *MES* 63. The first part of the exemplum, in English, takes the anecdote to the point where the Jew asks the clerk in which part of his body he has put the Host. The exemplum is then retold in Latin and continues to its conclusion with the bracketed material (translation mine). The double bracketed material, omitted from the *MES* exemplum, occurs in the condensed version in Cambridge Trinity College Library MS 262, B.11.23, fol. 104, a fifteenth-century *Manuale sacerdotis* primarily concerned with instructing priests in their duties regarding absolution. *IE* no. 2689 c.

15. *MES* 129–30. *IE* no. 2641. Variants tell of an ass adoring the Host given it by a heretic and cattle kneeling before the Host.

16. *Speculum Laicorum* no. 269. My translation is from Charbonnier "Recherches," 8. *AT* no. 312 tells it of a smith, not a Jew, and cites Jacques de Vitry, but I cannot locate it in Crane's edition. *IE* no. 2687.

17. *Festial* 108–09. *IE* omits this precise motif but lists a similar one, no. 3049, "Lilies prove Mary's virginity."

18. *Festial* 248–49. According to Herbert *Cat. of Rome.* 3.707, Mirk's source was probably the *Speculum historiale* 7.3. The localizing of the events in England does not occur in all versions. *IE* no. 2790.

19. *Festial* 301. *IE* no. 2419 cites variants of the first portion of the exemplum told of Pope Leo, and some romance analogues. A plethora of romance motifs had collected around the figure of St. John Damascene probably due to his position as the vizier to the caliph of Damascus before becoming a monk. This tale contains several salient features associated with the "ill treated heroine," "heroine flight," and "outcast heroine" incidents of the Catskin cluster of the "Cinderella" tale type, for which see Cox *Cinderella* xlivff. These are the abandonment of the protagonist in a foreign land, the slanderous letter of an envious peer that the protagonist has betrayed the ruler, the mutilation of a hand and its miraculous restoration (a motif that also occurs in apocryphal narratives of the Jews attacking the funeral bier of the Virgin), the reunion of the slandered protagonist with the ruler, the ultimate discovery and punishment of the slanderer and the intervention of a "fairy godmother" figure, here the Virgin, the special enemy of the Jews, in the denouement. The first portion of the tale occurs in *AT* no. 381 and *JW* 277, both following *AN* in identifying Mirk's unnamed monk as John Damascene. *Speculum historiale* 18.103–5 may have been the *AN*'s direct source. I cannot locate any other version that includes the conversion of the Jew by a miraculous portrait of the Virgin, but the motif of such a painting by St. Luke is listed in *IE* no. 3576 and is referred to in *AT* no. 471, in an attribution to St. Gregory. According to *GL* St. Gregory 1.174, Luke's painting of the Virgin, "a perfect likeness," was kept in the church of Saint Mary Major in Rome and carried in procession against the plague.

20. *AT* no. 308. According to Herbert *Cat. of Rome.* 2.629, no. 5; 656, no. 3; and 732, the probable original of the *AN*'s exemplum was either *GL* Assumption of the Blessed Virgin Mary 2.87–88 or de Beauvais's *Speculum historiale*, both of which omit the Bourges locale. *Festial* 277. follows *GL*. For the early history of the core motif, see Parkes *Conflict* 296, 336. The analogue of "the little chorister" appears in *DM* 8. 1.67.3, in a section on miracles of the Virgin. The thirteenth-century Spanish collection of Marian miracles *Cantigas de Santa Maria* includes both "the little chorister" and "the Jew of Bourges," for which see Goldberg "Medieval Commonplaces" 106.

Notes

Chapter One: Introduction

1. *New Catholic Encyclopedia*, S.V. "Lateran Council." Wenzel "Seven Deadly Sins" states that the "capital vices" or deadly sins were the most widely used scheme upon which the priest instructed his penitents to examine their consciences in preparation for taking Communion (13).

2. According to Wenzel, the homilist was not only to provide "abstract, systematic analysis of the sins, but also portrayals of such sinners" (ibid. 17); hence the legitimation of a wide variety of narratives within or concluding the sermon proper and the authorship by highly placed churchmen of exempla collections for use by preachers.

3. In *The Revised Medieval Latin Word-List*, ed. Ronald Latham (London: Oxford University Press, 1965), *exemplum* is defined as "to serve as example." For some medieval ambiguity in the definition of "exemplum" see the prologue to Jacques de Vitry's sermons in JdeV Crane xxli–xlii; Odo de Cheriton's prologue in *Etude sur les fables* (ed. Hervieux) 4.175; Etienne de Bourbon's prologue in *Anecdotes historiques* (ed. la Marche) 2; Humbert de Roman's remarks on the purpose of exempla in Welter, *L'Exemplum* 70–72; Arnold of Liège's prologue in Herbert *Cat. of Rom.* 3.428–29; and the remarks of the preacher in *MES* 203. Modern scholars faced with the bounty of medieval material to which the term *exemplum* was applied have generally reserved the term for illustrative material shaped into narrative form. For an extensive current discussion of the exempla as narrative, see Bremond, Le Goff, and Schmitt, *L'Exemplum*, esp. chap. 2.

4. See Crane on the first use of exempla in popular preaching by St. Gregory (JdeV xviii).

5. Interesting illustrations of the informal methods of oral transmission by which exempla circulated throughout Europe are provided by the introductions to many of Caesar of Heisterbach's tales. See, for example, the Host profanation by a Jewish boy in Wrocaw (*IE* no. 2689), which is discussed by Geremek "L'Exemplum" 169–70.

6. Crane asserts that because of de Vitry's fame in utilizing sermon stories to great effect in the campaigns against heresy and in support of the crusades, his name was frequently attached to narratives that do not appear in the canon of his sermons, as far as it can be authenticated (JdeV, xxxiv–vi).

7. Exempla citations of Humbert's narratives often are abbreviated as "Humbert" or "*de dono timoris.*" For a discussion of Humbert's collection (not available in printed form), see Berlioz, "Le récit efficace."

8. Herbert, *Cat. of Rom.* 3.428–29.

9. Berlioz "Le récit efficace" 122.

10. Lines 45–50. Robert Mannyng states that he wrote in English and included "tales and rhymes" to draw the common people away from the wickedness they fall into at games, feasts, and drinking bouts and provide them with a more constructive way to spend their time.

11. Berlioz "Le récit efficace" 131.

12. Ibid.

13. Tubach "Exempla in the Decline" 417.

14. Berlioz "Le récit efficace" 121.

15. Ibid.

16. *IE* no. 4237.

17. Stierle "L'Histoire" 183.

18. For much of this discussion I am indebted to the exhaustive and enlightening analysis of the rhetorical style of *Jacob's Well* made by Wilfred Lister in his dissertation, particularly chap. 6. See also Gregg "Exempla of Jacob's Well" 372–80.

19. For a discussion of the current scholarly debate about the extent to which the church exerted hegemony over the medieval mentality, see Charles Haskins "Spread of Ideas" and Lee Patterson *Negotiating the Past*, which takes issue with the views of D. W. Robertson, Jr. For Robertson's views see his *Essays in Medieval Culture.*

20. Sander L. Gilman, in his invaluable study *Difference and Pathology: Stereotypes of Sexuality, Race, and Madness*, notes that the stereotypical representations of the Other as construed in cultural texts are "inherently bipolar, generating pairs of antithetical signifiers." Group identity protects the "insider" and defines and excludes the Other as its antithesis (25–26).

21. The contextualization of the exemplum as a battle between good and evil is deeply rooted in medieval theology. As Gilman asserts, stereotyped representations derive from "the models from our social world . . . [they] are never randomly chosen." Models of the Other (such as we find in the exempla) are "potent and enduring" because, as the products of a specific culture and history, they can be "perpetuated, resurrected and shaped [through texts] containing the fantasy life of a culture, quite independent of the existence or

absence of the group in a given society" or "the real actions of the sterotyped groups" (ibid. 20). Although my analysis here develops independently of Gilman's particular examples, his words describe popular pulpit literature precisely in regard to women and Jews and their association in medieval times with the devil.

22. Again, while Gilman makes no specific reference to exempla literature, his declaration that images of the Other in a wide variety of texts "function as structured expressions of the inner world in our mental representations" (ibid. 26) may be aptly applied here. His comments regarding the means by which we invest the Other with all the evil qualities that we fear in ourselves speak directly to the two major exempla types of demon-inspired sinners under discussion—women and Jews—whose lecherous and perifidious conduct good Christians must eschew.

23. Freud *Basic Writings* 854–55, 858. Gilman discusses projection as a means of controlling the intolerable anxiety that arises from the repression of unwanted psychic impulses and helping to move the threatened personality towards the integration necessary for functioning. That integration is largely illusory, however, since it has been obtained at the expense of the Other onto whom the unwelcome material is projected and it operates in spite of any incongruencies that may exist between the projected patterns and the external reality. (See *Difference and Pathology* introduction and 21.)

24. Todorov *Conquest of America* 248–49.

Chapter Two: Devils in Medieval Exempla

1. Le Goff *La Civilization* 205, 419.

2. Pagels asserts that the Gospels created "a supernatural drama" that interpreted the story of Christ as "a struggle between God's spirit and Satan" and the demons, who belong to Satan's kingdom (*Origin of Satan* xvii, xxiii).

3. Augustine *City of God* 8.20–22.

4. Fox *Pagans* 7.

5. Ivanits *Russian Folk Belief* 10.

6. Pagels *Origin of Satan* 120, 124, 131.

7. Ibid. 39–40.

8. The Latin name Lucifer, "light-bearer," is a reference to the figure in Isaiah 14:12 called "son of morning," i.e., a bright star. In the scriptural passage it is a symbolic representation of the tyrannical king of Babylon in his splendor and eventual fall, from whence it was applied to Satan in his fall from heaven, and so employed in Christian imagery from St. Jerome on.

9. See, for example, Rev. 8:10, 9:1; Luke 10:18; and Acts 5:3.

10. Augustine *City of God* 14.3, 2.25.

11. Ibid. 19.13.

12. Ibid. 8.22. This notion had been articulated by early Christians before St. Augustine. In the second century, Tatian, a Syrian convert and pupil of Justin Martyr, wrote in his "Address to the Greeks" of demons as rebels who were fallen angels too weak to destroy God's universe, who were "inspired by hostile malice" to tyrannize human beings "through dreams and fantasies" (Pagels *Origin of Satan* 131–32).

13. Augustine *City of God* 9.18–22.

14. See *IE* no. 2138 for a brief tale originating in *DM* 5.10 and retold in *AT* no. 253, which is an exception to the lack of regret generally expressed by devils in regard to their fall from heaven.

15. The Last Judgment scenes in a multitude of medieval European churches are a bountiful source of the most grotesque depictions of the devil. In Taddeo di Bartolo's fresco (1396) in the Cathedral in San Gimignano, for example, the devils of Avarice are horned, winged, and bushy-tailed creatures with the faces of apes, goats, and pigs; and those of Anger are horned, black, and green-colored creatures with serpent-like tails, bulging eyes, toothy grins, and fangs protruding from their mouths and heads. In Florence's Baptistry of St. John, the chief devil is blue, horned, bald, and bearded; other devils, in the act of devouring the souls of sinners, are portrayed in the form of toads and serpents. An interesting secular depiction is that of a fifteenth-century Jewish medical treatise illustrating St.-John's-wort with a horned, pointy-eared devil having five-clawed arms, a hairy body, and a rudimentary penis.

16. See Pagels *Origin of Satan* 100.

17. In the Hebrew Bible see Job 8:3–6; in the Christian Bible see, for instances, Matt. 9:24 and 34; Luke 22:53; and John 12:31, 14:30, and 16:11.

18. The ambiguity associated with black skin is evidenced in an exemplum in which benign black-skinned men chase away demons annoying churchgoers at confession: *IE* no. 664. Granger Ryan notes in his translation of *The Golden Legend* that "*Aethiops*, in Jacobus' [de Voragine's] time, meant a black man, the color black standing for evil as white for virtue," following patristic exegesis of biblical passages (1.283 n. 10). Early Christian perceptions of "black" or "blue" skinned "Ethiopians" or "men of Ind [India]" as alien, demonic, and symbolic of paganism merit further study.

19. See *IE* no. 4773 for references.

20. *VP* (PL 21, col. 455). For an Indian demon as "an Ethiopian blacker than soot," see *GL* St. Bartholomew 2.112; for devils as "deformed Moors" and "Ethiopians," see the exemplum of Peter the Tax Collector [Toller] in the Life of St. John the Almsgiver in *VP* (PL 73, col. 356, chap. 21.); for devils as little blue men of India, see *AT* no. 591. For similar descriptions see JdeV Crane 81 and Bourbon *Anecdotes historiques* nos. 219, 461.

21. *GL* 1.182–83.

22. *Festial* 238, and see above n. 21.

23. *Dial*. 2.4, listed in *IE* as no. 1534. See also *AT* no. 110 and *DM* 5.12.

24. JdeV (Crane) 88; see *IE* no. 1490. For other black animals associated with the devil see JdeV (Crane) 114 and *DM* 11.41. Also associated with the devil, particularly his ability to take possession of a body, is the pig, following the Gospels' narrative of the Gadarene swine (Matt. 8:32 and Mark 5:13). See the *Festial*'s tale of a devil-possessed pig that ran around a church and then disappeared (278).

25. A sinner's black arm: *GL* St. Laurence 2.69; a sinner's black body: *IE* no. 2414; a black spot on a sinner's hand: Schmitt *Prêcher* 91; a usurer in black robes: *DM* 12.24; feet turn black: Herbert *Cat. of Rom.* 3.502, no. 303; Satan's black book: *AT* no. 30.

26. The devil's hideousness can kill: *DM* 5.29; the devil has no back: *DM* 3.6.

27. *DM* 11.39; see also JdeV (Crane) 168; *IE* no. 2489 and no. 2738.

28. Augustine *City of God* 8.20–22.

29 Demon union with human beings produces exceptional child: *DM* 3.11; human female's intercourse with male devil:*DM* 3.9; human male's intercourse with female devil: *DM* 3.10.

30. See other analogues of this widely disseminated Koranic tale in *DM* 18.1.29; Herbert *Cat. of Rom.* 3.446, no. 22; *GL* St. Nicholas 1.26; *JW* 285–87. *IE* no. 2558.

31. Herbert *Cat. of Rom.* 3.662, no. 214.

32. For devil as Virgin: *IE* no. 1565 and no. 280; as Christ: *IE* no. 1536.

33. See, for instance, *AT* no. 662 (*IE* no. 2717) in which the devil obstructs a bishop's prayers for a soul trapped in a block of ice by instigating quarrels in the bishop's household that demand his attention.

34. *Summa theologica*, pt. 1, question 114, art. 1 (583).

35. *DM* 5.52

36. JdeV (Crane) 19. For other exempla of carelessness in saying Mass see *AT* no. 122 and no. 150. Cursing objects and people: JdeV (Crane) no. 295 and *DM* 5.26; devil rebuking a gambler: *Cat. of Rom.* 3.700, no. 26.

37. Augustine *City of God* 14.2.

38. Christian scriptural derogations of wealth are many, as for instance Matt. 6:19–21: "Do not lay up for yourselves treasures on earth . . . For where your treasure is, there your heart will be also." For the Hebrew Bible's injunctions against usury see Lev. 25:36–37, Deut. 23:20, and Exodus 22:24.

39. Peasant refuses alms: *IE* no. 939; saying about usurer: *Speculum Laicorum* no. 578, cited in Charbonnier "Recherches" 66.

40. Toad feeds usurer his money: *IE* no. 4889; usurer eats gold in hell: *IE* no. 5039.

41. *Tabula exemplorum* no. 224, cited in Charbonnier "Recherches" 201.

42. *DM* 5.34.

43. Chief devil denied contrite man's soul: *AT* no. 178; original in *JdeV* (Crane) no. 303; *IE* no. 1194 omits *AT*. Confessions made to devil: Herbert *Cat. of Rome*. 3.260, no. 83; *DM* 2.38.

44. Le Goff *La Civilization* asserts that "all thought, all the behavior of medieval man was dominated by a more or less conscious Manicheism [struggle between the forces of evil and good]. For them, on one side was God, on the other, the Devil. This great division dominated moral life, social life, political life. Humanity was pulled between two powers, which men [did not] under[stand] . . ." (205, translation mine). See also p. 419 of Le Goff for a similar comment.

45. *Tabula exemplorum* no. 270, cited in Charbonnier "Recherches" 29.

46. In the Epistle of Jude, chap. 9, the Archangel Michael contends with the devil for the soul of Moses, one of the seminal images upon which medieval depictions of the contest between the saints (usually St. Michael) and the devil for the souls of men were based.

47. *GR* 62 (addit. MS 9066) 379.

48. Augustine *City of God* 18.18.

49. Ibid. 51.

50. *Summa theologica* pt. 1, question 114, art. 1 (582).

51. Geremek "L'Exemplum," 174.

52. For devils speaking in tongues see, for instance, JdeV (Crane) 233; for demonic transport over long distances, see *DM* 8.59 and *IE* no. 2996; for devils uncovering secrets, see *DM* 3.5, 6.

53. For the notion of Satan as an "intimate" enemy and an illuminating discussion of this concept, see Pagals *Origin of Satan* 49.

Chapter Three: Women in Medieval Exempla

1. For a cogent study of this theme in medieval Spanish homiletic literature see Goldberg "Medieval Commonplaces," which specifically links medieval antifeminism and anti-Judaism; for some salient narrative illustrations, see particularly pp. 95–97. See also Parkes *Conflict* 375, for the characteristics of betrayal, carnality, and abandonment by God linking women and Jews.

2. *AT* no. 499, derived from *GL* On the Commemoration of All Soul's Day 2.286. The original is from *On Miracles*, a tract by the reformist abbot Peter of Cluny (d. 1156), who is cited in later analogues. *IE* no. 3892 omits the reference to the tale in *HS* lines 10729–86.

3. Pernoud "La femme" traces the antifeminist attitudes that developed in the fourteenth century largely to the influence of the mendicant orders of monks such as Dominicans and Franciscans, and notes secular literature such as Eustace Deschamp's *Mirror of Marriage*, Jean de Meung's *Romance of the Rose*, and Gilles Bellemère's *Fifteen Days of Marriage* as examples of this new misogyny (269–71).

4. *KTL* 60.78, 62.82.

5. In Jewish folklore, Lilith, Adam's first wife before Eve's creation, was turned out of Eden because she would not submit to Adam's authority, but she had sexual intercourse with him after his expulsion and gave birth to evil spirits, called *jinn*. Other, later Semitic myths characterize her as a succubus, a demon who caused nocturnal emissions with the resultant birth of witches and demons called *lilim*. Lilith was supposed to dwell in deserted places and believed to steal and kill children. See Brunel *Companion to Literary Myths*, 720–24.

6. Chaucer's Wife of Bath was well aware of the clerical bias: "Thou seyst also that if we make us gay / with clothing, and with precious array / That it is peril of oure chastitee" (Chaucer *Works* lines 336–39). Robert Mannyng was one of those who cited women's apparel as part of their fiendish temptation of men into sin, calling their "gay kerchiefs" worn to church "the devils sails" (*HS* lines 8881–92).

7. *Saints and She-Devils* 145–49 traces the theme of Magdalene in medieval art as well as literature. Warner *Alone of All Her Sex* discusses the figure and legend of St. Mary of Egypt, another reformed prostitute analogous to Mary Magdalene, "who so neatly condenses Christianity's fear of women, its identification of physical beauty with temptation, and its practice of bodily mortification" (232).

8. *IE* no. 1268 notes this motif in *AT* no. 132; *DM* 8.2.52; and JdeV (Crane) 245, all of which ultimately derive from *VP* (PL 73), cols. 744, 878.

9. Phipps, "Menstrual Taboo," 300.

10. Carroll *Cult of the Virgin Mary* follows Freudian theory in asserting that "the content of religion is shaped by impulses and desires found in the male unconscious," particulary of the Oedipal period (57). For a summary of Freud's views, see Freud *Basic Writings* pp. 614–18 and n. 1.906–9, 954. I follow Carroll's very convincing argument here (50–58); for the pertinent economic details see particularly pp. 80–84.

11. Augustine *City of God* 22.17. Augustine's beliefs about the transmission of original sin through sexual intercourse are stated as follows: "The seminal nature was there from which we were to be propagated; and this [was] vitiated by sin, and bound by the chain of death . . ." and "Now we bear the image of the earthly man by the propagation of sin and death which pass on us by

ordinary generation" (13.14, 23). See for comment, Pagels *Adam, Eve, and the Serpent* 109, 131.

   12. Augustine *City of God* 22.17.

   13. No. 364, narrated by Charbonnier "Recherches" 182 n. 1. For an interesting discussion of exempla in which adulteresses symbolically kill their lovers by bringing their souls to damnation, see Sinicropi "Chastity and Love" 109–13.

   14. Chaucer *Works* 11.693–96.

   15. *HS* lines 7925–29. These very thoughts are echoed in a complaint by Chaucer's Wife of Bath that "thou [men] liknest eek wommenes love to helle / to bareyne lond, ther water may not dwell. / Thou liknest it also to wilde fyr; / The moore it brenneth, the moore it hath desir / To consume every thyng that brent wole be" (lines 371–75).

   16. Cited in Warner *Alone of All Her Sex* 58–59.

   17. See Gies and Gies *Marriage and the Family* 65, for an analysis of medieval occurrences of incest. Humbert de Romans's father-daughter incest exemplum is described in Berlioz "L'récit efficace" 131. As exempla of daughter-father incest, *IE* lists no. 2731, this tale; nos. 2729 and 2739 also portray a daughter as the murderer of her parents and child/children. Contrition saves the daughter in all these cases, but no mention is made of the culpability of the father, who in real life is commonly the initiator of such incest. Only in *IE* no. 2732, a different tale also involving father-daughter incest, is there any hint of the father's guilt. The point of father-daughter incest exempla (many fewer than the reverse) appears to be that the female is a perpetrator rather than a victim and that sincere contrition washes away even the most heinous sins.

   18. For elucidation of this notion, see Freud *Basic Writings* 617–19. The psychological defense mechanism of "splitting," especially in regard to the "good mother/bad mother" is relevant here. A useful summary of object splitting is found in Grotstein, *Splitting and Projective Identification;* some key comments illuminate my future references to this phenomenon: "In the perceptual or cognitive sense, an act of discriminative separation is involved [in splitting] . . . by which the ego can split an object into two or more objects in order to locate polarized, immiscible qualities separately. Perceptual cognitive splitting is linked to an object, of whom the mother is primary" (3). Grotstein summarizes the seminal work in this area of Melanie Klein, who described splitting as a defense which "constitutes a phantasy whereby the subject may experience . . . a splitting in the object that confronts him." Splitting derives from the ego's need to distinguish between two separate beings within one parental object; the most common split object being what Klein calls "the good breast" and "the bad breast" (9), i.e., the mother.

For a discussion of the bad mother/good mother dichotomy in the religious
dynamic of Hinduism that illuminates this point, see Nanda "Hijaras" 405–8.

19. De Bourbon (no. 299): cited in Charbonnier "Recherches" 30 n. 1.
Tertullian: cited in Warner *Alone of All Her Sex* 58.

20. *VP* (PL, 73), col. 879.

21. Gower *Complete Works* vol. 1, lines 17899–904 (p. 208). Exempla referring to women's beauty suggest similar problems. *AT* no. 728, for example, in
advising men not to wed, proffers many reasons, including the cost of sup-
plying their material needs, their untrustworthiness, and, in the case of beautiful wives, the problem of defending their chastity from the suitors whom
they attract.

22. *Reaction formation* is a Freudian term for repressed impulses that in the
course of the individual's development evoke a feeling of unease, thus awak-
ening a psychic counterforce (reactions) that build up shame and disgust
(Freud *Basic Writings* 584). See Anson "Transvestite in Monasticism" 213–14,
for illuminating comment on the role of reaction formation in the instances of
transvestism in hagiographies of female saints such as Theodora.

23. The woman who painted herself: *KTL* 53.69. See also 65–68 and 70 for
similar instances. The woman who was late for Mass: Charbonnier
"Recherches" 264 n. 1.

24. See *Malleus maleficarum* pt. 1, question 9 for a discussion of whether
witches can, with the help of devils "truly and actually remove men's members." The response is that "when it [removal of the member] is performed by
witches, it is only a matter of glamour; although it is no illusion in the opinion
of the sufferer" (58). Devils, however, with God's permission, "can take off that
member as well as others, truly and actually" (61). The *Malleus maleficarum*
returns to this issue later in pt. 2, question 1, chap. 7, with exempla illustrating
the rubric "How, as it were, they [witches] deprive Man of his Virile Member"
(118–19).

25. Ibid. pt.1, question 11, chap. 13, and pt. 2, question 1, for this point.
Also see *HS* lines 9620–70.

26. Ibid. pt. 2, question 1, chap. 4: "in times long past the Incubus devils
used to infest women against their wills . . . But they do not now subject themselves unwillingly . . ." (111).

27. The witch's "topsy turvey" world, a phrase used in *Saints and She-
Devils*, describes what many scholars of witchcraft perceive was its central
threat to clerical authority: its reverse images and false presentations of the
real world, including parodies of religious rituals (68). See also Hurtig "Witch
Craze" (138).

28. *Malleus maleficarum* pt. 1, question 6 (43).

29. Tertullian cited in Warner *Alone of All Her Sex* 58; St. Ambrose cited in Goldberg "Medieval Commonplaces" 104. Adam's rib, *Tabula exemplorum* no. 155, cited in Charbonnier "Recherches" 29 n. 2.

30. *VP* (PL, 73) col. 894; *AT* no. 2; see *IE* no. 4750 for analogues. For the early Christian conflation of pagan gods with demons in the Christian sense, see Pagels *Origin of Satan* 121.

31. Hurtig "Witch-Craze" 52 employs the term "nature out of control," from Andreas Huyssen's *After the Great Divide*. Huyssen, in speaking of women as modernism's "other," could well be characterizing the medieval situation: "The fear of the masses in this age . . . is always a fear of woman, a fear of nature out of control, a fear of the unconscious, of sexuality, of the loss of identity and stable ego boundaries in the mass" (133–40).

32. *KTL* 27.23.

33. See Goldberg "Medieval Commonplaces" 95–98, for exempla that conflate women's inability to keep a secret and their treachery in disclosing secrets to the enemies of their state. The notion of women as unable to keep secrets is found as far back as the Romans. Plutarch, in his Life of Marcus Brutus, has Brutus's wife Portia slash her thigh in order to distinguish herself from other women, who are "too weak to keep a secret safely" (Plutarch, *The Lives of the Noble Grecians and Romans*, Dryden translation. Great Books of the Western World, vol. 14. [Chicago: Encyclopedia Britannica, 1952], 807). Whitney Chadwick interprets a Rennaissance painting of this episode that includes gossiping women as depicting the notion that women's volubility was seen as a "defect" in their nature that was a metaphor for their uncontrolled sexual desire (*Women, Art, and Society* 92).

34. Chaucer's Wife of Bath suggests as much in describing her "gossib" Alisoun "[who] knew myn herte, and eek my privetie / Bet than oure parisshe preet, so moot I thee!" (lines 529–32). The Wife continues that she disclosed everything her husband did, from his "pissing on a wall" to committing a capital crime, not only to her dear friend Alisoun, but to "another worthy wyf" and to her niece, whom she loved dearly. Her husband was often furious at himself for ever revealing his misdeeds to her, as she never kept them secret.

35. The example of St. Jerome: *HS* lines 7903–38. Such sentiments were commonplace; one especially vituperative version is stated in the official documents of the newly formed Premonstratensian order: "The poisons of vipers and dragons are healthier and less harmful for men than familiarity with women" (cited in *Her Story*, ed. Barbara Q. MacHoffie, 50).

36. *KTL* 47–49.66.

37. The importance of virginity as a mediating category whereby early and medieval Christian women could transcend their inferior nature is a central theme treated by scholars. For example, Rosemary Ruether asserts that "as

ascetics, [women] were freed from the 'curse of Eve' . . . bearing children in sorrow and being subject to their husbands" (*Women in Spirit* 72). Elsewhere she comments that "through holiness and ecstasy, a woman transcends nature and participates in the eschatological sphere [in which] sex hierarchy is abolished for that asexual personhood in which there is neither 'male not female' . . . For most of Christianity this dissolution of sex heirarchy was linked with celibacy" (22). See also Pagels *Adam, Eve, and the Serpent*, where celibacy is linked with freedom as the paradoxical cornerstone of the first four centuries of Christianity (78). MacHoffie, *Her Story*, notes that while male celibates could retain their masculine natures, that is, their superior intellectual and spiritual qualities while denying their sexuality, women celibates had to *erase* their essential nature, that is, their procreative functions, in order to achieve an exalted spiritual state (51).

38. Pagels *Adam, Eve, and the Serpent* asserts that "Jesus radically challenged the [Jewish] consenus that 'one must accept whatever facilitates procreation, including divorce and polygamy; and that one must reject whatever hinders procreation—even a marriage itself'" (13). For examples of other carnal qualities attributed to the Jews as an extention of their sexual indulgences see Goldberg "Medieval Commonplaces" 88, 90–91.

39. *KTL* 62.83.

40. *Saints and She-Devils* 93. See the specific exemplars of St. Barbara and St. Catherine (91–95). Ruether asserts that "medieval monasticism continually suggested that the bridal relation to Christ allows a woman to reject her physical subordination to sexual roles in society" (*Women of Spirit* 24). Eleanor McLaughlin analyzes the Life of the twelfth-century saint Christina Markyate, who "vowed to be the spouse of Christ and no other," found "manly courage" to escape her persecutors, and escaped her marriage disguised as a boy, "mount[ing] her horse like a man" to flee to an eremetic existence (ibid. 111–13).

41. For an illuminating and persuasive psychoanalytic approach to cross-dressing in hagiography, see Anson "Transvestite in Monasticism" which asserts that in a male society dedicated to celibacy as the highest virtue and so not surprisingly given to excesses of antifeminism, the fantasy of a holy woman disguised among their number represented ". . . a psychological opportunity to neutralize the threat of female temptations" (5). In his analysis of the exemplum of St. Theodora in this context, Anson declares that her male "disguise rescues the [monastic] community by rendering finally harmless the threatening vision of woman" so that the tale becomes a "wish fulfillment dream of the domestication of the demonic seductress" (17).

42. Augustine *City of God* 1.17, 20, 26.

43. Warner *Alone of All Her Sex* chap. 4 discusses in detail the oral and written traditions that were combined and elaborated over the centuries to con-

struct the figure of the Virgin Mary, and she links the church's promulgation of the tenets of Mary's Assumption and Ascension to its continuing concern that bodily purity be seen as central to spiritual purity.

44. In a summary of Melanie Klein's "good mother/bad mother" theory (see above, n. 18), H. J. S. Guntrip's comments in *Psychoanalytic Theory, Therapy, and the Self* illuminate the concept of the Virgin as "the good mother." Klein postulated three basic maternal fantasy figures "who can appear in many guises." One is the tantalizing mother, who excites needs; one is the authoritarian, antilibidinal mother who denies satisfaction; and one is the "morally idealized" mother with whom "conformity is accepted in hope of at least approval . . . The exciting and rejecting objects are both bad and are repressed . . . The ideal[ized] object is projected back . . ." (98). Without oversimplifying or distorting the original psyshoanalytic arguments, it is not difficult to see how such a theory enhances our understanding of the medieval concept of the Virgin among her monkish devotees.

45. The medieval tradition of the Virgin as the special enemy of the devil derives from St. Jerome's Vulgate Latin translation of Genesis 3.15: "I will put enmity between thee and the woman, and thy seed and her seed; she shall crush thy head and thou shall lie in wait for her heel," which was interpreted as a prefiguration of Mary defeating evil, particularly the evil of carnality. As the serpent had over time become assimilated to the figure of the devil, the image of a physically uncorrupted Mary victorious over him, sometimes with the assistance of St. Michael and his scales of judgement, became very popular in religious literature and art.

46. Grotstein *Splitting and Projective Identification* examines a specific facet of the split between two aspects of the same object based on Melanie Klein's work that is germane here: "a very deep split between the two aspects of the object indicates that it is not the good and bad object that are being kept apart, but an idealized and extremely bad one. So deep and sharp a division reveals that destructive impulses, envy, and persecutory anxiety are very strong and that idealization serves mainly as a defense against these emotions . . . excessive idealization denotes that persecution is the main driving force" (33).

47. "Ave Maria" saves a monk: IE no. 2094; "Theophilus," see chapter 4, exemplum J9; a knight saved from a demonic bargain: IE no. 5133 (also AT no. 555 from DM 2.12); the pilgrim to St. James: see chapter 2, exemplum D24.

48. Warner *Alone of All Her Sex* asserts that Mary's loyalty to her women devotees even outweighs justice and cites a devil in one tale who complains that "It is she who does us the most harm. Those whom the Son in his justice casts away, the mother in her superfluity of mercy brings back again to indulgence (325 and n. 19).

49. Cox *Cinderella* xxxvii, xliii–xliv, xvi; see esp. xlix–lxvi for religious analogues. An interesting blend of religious and romance motifs is the Tuscan folktale "Olive," which tells how a Jewish girl, given to a Christian foster family by her father, defeats his attacks on her through her devotion to the Virgin Mary. After suffering through many of the episodes attached to the Catskin group of motifs, the Jewish girl is saved by the Virgin. Italo Calvino, the editor of this tale, notes analogues in the *Arabian Nights* and various European collections, in romances of both secular and religious heroines: Orlanda, Florencia, St. Gugliema, the princess of Dacia, the Queen of Poland, Crescenzia, and St. Olive (*Italian Folktales* no. 71).

Chapter Four: Jews in Medieval Sermon Stories

1. Ellison *Invisible Man* 3.

2. For specific instances see Ben-Sasson *History* 418–19, 480–82; Poliakov *History* 1.113; and Ginzburg *Ecstasies* 50–51, 68.

3. The last four decrees promulgated by the Fourth Lateran Council specifically concerned the Jews. Canons 67–69 sought to restrict Jewish moneylending, compel Jews to pay tithes and ecclesiastical dues, prevent miscegenation between Jews and Christians, confine Jews to their houses during Holy Week through Easter Sunday, and debar them from public office. Secular rulers were enjoined to enforce these canons by Pope Innocent III, although in practice his authority was limited. Canon 70 exhorted Jews to reject Judaism and convert to Christianity.

4. See, for example, the Jewish poetry in response to the massacres of the Crusades described by Ben-Sasson *History* 412–17 and Jewish travel diaries in *Jewish Travellers*, ed. Elkan Adler.

5. For the expulsion of Jews from various European communities, see Ben-Sasson *History* 462–67; Poliakov *History* 1.118–19; Langmuir *Definition* 303.

6. *Jewish Travellers* 197–98.

7. Mirk *Instructions* lines 41–42.

8. For the link between Jews and lepers in antique times, see Ginzburg *Ecstasies* 35–36. Tacitus devotes sections 1–5 of bk. 5 of his history to derogation of the Jews in his discussion of Titus's governance of Judea. (Tacitus *The Histories* [trans. Alfred John Church and William Jackson Brodribb]). Two accessible full length studies are Sevenster, *Roots of Pagan Antisemitism* and Stern, *Greek and Latin Authors.*

9. Martens "Miroir du meutre" 68–70.

10. Mélèze-Modrzejewski "Sur l'antisemitism païen" 411.

11. Ruether *Faith and Fratricide* 2.

12. A fascinating modern example of the belief that Christ lives in his statues is a 1991 report of an assault on a crucifix statue in the Church of S. Maria de Ricci in Florence, Italy. Apparently, in February 1978, according to a handout at the church, a "sacrilegious person" broke the arms and legs of the church's great crucifix, at which moment the formerly serene face of Christ became contorted into a horrible grimace of pain. A photograph was taken of the new visage and a copy of the two faces side by side accompanies the text describing this "miraculous" occurrence.

13. Trachtenberg *Devil and Jews* 50–51 cites a sixteenth-century list of uniquely Jewish diseases, each attributed to a particular tribe of Israel for its particular sin in connection with the Passion. Thus, for example, because Levi slapped Jesus and spat on him, members of this tribe have difficulty bringing up phlegm. Gilman *Difference and Pathology* places this motif within the context of otherness (151).

14. Mute Jew regains speech through baptism: Parkes *Conflict* 297; Jew regains sight with monk's blood: ibid. 296.

15. For scriptural images of Jewish blindness and darkness, see Gospel of John 3:19–21; Revelation 1:13, 21–23, 22:5; and Romans 11:7–8. For Jews blind or blindfolded as emblematic of their spiritual condition see Ben-Sasson *History* 556 and Blumenkranz "Le juif" 76. For the Pauline formulation of the Jewish "veil," see Ruether *Faith and Fratricide* 35–36.

16. Augustine *City of God* 7.32, and 8.46. For comments, see Talmage *Disputation and Dialogue* 18–19, 31.

17. Augustine *City of God* 7.32, and 8.46.

18. Jew lends money: Parkes *Conflict* 294. Analogues appear in Herbert *Cat. of Rom.* 3.529, no. 12 and 3.677, no. 12.

19. Parkes *Conflict* 294–95 offers several examples.

20. *JW* 301. This material does not appear in the English sermoner's source, the *AN* (*AT* no. 376 and no. 799).

21. A useful compendium of psychological theories of anti-Semitism is found in Nathan W. Ackerman and Marie Jahoda, *Anti-Semitism and Emotional Disorder: A Psychological Interpretation.* For the roots of anti-Judaism in xenophobia, Christian doubt, and economic scapegoating, see Gavin Langmuir's *History, Religion and Antisemitism.* For sociological factors in historic anti-Semitism, see Gordon Allport *The Nature of Preudice* 249 and 386.

22. Abrahams *Jewish Life* 62–82 offers a useful summary of Jewish residential restrictions and medieval ghettoization. See also Ben-Sasson *History* 563–65 for pertinent comments on Jewish residential arrangements. Metzger and Metzger *Jewish Life* 55 interprets fourteenth- and fifteenth-century Jewish illustrations of Jewish buildings with ramparts, moats, and fortified closed gates as signifying the hostility Jews perceived directed against them by

Christians. See also the description of the Jewish community in fifteenth-century Palermo by the Jewish traveller Obadiah da Bertinor (*Jewish Travellers* 211) and Jewish communities in the eastern Mediterranean by Meshullam Ben R. Menahem (ibid. 201, 203).

23. Abrams *Jewish Life* 66.

24. An interesting counterpoint to Christian isolatory regulations against the Jews is the observation of the Jewish traveller Obadiah da Bertinoro that in Alexandria, where there are Christian merchants of all the European nations, "the Christians are obliged to shut themselves in their houses every evening; the Arabs close up the streets from without, and open them again every morning. It is the same on Friday from noon til the evening; while the Arabs tarry in the house of prayer, the Christians have to stay in their houses, and whoever is seen in the street has himself to blame if he is ill-treated" (*Jewish Travellers* 223).

25. Quoted in Poliakov *Anti-Semitism* 25.

26. See *IE* no. 147 and Herbert *Cat. of Rom.* 3.325, no. 19; and 3.390, no. 292.

27. Richardson, *Angevin Kings* 181. See also Ben-Sasson *History* 484–85. Obadiah da Bertinoro, again, in describing Palermo, notes "As a mark of distinction [the Jews] are obliged to wear a piece of red cloth, about the size of a gold coin, fastened on the breast" (*Jewish Travellers* 211). Metzger and Metzger *Jewish Life* 143–46 discuss the distinctive articles of Jewish clothing and the badges of infamy, with accompanying manuscript illustrations.

28. Quoted in Poliakov *History* 25.

29. Ruether *Faith and Fratricide* 128, 136.

30. Abrams *Jewish Life* notes the coupling of Jews and harlots in anti-Jewish statutes (408 n. 2) and legislation which located brothels in the Jewish quarters (68). Garber *Vested Interests* comments on the linking of Jews and women as exemplars of "looseness" and the subjects of the same sumptuary laws (25–28). Garber's observations here follow those of Diane Owen Hughes "Distinguishing Signs" 17–18, 37, 47. For a typical artistic rendering of the theme of a wanton woman symbolizing the synagogue, see Blumenkranz *Le Juif* 108 fig. 123.

31. I am indebted to Garber *Vested Interests* 271 for a cogent analysis of this theme; the "Buck" and "Sambo" splitting in white southern American views towards African American males is also noted in Fox-Genovese *Plantation Household* 291–92.

32. For proto-Shylock exempla with the motif of the emasculated Jew, see *IE* no. 2800, 2804; Herbert *Cat. of Rom.* 3.659, no. 176. Brown "Medieval Prototypes" 228–29 and n. 4 provides insightful comments about these exempla.

33. From the Jewish perspective, this theme takes on a reversed aspect. See Isaac Chelo's account of miscegenation in the Holy Land between "A young

Israelitish girl of great beauty" and a Christian crusader, who eventually married the girl and converted to Judaism (*Jewish Travellers*, 14).

34. Blumenkranz *Le juif* 81–82; figs. 87–88.

35. Herbert *Cat. of Rom.* 3.329, no. 15; and 3.684, no. 32.

36. Ruether *Faith and Fratricide* 155. Jewish dietary laws originate in the Hebrew scriptures: Leviticus 3:17, 7:6, 19:26; Deuteronomy 12:16. The ethical, historical, pragmatic, and anthropological reasons for kosher laws are still an open question. The inability to distinguish between "food" and "nonfood" in regard to the Host was also attributed to sinful, i.e., skeptical, Christians, for an example of which see *IE* no. 2685 of a woman who tested the Host by baking it in an oven.

37. *GL* Assumption of the Virgin 2.94–95 describes how "some Jews, hardened in their old malevolence," accompanied Mary's bier, and one, "a true limb of Satan" laid hands on the litter. In this version, the Jew's hands "fell off as dry as a stick" until he repented and had his hand restored by touching Mary's body.

38. See Ward *Cat. of Rom.* 2.658, no. 16; 2.732, no. 35. See also the reference in Frank "Miracles of the Virgin" 295 n. 4.

39. See *IE* nos. 2806, 441.

40. For "splitting" as a projective phenomenon in ambivalent object relations, see chapter 3, nn. 18, 44. "Splitting" in regard to Jews also occurs in the popular medieval drama and art, where the Jewish prophets are represented as holy men, forerunners of Christianity, whereas contemporary Jews are represented negatively, in their mandatory garb, as enemies of Christianity.

41. See Poliakov *History* 135; Blumenkranz *Le Juif* 64; Parkes *Conflict* 164; Trachtenberg *Devil and Jews* 162 for instances. Ruether *Faith and Fratricide* quotes Chrysostom's elaboration of the prophets' descriptions of Israel as calves and cows with the remark that animals unfit for work are marked for slaughter, a condition that applies to the Jews (179).

42. Parkes *Conflict* 144, 133.

43. Ibid. 165.

44. Quoted in Langmuir *Definition* 207.

45. *DM* 10.69.

46. The identification of the Jews with the devil had been a staple of the patristic *adversos Judaeos* tradition and was a commonplace in medieval homiletics, literature, drama, and the plastic arts. Chaucer's Prioress, for example, calls the Jew "our firste fo, the Serpent Sathanas, that hath in Jews herte his waspes nest" (line 1748). See Trachtenberg *Devil and Jews* 23–26 for the complicity between Satan and the Jews in several French passion plays and exempla. In *N-Town Plays* (ed. Stephen Spector), Satan, in his prologue to Passion Play 1 (no. 26), details his malicious role in human history, stating that he set in motion "the

new engines of malicious conspiracy [against Christ]," by instigating "his pepyl" (i.e. the Jews) to testify against Jesus (lines 49–52); see also Spector's nn. 26, 49–60 (2.490). Similarly, in the *Carmina Burana*, a fifteenth-century Christmas musical drama from the cycle "Prophets' Plays," the Jews are depicted as allies of the devil through the character "Archisynagogues." I am grateful to Margot E. Fassler (Yale University Institute of Sacred Music), whose lecture "Anti-Jewish Themes in Medieval Prophets' Plays" placing this material in the framework of medieval anti-Judaic polemic was delivered to the Medieval Club of New York, May 12, 1995. Blumenkranz *Le juif* notes numerous examples in medieval manuscript illustrations, including one that shows the Jews in Hell with Eve and the Devil of Temptation, making explicit the theme of devils, women, and Jews as an "unholy trinity" of the damned.

47. *Tabula exemplorum* no. 57, cited in Charbonnier "Recherches" 301 n. 1.

48. Quoted in Langmuir *Definition* 201.

49. Poliakov *History* 25. See also Parkes *Conflict* chap. 9, "Jews in the Theologians." William of Malmesbury in his account of Pope Sylvester, refers to a "Jew-Necromancer" (Chronicle 181); in the *Malleus maleficarum* pt. 1, question 10, the query of whether witches use magic to change men into beasts is answered with an exemplum of a woman whose "shameful act caused a Jew to work a charm against her by which she was changed into a filly." *IE* no. 2627 is a variant minus the Jew. Jews themselves acknowledged, but did not necessarily critize the supernatural power of some of their number, for which see *Jewish Travellers* 91.

50. *IE* nos. 2800, 2804.

51. Trachtenberg *Devil and Jews* 203.

52. Herbert *Cat. of Rom.* (*Speculum laicorum* 3.484, no. 70, and 399, no. 465.

53. Ibid. 675, no. 18. *Speculum laicorum* no. 269 presents a clerical necromancer instead of a Jew (narrated in Charbonnier "Recherches" 94 n. 1).

54. See Ward *Cat. of Rom.* 2.638, no. 10 for an extensive history of this tale, whose first appearance in a tenth-century semon in Constantinople involves one "Abram the usurer." *IE* no. 2797 includes incorrect cites: Herbert 505, no. 31 and Ward 2.601 are "The Jew of Bourges." Parkes *Conflict* 294 gives a full summary of the original, which ends with the conversion of the Jewish usurer. Artistic renderings of Jews, however, promoted the identification of Jews as moneylenders. Blumenkranz *Le juif* offers many examples such as an illustration for Jeremiah's Lamentations in the *Bible moralisée* accompanying the text "All our people sigh . . . give their precious goods for nourishment" that shows a Jewish moneylender/pawnbroker in contemporary dress (76).

55. Richardson *Angevin Kings* 225–29.

56. *IE* no. 2799.

57. Ben-Sasson *History* 563, 575–76.

Abbreviations

Works most frequently cited in the Notes have been identified by the following abbreviations:

AN   Arnold of Liège. *Alphabetum narrationum.* British Museum Harley MS 268.

AT   *An Alphabet of Tales: An English 15th Century Translation of the Alphabetum Narrationum.* Edited by Mary Banks. Early English Text Society, OS, 126 and 127. London: Paul, Trench, Trübner & Co., 1904–5.

Cat. of Rom.   Herbert, John, and Harry Ward. *Catalogue of Romances in the Department of Manuscripts in the British Museum.* 3 vols. London: Printed by the Order of the Trustees, 1883–1910.

Dial.   Gregory the Great. *Dialogues.* Translated by Odo John Zimmerman. New York: Fathers of the Church, 1959.

DM   Caesar of Heisterbach. *Dialogue of Miracles.* Translated by Charles Bland and Henry Scott. 2 vols. London: Routledge & Sons, 1929.

EETS   Early English Text Society. OS: Original Series. ES: Extra Series.

Festial   Mirk, John. *Mirk's Festial: A Collection of Homilies.* Edited by Theodore Erbe. Early English Text Society, ES, 96. London: Paul, Trench, Trübner & Co., 1905.

GL   Jacobus de Voragine. *The Golden Legend: Readings on the Saints.* 2 vols. Translated by William Granger Ryan. Princeton: Princeton University Press, 1993.

GR   *The Early English Versions of the* Gesta Romanorum. Edited by Sidney Herrtage. Early English Text Society, ES, 33. London: Trübner, 1889.

HS Mannyng, Robert. *Robert of Brunne's* Handlyng Synne *with William of Waddington's* Manuel des Péchiez. Edited by Frederick Furnival. Early English Text Society, OS, 119 and 123. London: Paul, Trench, Trübner & Co., 1909.

IE Tubach, Frederic. *Index Exemplorum: A Handbook of Medieval Religious Tales.* Folklore Fellows Communications 86, no. 204. Helsinki: Suomalainen Tiedeskatemia Akemia Scientiarum Fennica, 1969.

JdeV, Crane Jacques de Vitry. *The Exempla; or, Ilustrative Stories from the Sermones Vulgares.* Edited by Thomas Crane. Publications of the Folklore Society, 26. London: Folklore Society, 1890.

JW *Jacob's Well.* Pt. 1. Edited by Arthur Brandeis. Early English Text Society, OS, 115. London: Paul, Trübner & Co., 1900.

KTL Tour Landry, Geoffroy de la. *The Book of the Knight of Tour Landry.* Edited by Thomas Wright. Early English Text Society, OS, 33. London: Trübner, 1906.

MES *Three Middle English Sermons from the Worcester Chapter Manuscript F. 10.* Edited by D. M. Grisdale. Leeds: School of English Language in the University of Leeds, 1939.

PL Patrologiae cursus completus, series latina. Edited by Jacques P. Migne. Paris: J. P. Migne, 1844–1864.

VP *Vitae patrum sive historiae eremiticae libri decem.* Edited by Herbert Rosweyd. Patrologiae cursus completus, series Latina, vol. 73. Paris: J. P. Migne, 1849.

* All references from the Hebrew and Christian Bible are from the King James version.

Bibliography

Primary Sources

Alphonsi, Petrus. Disciplina Clericalis: *An Anonymous Middle English Translation.* Edited by William Hulme. Western Reserve University studies in English, 5. Cleveland: Western Reserve University Press, 1919.

An Alphabet of Tales: An English 15th Century Translation of the Alphabetum Narrationum. Edited by Mary Banks. Early English Text Society, OS, 126 and 127. London: Paul, Trench, Trübner & Co., 1904–5.

Arnold of Liège. *Alphabetum narrationum.* British Museum Harley MS 268.

Augustine. *City of God.* Translated by Marcus Dods. Great Books of the Western World, vol. 18. Chicago: Encyclopaedia Britannica, 1952.

Barlaam and Joasaph. Translated by Harold Mattingly and George Woodward. New York: Macmillan, 1914.

Bourbon, Etienne de. *Anecdotes historiques: Légendes et apologues tirés du recueil inédit de Etienne de Bourbon.* Edited by Lecoy de la Marche. Librairie de la Societe de l'Histoire de France, 185. Paris: Librairie Renouard, 1877.

Boyd, Beverly. *Middle English Miracles of the Virgin.* San Marino, Calif.: Huntington Library, 1964.

Budge, Wallis. *One Hundred and Ten Miracles of Our Lady.* London: Medici Society, 1874.

Caesar of Heisterbach. *Dialogue of Miracles.* Translated by Charles Bland and Henry Scott. 2 vols. London: Routledge & Sons, 1929.

Cheriton, Odo de. *Etude sur les fables et les paraboles d'Eudes de Cheriton.* Edited by Leopold Hervieux. Les Fabulistes Latin depuis le Siècle d'Auguste jusqu'àla Fin du Moyen Age, 4. 1898. Burt Franklin Research and Sourcework Series, 99. Reprint, New York: Burt Franklin, 1965.

Delehaye, Hippolyte. *The Legends of the Saints.* Translated by Donald Attwater. New York: Fordham University Press, 1962.

The Early English Versions of the Gesta Romanorum. Edited by Sidney Herrtage.
    Early English Text Society, ES, 33. London: Trübner, 1889.
English Metrical Homilies from Manuscripts of the Fourteenth Century. Edited by
    John Small. Edinburgh: W. Patterson, 1862.
Fabliaux ou Contes, Fables, et Romans du XIIe et du XIIIe siècle. Edited by Pierre
    Le Grand d'Aussy. 3rd ed. Paris: J. Renouard, 1829.
Fons Jacobi (Jacob's Well). Salisbury Cathedral Library MS 103.
Gerould, Gordon. *The North English Homily Collection: A Study of the Manuscript
    Relations and the Sources of the Tales.* Oxford University Press, 1902.
Gesta Romanorum. Translated by Charles Swan. Revised by Wynnard Hooper.
    New York: Dutton, 1905.
Gregory the Great. *Dialogues.* Translated by Odo John Zimmerman. New York:
    Fathers of the Church, 1959.
Jacob's Well. Pt. 1. Edited by Arthur Brandeis. Early English Text Society, OS,
    115. London: Paul, Trübner & Co., 1900.
Jacobus de Voragine. *The Golden Legend: Readings on the Saints.* Translated by
    William Granger Ryan. 2 vols. Princeton: Princeton University
    Press, 1993.
————. *The Golden Legend as Englished by William Caxton.* London: J. M.
    Dent, 1900.
Jacques de Vitry. *The Exempla; or, Illustrative Stories from the* Sermones Vulgares.
    Edited by Thomas Crane. Publications of the Folklore Society, 26.
    London: Folk-lore Society, 1890.
Jewish Travellers in the Middle Ages: 19 First Hand Accounts. Edited by Elkan
    Nathan Adler. New York: Dover Publications, 1987.
Kramer, Heinrich, and James Sprenger. *Malleus Maleficarum.* Translated by
    Montague Summers. New York: Dover Publications, 1971.
The Lay Folks Catechism. Edited by Henry Nolloth and Thomas Simmons. Early
    English Text Society, ES, 118. London: Paul, Trench, Trübner &
    Co., 1901.
Liber exemplorum. Edited by Andrew Little. Oxford: Society for Franciscan
    Studies, 1903.
Mannyng, Robert. *Handlyng Synne.* Edited by Idelle Sullens. Binghamton:
    Center for Medieval and Early Rennaissance Studies, State
    University of New York at Binghamton, 1983.
————. *Robert of Brunne's* Handlyng Synne *with William of Waddington's* Man-
    uel des Péchiez. Edited by Frederich Furnival. Early English Text
    Society, OS, 119 and 123. London: Paul, Trench, Trübner & Co., 1909.
Middle English Sermons from MS Royal B. XXIII. Edited by Woodward Ross.
    Early English Text Society, OS, 209. London: Oxford University
    Press, 1940.

Mirk, John. *John Mirk's* Instructions for Parish Priests. Edited by Gillis Kristensson. Lund Studies in English, 49. Lund: CWK Gleerup, 1974.

————. *Mirk's* Festial: *A Collection of Homilies.* Edited by Theodore Erbe. Early English Text Society, ES, 96. London: Paul, Trench, Trübner & Co., 1905.

N-Town Plays. Edited by Stephen Spector. 2 vols. Early English Text Society, SS, 11. Oxford: Oxford University Press, 1991.

Political, Religious, and Love Poems. Edited by Frederick Furnival. Early English Text Society, OS 15. London: Trübner, 1866.

Speculum sacerdotale. Edited by Edward Weatherly. Early English Text Society, OS, 200. London: Oxford University Press, 1936.

Three Middle English Sermons from the Worcester Chapter Manuscript F. 10. Edited by D. M. Grisdale. Leeds: School of English Language in the University of Leeds, 1939.

Tour Landry: Geoffroy de la. *The Book of the Knight of Tour Landry.* Edited by Thomas Wright. Early English Text Society, OS, 33. London: Trübner, 1906.

Vitae patrum sive historiae eremiticae libri decem. Edited by Herbert Rosweyd. Partologiae cursus completus, series Latina, vol 73. Paris: J. P. Migne, 1849.

Waddell, Helen. *The Desert Fathers.* London: Constable & Co., 1987.

William of Malmesbury. *Chronicle of the Kings of England.* Translated by J. A. Giles. London: Henry G. Bohn, 1947.

Secondary Sources

Abrahams, Israel. *Jewish Life in the Middle Ages.* Philadelphia: Jewish Publication Society of America, 1896. Reprint, New York: Atheneum, 1978.

Ackerman, Nathan W., and Marie Jahoda. *Anti-Semitism and Emotional Disorder: A Psychological Interpretation.* New York: Harper, 1950.

Allen, Hope Emily. "The *Speculum Vitae*: Addendum." *PMLA* 31, no. 2 (1917): 133–62.

Allen, Roland. "Gerbert, Pope Sylvester II." *English Historical Review* 7, no. 28 (October 1892): 625–88.

Allport, Gordon. *The Nature of Prejudice.* Newton, Mass.: Addison-Wesley, 1978.

Anson, John. "The Female Transvestite in Early Monasticism: The Origin and Development of a Motif." *VIATOR: Medieval and Rennaissance Studies* 5 (1974): 1–32.

Arnould, Emile. Le manuel des péchés: *Etude de littérature religieuse anglo-nor-mande (XIIIe siècle)*. Paris: E. Droz, 1940.

Baron, Salo Wittmayer. *A Social and Religious History of the Jews*. Vol. 9, *The Late Middle Ages and the Era of European Expansion, 1200–1650*. New York: Columbia University Press, 1965.

Bennett, Henry. "The Author and his Public in the 14th and 15th Centuries." *Essays and Studies by Members of the English Association* 23 (1938): 7–24.

———. "Fifteenth Century Secular Prose." *Review of English Studies* 21 (1945): 257–63.

———. "The Production and Dissemination of Vernacular MSS. in the Fifteenth Century." *The Library*, 5th ser., 1, nos. 3–4 (1946–47): 167–78.

Benore, Gretchen. "The Appeal of the Cult of the Virgin." *Student Scholar* (Ohio Wesleyan University) 1988–89: Abstract 22, 43–44.

Ben-Sasson, H. H. *The Middle Ages*. Pt. 5 of *A History of the Jewish People*, edited by H. H. Ben-Sasson. Cambridge: Harvard University Press, 1976.

Berger, Harry, Jr. "Ecology of the Medieval Imagination: An introductory Overview." *Centennial Review* 12, no. 3 (1968): 278–313.

Berlioz, Jacques. "Introduction bibliographique: Moyen age." *Mélanges de l'ecole francaise de Rome* 92 (1980): 23–31.

———. "Le récit efficace: L'Exemplum au service de la predication (XIIIe–XVe siècles)." *Mélanges de l'ecole francaise de Rome* 92 (1980): 113–46.

Blench, John. *Preaching in England in the Late Fifteenth and Sixteenth Centuries*. New York: Barnes and Noble, 1964.

The Blood Libel Legend: A Casebook in Anti-Semitic Folklore. Edited by Alan Dundes. Madison: University of Wisconsin Press, 1991.

Blumenkranz, Bernhard. *Le juif médiéval au miroir de l'art chrétien*. Paris: Etudes Augustiniennes, 1966.

Bremond, Claude, Jacques Le Goff, and Jean-Claude Schmitt. *L'exemplum*. Belgium: Turnhout, 1982.

Brown, Beatrice. "Medieval Prototypes of Lorenzo and Jessica." *Modern Language Notes* (April 1929): 227–32.

Brunel, Pierre, ed. *Companion to Literary Myths, Heroes, and Archetypes*. Translated by Wendy Allatson, Judith Hayward, and Tricia Selous. New York: Routledge, 1992.

Calvino, Italo, ed. *Italian Folktales*. Translated by George Martin. New York: Harcourt Brace Jovanovich, 1980.

Capes, William. *The English Church in the Fourteenth and Fifteenth Centuries*. London: Macmillan, 1901.

Caplan, Harry. "Classical Rhetoric and Medieval Theories of Preaching." *Classical Philology* 28 (1933): 73–96.

————. "Rhetorical Invention in Some Medieval Tractates on Preaching." *Speculum* 2 (1927): 284–95.

Carroll, Michael P. *The Cult of the Virgin Mary: Psychological Origins*. Princeton: Princeton University Press, 1986.

Carver, James. "The Northern English Homily Cycle." Diss., New York University, 1938.

Chambers, John. *Divine Worship in England in the Thirteenth and Fourteenth Centuries*. London: Pickering, 1877.

Charbonnier, Claudine Nore. "Recherches sur le personnage du diable dans les exempla (XIIIe siècle)." Thèse, L'Université de Paris IV, 1974 (dactyl 1975).

Chaucer, Geoffrey. *The Works of Geoffrey Chaucer*. Edited by F. N. Robinson. 2nd ed. Boston: Houghton Mifflin, 1957.

Cox, Marian Roalfe, ed. *Cinderella: Three Hundred and Forty-Five Variants*. Publications of the Folklore Society 31. 1982. Reprint, Nendeln, Liechtenstein: Kraus Reprint, 1967.

Crane, Thomas. "Medieval Sermon Books." *Proceedings of the American Philosophical Society* 21, no. 114 (1883): 49–98.

————. "Medieval Sermon Books Since 1883." *Proceedings of the American Philosophical Society* 56 (1917): 369–402.

————. "Medieval Story Books." *Modern Philology* 9 (1919): 235–37.

Cutts, Edward. *Parish Priests and Their People in the Middle Ages*. London: London Society for Promoting Christian Knowledge, 1898.

Deansley, Margaret. "Vernacular Books in England in the Fourteenth and Fifteenth Centuries." *Modern Language Review* 15 (1920): 353–65.

De Gandillac, Maurice. "Juif et judeite dans le 'Dialogue' d'Abelard. In *Pour Leon Poliakov: le racisme, mythes et sciences*, edited by Maurice Olender, 385–401. Brussels: Editions Complexe, 1981.

Dickinson, Roland. "Didacticism in the Fifteenth Century Novella and Folktale." *Southern Folklore Quarterly* 30 (1966): 264–70.

Disputation and Dialogue: Readings in the Jewish-Christian Encounter. Edited by Frank Talmage. New York: KTAV Publishing House, 1975.

Ellison, Ralph. *Invisible Man*. New York: Random House, 1990.

Elsasser, Albert. "The Exempla of Mirk's Festial." Diss. Princeton University, 1924.

Emery, Richard W. "Le Prêt d'argent juif en Languedoc et Roussillon." *Juifs et judaisme de Languedoc: Cahiers de Fanjeaux: Collection d'histoire religieuse du Languedoc au XIIIe et au début du XIVe siècles* 12 (1976).

Fassler, Margot E. "Anti-Jewish Themes in Medieval Prophets' Plays." Lecture delivered to the Medieval Club of New York, May 12, 1995.

Fittabile, Leo. "An Introduction, Glossary, and Index for an Alphabet of Tales," Diss. Boston University, 1957.

Fox, Robin Lane. *Pagans and Christians*. New York: Harper & Row, 1988.

Fox-Genovese, Elizabeth. *Within the Plantation Household: Black and White Women of the Old South*. Chapel Hill: University of North Carolina Press, 1988.

Frank, Robert Worth, Jr. "Miracles of the Virgin, Medieval Anti-Semitism, and the 'Prioress' Tale.'" In *The Wisdom of Poetry: Essays in Early English Literature in Honor of Morton W. Bloomfield*, edited by Larry D. Benson and Sigfried Wenzel, 290–97. Kalamazoo: Medieval International Publications, Western Michigan University, 1982.

Freud, Sigmund. *The Basic Writings of Sigmund Freud*. Translated and edited by A. A. Brill. New York: Random House, 1938.

Garber, Marjorie. *Vested Interests: Cross-Dressing and Cultural Anxiety*. New York: Harper Collins, 1992.

Geremek, Bronislaw. "L'Exemplum et la circulation de la culture au Moyen Age." *Mélanges de l'ecole francaise de Rome* 92 (1980): 153–79.

Gies, Frances, and Joseph Gies. *Marriage and the Family in the Middle Ages*. New York: Harper & Row, 1987.

—————. *Women in the Middle Ages*. New York: Harper & Row Publishers, 1978.

Gilles, Henri, "Commentaires méridionaux des prescriptions canoniques sur les juifs." *Juifs et judaisme de Languedoc: Cahiers de Fanjeaux: Collection d'histoire religieuse du Lanugedoc au XIIIe et au début du XIVe siècles* 12 (1976): 23–50.

Gilman, Sander L. *Difference and Pathology: Stereotypes of Sexuality, Race, and Madness*. Ithaca: Cornell University Press, 1985.

Gimpel, Jean. *Les Bâtisseurs de cathedrales*. Paris: Sevil, 1980.

Ginzberg, Carlo. *Ecstasies: Deciphering the Witches' Sabbath*. New York: Pantheon Books, 1991.

Goldberg, Harriet. "Two Parallel Medieval Commonplaces: Antifeminism and Antisemitism in the Hispanic Literary Tradition." In *Aspects of Jewish Culture in the Middle Ages*, edited by Paul E. Szarmach, 85–119. Albany: State University of New York Press, 1979.

Gower, John. *The Complete Works of John Gower*. Vol. 2. Edited by G. C. Macaulay. Oxford: Clarendon Press, 1899.

Gregg, Joan. "The Exempla of 'Jacob's Well': A Study in the Transmission of Medieval Sermon Stories." *Traditio* 33 (1977): 359–80.

Grotstein, James S. *Splitting and Projective Identification*. New York: Jason Aronson, 1981.

Guntrip, H. J. S. *Psychoanalytic Theory, Therapy, and the Self.* New York: Basic Books, 1971.

Haskins, Charles. "The Spread of Ideas in the Middle Ages." *Speculum* 1 (1926): 19–30.

Heath, Peter. *The English Parish Clergy on the Eve of the Reformation.* London: Routledge & Sons, 1961.

Herbert, John. "The Authorship of the *Alphabetum Narrationum.*" *The Library*, 2nd ser., 6, no. 21 (1905): 94–101.

Herbert, John, and Harry Ward. *Catalogue of Romances in the Department of Manuscripts in the British Museum.* 3 vols. London: Printed by Order of the Trustees, 1883–1910.

Hinnebusch, William. *The Early English Friar Preachers.* Rome: S. Sabinae, 1951.

Hurtig, Janise. "Engendering the Witch-Craze: Notes toward a Decentered Interpretation. *Michigan Discussions in Anthropology* 9 (Spring 1990): 133–39.

Huynes, Diane Owen. "Distinguishing Signs: Ear-Rings, Jews, and Franciscan Rhetoric in the Italian Renaissance City." *Past and Present* 112 (August 1986): 3–59.

Huyssen, Andreas. *After the Great Divide: Modernism, Mass Culture, Post-modernism.* Bloomington: University of Indiana Press, 1986.

Ivanits, Linda J. *Russian Folk Belief.* New York: M. E. Sharpe, 1989.

Jarret, Bede. *The English Dominicans.* London: Bournes, Oates & Washbourne, 1921.

Jofen, Jean. "The Jewish Law of Usury as Seen in Elizabethan Literature." *The Jewish Law Annual*, 8 (1989), 147–57.

Kennedy, Charles W. *Early English Christian Poetry.* New York: Oxford University Press, 1952.

Krappe, Alexander, H. "Les Sources du *Libro de exemplos.*" *Bulletin Hispanique* (1937): 5–54.

La Garde, Andre. "De Manuel du Confessor au XIe Siècle." *Revue d'histoire et de littérature religieuses* 2, no. 5 (September–October 1911): 542–50.

Langmuir, Gavin I. "L'Absence d'accusation de Meurte Rituel a l'ouest du Rhone." *Juifs et judaisme de Languedoc, 4: Cahiers de Fanjeaux: Collection d'histoire religieuse du Languedoc au XIIIe et au début du XIVe siècles* 12 (1976): 236–49.

———. "Historiographic Crucifixion." In *Les juifs au regard de l'historire: Mélanges en l'Honneur de Bernhard Blumenkranz*, edited by Gilbert Dahan, 106–27. Paris: Picard, 1985.

———. *History, Religion, and Antisemitism.* Berkely and Los Angles: University of California Press, 1990.

———. *Towards a Definition of Antisemitism.* Berkely and Los Angeles: University of Calif. Press, 1990.

Le Goff, Jacques. *La Civilization de l'Occident Médiéval*. Paris: Arthaud, 1965; Paris: Universitaires de France, 1969.

————. "Le Juif dans les exempla médiévaux: le cas de l'*Alphabetum Narrationum*." In *Pour Leon Poliakov: Le racisme, mythes et sciences*, edited by Maurice Olender, Brussels: Editions Complexe, 1981.

————. "Réalities sociales et codes idéologiques au debut du XIIIe siècle: un exemplum de Jacques de Vitry sur les turnois." In *Europaische Sachkultur des Mittelalters: Gedenkschrift aus Anlass des Zehnjahrigen Bestehens des Institutes für Mittelalterliche Realienkunde Osterreichs*, 101–12. Vienna: Verlag der Osterreichischen Akademie der Wissenschaften, 1980.

Lister, Wilfred, "A Stylistic Analysis of *Jacob's Well* (Chapters 1–50)." Diss. University of Southhampton, England, 1986.

Lohr, Evelyn. "Patristic Demonology in Old English Literature." Diss. New York University, 1947.

Louis, Andre. "Le Conte Populaire, En Face Des Apports Divers Des Mass-Media, a-t-il Encore Dans La Tunisie D'Aujourd'hui une Fonction Culturelle?" Helsinki: Folk Narrative Congress, 1974.

Macculloch, John. *Medieval Faith and Fable*. Boston: Marshall Jones, 1932.

MacHoffie, Barbara Q. *Her Story*. Philadelphia: Fortress Press, 1986.

Manning, Bernard. *People's Faith in the Age of Wycliff*. Cambridge: Cambridge University Press, 1919.

Martens, Frances. "Le miroir du meurtre ou le synagogue dévoilée." In *Pour Leon Poliakov: Le racisme, mythes et sciences*, edited by Maurice Olender, 61–72. Brussels: Editions Complexe, 1981.

Martin, C. Trice. "Clerical Life in the Fifteenth Century." *Archeologia*, pt. 2, 60 (1907): 359–80.

Mélèze-Modrzejewski, Jules Isaac. "Sur l'antisemitisme païen." In *Pour Leon Poliakov: Le racisme, mythes et sciences*, edited by Maurice Olender, 411–39. Brussels: Editions Complexe, 1981.

Metzger, Therese, and Mendel Metzger. *Jewish Life in the Middle Ages: Illuminated Hebrew Manuscripts of the Thirteenth to the Sixteenth Centuries*. Fribourg, Switzerland: Office du Livre, 1982. Reprinted, Secaucus, N.J.: Chartwell Books, n.d.

Michelet, Jules. *Satanism and Witchcraft: A Study in Medieval Superstition*. Translated by A. R. Allinson. New York: Citadel Press 1939.

Mosher, Joseph. *The Exemplum in the Early Religious and Didactic Literature of England*. New York: Columbia University Press, 1911.

Nanda, Serena. "Hijaras: An Alternative Sex and Gender Role in India." In *Third Sex, Third Gender: Beyond Sexual Dimorphism in Culture and History*, edited by Gilbert Herdt, 405–8. New York: Zone Books, 1994.

Neale, John M. *Medieval Preachers and Medieval Preaching*. London: J. C. Mozley, 1856.

Nelli, Rene. "Exempla et mythes cathares (lre serie)." *Folklore: Revue d'Ethnographie méridionale* 23, no. 3 (autumn 1970).

Oldrieve, Susan. "Marginalized Voices in 'The Merchant of Venice.'" *Cardozo Studies in Law and Literature* 5, no. 1 (1933): 87–105.

Owst, Gerald. *Literature and Pulpit in Medieval England*. Cambridge: Cambridge University Press, 1933.

————. *Preaching in Medieval England*. Rev. ed. New York: Russell & Russell, 1965.

Pagels, Elaine. *Adam, Eve, and the Serpent*. New York: Vintage Books: 1989.

————. *The Origin of Satan*. New York: Random House, 1995.

Pantin, William. *The English Church in the Fourteenth Century*. Cambridge: Cambridge University Press, 1995.

Parkes, James. *The Conflict of the Church and the Synagogue: A Study in the Origins of Antisemitism*. New York: Atheneum, 1969.

Patterson, Lee. *Negotiating the Past*. Madison, Wisconsin: University of Wisconsin Press, 1987.

Pernoud, Regine. *La femme au temps des Cathédrales*. Paris: Stock, 1980.

Pfander, Homer. "The Medieval Friars and Some Alphabetical Source Books for Sermons." *Medium Aevum* 3, no. 1 (February 1934): 19–29.

————. "The Popular Sermon of the Medieval Friar in England." Diss. New York University, 1937.

————. "Some Medieval Manuals of Religious Instruction in England." *Journal of English and German Philology* 35 (1936): 243–58.

Phipps, William. "The Menstrual Taboo in the Judeo–Christian Tradition." *Journal of Religion and Health* 19 (Winter 1980): 298–303.

Poliakov, Leon. *The History of Anti-Semitism*. Vol 1. Translated by Richard Howard. New York: Vanguard Press, 1965.

Richardson, Henry G. *The English Jewry under Angevin Kings*. London: Methuen, 1960; Westport: Greenwood Press, 1983.

Robertson, D. W., Jr. *Essays in Medieval Culture*. Princton: Princeton University Press, 1980.

————. "Frequency of Preaching in Thirteenth Century England." *Speculum* 24 (1949): 376–88.

Rosenthal, Constance. *The Vitae Patrum in Old and Middle English Literature*. Philadelphia: University of Penn. Press, 1936.

Ruether, Rosemary. *Faith and Fratricide: The Theological Roots of Antisemitism*. New York: Seabury Press, 1974.

Russel, J. C. "The Clerical Population of Medieval England." *Traditio* 2 (1944): 177–212.

Saints and She-Devils: Images of Women in the 15th and 16th Centuries. Edited by
Lene Dresen-Coenders. London: Rubicon Press, 1987.

Sanford, Eva K. "The Use of Classical Latin Authors in the *Libri Manuales.*"
Transactions of the American Philosophical Association 55 (1924):
190–248.

Sartre, Jean-Paul. *Anti-Semite and Jew.* Translated by George J. Becker. New
York: Schocken Books, 1948.

Schmitt, Jean-Claude. "'Jeunes' et Danse des Chevaux de Bois: Le Folklore
Méridional dans la Littérature des Exempla (XIIIe-XIVe siècles)."
*La Religion populaire en Languedoc du XIIIe siècle a la moitie du XIVe
siècle: Cahiers de Fanjeaux* 11 (1976): 127–58.

———. *Prêcher d'exemples: Récits de prédicateurs du Moyen Age.* Paris:
Stock, 1985.

Scholderer, Victor. "The Legend of Archbishop Udo." *The Library*, n.s., 36, 9
(1908): 337–52.

Schwarzbaum, Haim. "International Folk Motifs in Petrus Alfonsi's *Disciplina
Clericalis.*" *Sefarad* 21 (1961): 267–99; 22 (1962): 321–44; 23 (1963):
54–73.

Sevenster, J. N. *The Roots of Pagan Antisemitism in the Ancient World.* Leyden:
E. J. Brill, 1975.

Sinicropi, Giovanni, "Chastity and Love in the *Decameron.*" In *The Olde Daunce:
Love, Friendship, Sex, and Marriage in the Medieval World,* edited by
Robert R. Edwards and Stephen Spector, 109–13. Albany: State
University of New York Press, 1991.

Smalley, Beryl. *English Friars and Antiquity in the Fourteenth Century.* Oxford:
Basil Blackwell, 1960.

Southern, R. W. "English Origins of the Miracles of the Virgin." *Medieval and
Rennaissance Studies* 4 (1958): 176–216.

Spector, Stephen. "Anti-Semitism and the English Mystery Plays." In *The Drama
of the Middle Ages,* edited by Clifford Davidson, C. J. Ganakaris, and
John H Stroupe, 328–41. New York: AMS Press, 1982.

———. "Empathy and Enmity in the *Prioress's Tale.*" In *The Olde Daunce:
Love, Friendship, Sex and Marriage in the Medieval World,* edited by
Robert R. Edwards and Stephen Spector, 211–28. Albany: State
University of New York Press, 1991.

Steckman, Lillian. "A Fifteenth-Century Festival Book." Diss. Yale University,
1934.

Stern, M., ed. *Greek and Latin Authors on Jews and Judaism.* Jerusalem: Israel
Academy of Sciences and Humanities, 1974.

Stierle, Karlheinze, "L'Histoire comme Exemple, l'exemple comme Histoire."
Poètique: Revue de théorie et d'analyze littéraires 9 (1972): 176–198.

Stover, Edna. "A Myrour to Lewde Men and Wymmen." Diss. University of Penn., 1951.

Suleiman, Susan. "Le Récit exemplaire: Parabole, fable, roman a thèse." *Poètique* 8, no. 32 (1977): 468–89.

Tardieu, Michel. "Prurit décrire et haine sociale chez les gnostiques." In *Pour Leon Poliakov: Le racisme, mythes et sciences*, edited by Maurice Olender, 167–76. Brussels: Editions Complexe, 1981.

Thompson, James. *The Medieval Library*. Chicago: University of Chicago Press, 1939.

Thompson, Stith. *The Folktale*. New York: Dryden Press, 1946.

Todorov, Tzvetan. *Conquest of America*. Translated by Richard Howard. New York: Harper & Row, 1984.

Toldo, Pietro. "D'All *Alphabetum Narrationum*." *Archiv fur das Studium der neuren Sprachen und Litteraturen* 117 (1906): 68–85, 287–303; 118 (1907): 69–81, 329–51; 119 (1907): 86–100, 351–71.

Trachtenburg, Joshua. *The Devil and the Jews: The Medieval Conception of the Jew and Its Relation to Modern Anti-Semitism*. Rev. ed. New Haven: Yale University Press, 1970.

Tubach, Frederic. "Exempla in the Decline." *Traditio* 18 (1962): 414–17.

————. *Index Exemplorum: A Handbook of Medieval Religious Tales*. Folklore Fellows Communications 86, no. 204. Helsinki: Suomalainen Tiedeskatemia Akemia Scientiarum Fennica, 1969.

Warner, Marina. *Alone of All Her Sex: The Myth and Cult of the Virgin Mary*. New York: Vintage Books, 1983.

Welter, J. Thomas. *L'Exemplum dans la littérature religieuse et didactique en moyen age*. Paris: Occitania, 1927.

Wenzel, Siegfried. "The Seven Deadly Sins: Some Problems of Research." *Speculum* 43, no. 1 (January 1968): 1–22.

Women in Medieval Society. Edited by Susan Stuard. Philadelphia: University of Penn. Press, 1976.

Women of Spirit: Leadership in the Jewish and Christian Traditions. Edited by Rosemary Ruether and Eleanor McLaughlin. New York: Simon and Schuster, 1979.

Wright, Thomas. *Essays on Subjects Connected with the Literature of England in the Middle Ages*. 2 vols. London: J. R. Smith, 1846.

Zink, Michel. "Le Traitement des 'sources exemplaires' dans les sermons occitans, catalans, premontais du XIIIe siècle." *La religion populaire en Languedoc du XIIIe siècle a la moitié du XIVe siècle: Cahiers de Fanjeau* 11 (1976): 161–86.

Index

Alphabet of Tales, An. See Alphabetum
   narrationum
Alphabetum narrationum (Arnold of
   Liège), 10
Alphonsi, Petrus. See Disciplina clericalis
Ambrose, Saint, 99, 211
angel, as soul's companion, 55, 56
anti-Judaism. See exempla, Jews in;
   Jews
Anthony, Saint, 100, 135
Arnold of Liège. See Alphabetum narrationum
Augustine, Saint
   on the devil, 26, 29, 32, 35, 61
   fear used by, 41
   on female sexuality, 92, 105
   on the Jews, 179, 188, 196–97
   on magic, 60
   on the transmission of original
      sin, 243–44n. 11
   on the will of God, 44

Babylon, as whore, 88
Bercheur, Pierre. See Gesta
   Romanorum
blackness and devils. See devils,
   black color; devils, darkness and
body versus soul, 42–43
Book of the Knight of Tour Landry, The,
   87

Bourbon, Etienne de, 95. See also
   Liber de septem donis
Bromyard, John, 14

Caesar of Heisterbach, 34, 37. See
   also Dialogue of Miracles
Chaucer's Wife of Bath, 83, 85,
   93, 101, 243n. 6, 244n.
   15, 246n. 34
Cheriton, Odo de. See Parables
Chrysostom, John, Saint
   on the Jews, 184, 186, 196–97,
      197–98
   on women, 93, 95, 99
Cinderella/Catskin motif, 108,
   146–47, 151, 166n. 28,
   235n. 19
confession–contrition–penance,
   41–42, 196
Constantine, 211
crucifix, 212, 250n. 12
Crusades, 7
Cynewulf, 211

Damascene, John, 228, 229, 235
Damien, Peter, 6
darkness and devils. See devils,
   darkness and
debate format, 68
devils, women, and Jews
   connections, 4, 19–20, 22, 35, 40,
      99, 109–10, 178, 186, 187